Elizabeth Taylor

Braemar Highlands

Their Tales, Traditions and History

Elizabeth Taylor

Braemar Highlands
Their Tales, Traditions and History

ISBN/EAN: 9783337120979

Printed in Europe, USA, Canada, Australia, Japan

Cover: Foto ©ninafisch / pixelio.de

More available books at **www.hansebooks.com**

BRAEMAR HIGHLANDS:

THEIR

TALES, TRADITIONS, AND HISTORY.

BY

ELIZABETH TAYLOR.

EDINBURGH:

WILLIAM P. NIMMO.

1869.

MURRAY AND GIBB, EDINBURGH,
PRINTERS TO HER MAJESTY'S STATIONERY OFFICE.

CONTENTS.

—o—

Part the First.

DESCRIPTION OF THE BRAEMAR HIGHLANDS.

CHAPTER I.

CHAPTER II.

CHAPTER III.

CHAPTER IV.

CHAPTER V.

CHAPTER VI.

CHAPTER VII.

𝔓art the Second.

EARLIEST TRADITIONS OF BRAEMAR.

CHAPTER I.

CHAPTER II.

CHAPTER III.

CHAPTER IV.

ℋart the ℱourth.

REBELLIONS OF "15' AND "45.'

PART THE FIRST.

DESCRIPTION OF THE BRAEMAR HIGHLANDS.

INTRODUCTORY REMARKS.

ITTLE apology will be needed for laying this volume before the public, as the locality of which it treats has excited no small degree of attention, since the publication of the 'Queen's Book' has opened up to us her quiet, simple life at *Balmoral.*

But, apart from the interest which royalty has thrown around *Braemar*, it possesses much to attract, —bracing air, magnificent scenery, and last, not least, some few historical associations, which, with a multitude of quaint old legends, form a medium through which we can obtain amusing, if not very correct, glimpses into the distant past.

The object of this volume has been to gather up these legends, reduce each to its own specific period, and so make them illustrate, in some measure, its obsolete practices and exploded beliefs. All tradi-

tions, it has been justly remarked, form themselves
into three classes : the first, those which are strictly
local and true ; the second being manifest inventions ;
the third, a mixture of truth and fiction.

Besides these general divisions, which appear pretty
clearly in the legends of *Braemar*, they still further
divide themselves, by cleaving, each one, to a distinct
period. The periods or centres round which they
culminate are three. The first includes all the early
traditions of *Braemar*, and has Malcolm Canmore
for its central figure. The second includes all those
respecting the rise of the Farquharson race, with
Finla, the founder of the clan, for its centre. The
third and last period includes the legends respecting
the Rebellions of ''15' and ''45,' with not one·indi-
vidual, but the House of Stuart, for its centre.

To form a sort of framework on which to hang
these legends, I have given some description of the
physical features of *Braemar :* this almost necessarily,
as not a mountain, hill, or stream, craggin or corry,
but bristles with some association or tradition striking
deeply into the dimness of antiquity. By means of
the figures attached to the places described, the reader
will be enabled to turn to the corresponding legend,
as the pages on which they occur will be given in a
fiy-leaf at the end of the volume.

Then, as to the sources whence I derived my information : almost solely, I may state, from parties

now or formerly resident in the district; and, in particular, to a few aged people, descended from the families whose history has been given, I am indebted for the bulk of the traditions and other interesting data found in this volume.

It was not until my collection, such as it is, was almost complete, that I became aware of the existence of a small volume, called *Legends of the Braes of Mar.* And since it came into my hands, occasionally, in reference to a date, etc., and frequently in regard to the correct orthography of several Gaelic phrases, I have availed myself of the help it afforded. This from necessity; as, though most of the people *speak* Gaelic with all the fluency of their mother tongue, very few can either *read* or *write* it. But in every other respect, during the preparation of this volume, I have pursued a thoroughly independent course.

In conclusion, while I wish to state that all pretence, even, to research or critical investigation, as to what is truth or otherwise in the traditions, is entirely disclaimed, yet, whenever a coincidence, or seeming coincidence, between them and any historical fact occurred to me, I have generally noted it; and when any phrase now obsolete, such as ' crop the causey,' etc., was used, if I could not get a satisfactory explanation from the narrator, I sought it from other sources, and put it in a footnote, or in the volume, as convenient. What I had in view—viz. the gathering up and putting in a readable form what I found ready to my hand in the minds of the people—is now accomplished ; and hope that this attempt to keep in remembrance the 'things that were' in an interesting locality, will be not wholly unacceptable.

CHAPTER I.

General Outline of the Braemar Highlands.

ABERDEENSHIRE, one of the most extensive and populous counties in the north
of *Scotland*, was anciently divided into
five districts : *Mar, Formartine, Buchan, Garioch,* and
Strathbogie.

Mar,[1] the first and largest of these divisions, was
again subdivided into two subordinate districts : *Mar*
proper, the lowland or level portion ; and *Braemar*,
the highland or mountainous.

Braemar was still further subdivided into six
parishes, which were, *St. Andrews, Crathie, Glengairn,
Glen Muich, Glen Taner,* and *Birse ;* the sixth, *Invernochty,* in *Strathdon*.

These arrangements, so far as merely arbitrary,
are now completely altered, as the ancient parish of
St. Andrews, known also as *Kindrochit,* now usurps
to itself exclusively the term *Braemar ;* and, besides,

---

[1] According to some authorities, *Mar* was divided into four districts :
Braemar, Cromar, Midmar, and *Foremar,* or *Formartine*.

7

this modern *Braemar* is no longer a distinct parish, but in union with *Crathie* forms one under the latter name.

In the following description of *Braemar*, I intend using the term in its widest sense, not in the modern or limited one. But before entering into the details of its particular localities, I will first endeavour to trace out briefly, but as distinctly as possible, the conformation of the great physical features which distinguish it.

As no other district in *Britain* can boast such an array of giant hills, they of course form its leading characteristic. In looking upon its mountains from any of the central peaks, they seem to rise up on every side, in interminable maze, their huge forms intersecting each other at every point. But notwithstanding these apparent irregularities, there *is* order in their disposition ; but it is only after continued observation that their natural classification into groups is recognised. However, therefore, local and merely arbitrary arrangements in *Braemar* may have altered, its mountains now, as in former days, resolve themselves into four distinct groups, geographically separated from each other by glens of sufficient width to interrupt the series.

Let the reader imagine a great square, or, more correctly, trapezoid. Its longest side, lying to the north, having an extension of some twenty miles from west to east, is formed by the *Cairngorm* and *Glengairn* ranges. Its parallel or southern side, extending also from west to east some sixteen or eighteen miles, is formed by the *Lochnagar* and *Glen Ey* ranges.

In the north-west corner is *Ben-Macdhui*, the highest point in the *Cairngorm* range ; while opposite, in the south-west corner, is *Cairn-Ecler*, the highest point in the *Glen Ey* range. A line drawn between them would be nearly straight, and give a length of some ten or twelve miles.

In the north-east corner is *Morven*, the highest summit in the *Glengairn* range ; while opposite, on the south-east, the classic *Lochnagar* raises its stately head. A line drawn between these two summits would make an angle somewhat acute, and give a length of from eleven to thirteen miles. The area within this supposed figure includes most of the district formerly known as *Braemar*, excepting perhaps the parish of *Invernochty*, in *Strathdon*.

These higher peaks do not, however, stand isolated. In the *Cairngorm* range or group there are five principal summits, all more than 4000 feet above the level of the sea ; while the huge forms of *Ben-Aun*, *Ben-a-Bhourd*, etc., which run out from them in an easterly direction, form, with the *Glen Ey* range, a continuous chain on the north side, with innumerable lesser heights sloping down from them towards a central valley or basin.

The *Lochnagar* range, which ranks next in height to the *Cairngorm* group, has a similar conformation, as the contiguous mountains are only separated from the central one by narrow ravines ; and, as on the north side of the valley, huge mountain masses connect the group with the *Glen Ey* range, and form a continuous chain on the south side.

As *Braemar* not only possesses the highest hills in Britain, but also the purest water, it naturally comes next under consideration. Its principal river is the *Dee*. In the north-west corner of the trapezoid, near the summit of *Brae-Riach*, in the *Cairngorm* range, it has its source at a height of some 4000 feet, in five springs of beautifully limpid water.

The stream formed by these springs runs into a corry or hollow, over the precipitous sides of which it again falls to a depth of at least 1000 feet. Recovering from this unceremonious descent, it hurries along its still descending course, gathering up innumerable rills and streams, as they come babbling down from the contiguous mountains.

The relative position of the *Dee* to the other mountain ranges can be conceived pretty correctly by recurring to our figure. From the north-west corner it flows southward some four or five miles through a glen of terrific grandeur, formed by the mountains of the *Cairngorm* group. Then, taking a sudden turn to the east, it flows right through the

central basin before described, and so continues to
flow until, its mission accomplished, it flows into the
German Ocean at *Aberdeen.* Briefly and beautifully
are the last two paragraphs epitomized by Professor
Blackie in his lines,

> ' The young river leaps from its sheer ledge,
>   Then sweeps with a full-flooded face to the sea.'

Along the beautiful valley locally termed *Strathdee,* the *Dee* lies like an extended back-bone, from
west to east ; while the glens, each with a tributary
stream, which open into it from north and south,
are like so many ribs, entering it sometimes almost
at right angles, but oftener oblique.

In addition to the highest hills and the purest
water, *Bracmar* also possesses the finest *pine forest*
in *Britain.* For nearly the last hundred years the
woodman's axe has by no means spared the trees,
yet a sufficiency of noble ones remain to justify its
claims to such pre-eminence.

On the north side of the *Dee* lies the forest of
Mar ; on the south, the *Balloch-buie.* Extensive as
both appear, they are but vestiges merely of the old
Royal Forest, or ' Sylva Caledonia,' where in days of
yore the kings of Scotland loved so well to chase
the deer. Besides the pine forests there are many
beautiful and extensive birch woods; but some notice
of their situation, etc., will come in more suitably
afterwards.

Thus far the characteristic features of *Braemar*. It has been pertinently remarked, that 'a correct geographical description of a locality often throws much light on its history.' I have endeavoured, therefore, to give as correct an outline of *Braemar* as possible, in the hope that it, with the more particular description which follows, will furnish a sort of key to the better understanding of the historical and traditional legends,—those shadowy footsteps of its earlier age.

CHAPTER II.

MORE minute description of the interesting localities of *Braemar* fittingly begins with the monarch of its mountains—*Ben-Macdhui*. As before stated, it is the highest summit of the *Cairngorm* range, being some 4297 feet.

The scenery from any part of it is very grand, often overpoweringly so, from the awe which the profound solitude of such a mountain wilderness induces. The prospect from its summit is a glorious one, but varies much both in extent and distinctness, according to the state of the atmosphere.

As several elaborate descriptions have been given of the wondrous panorama, and lately an exceedingly correct one by Her Majesty the Queen, it is unnecessary to give fresh details of it. I may just glimpse, instead, at the appearance of one or two of *Ben-Macdhui's* compeers,—*Cairn-Toul*, for instance, as its sugar-loaf shape particularly attracts attention ; or perhaps *Brac-Riach*, which is still more interesting, as from its steep brow the infant *Dee* is seen gushing like a long wavy line of silver.

To one standing on the western side of *Ben-Mac-dhui*, *Brac-Riach* presents the appearance of a long wall of precipice, said to be at least 2000 feet in height ; and so near does it appear, that one imagines it would be easy to throw a stone across the gorge to the top of it. This great wall extends several miles, and forms one side of the valley through which the *Dee* runs before it turns to the east. One beholding this tremendous precipice for the first time, will fully admit that they are indeed

> ' Grisly rocks, which guard
> The infant rills of Highland *Dee.*'

After the *Dee* has taken its abrupt turn to the east, if we follow its course along the road on the south side of the river some four or five miles, we come upon the *Linn of Dee*, one of the 'lions' of *Braemar*.

It does not at first sight strike you as anything extraordinary, as it is far more curious than grand, and the mind requires time to realize that. Before reaching the *Linn*, the river—it now deserves the name—appears very uneasy in its passage, giving the idea of a sensitive spirit, shrinking back from some not very clearly-defined ill in prospect. Then, as if resolved to brave the worst, it rushes forward with tremendous fury through the narrow gorge which the yawning rocks open to receive it.

After tumbling over a small height of some four or five feet, with increased desperation it rushes through a longer gorge of some four hundred yards. At length, clearing itself from all its conflicts, it steals away softly over the stones.

Round the *Linn* are some fine old trees, the remains of the 'Old Forest.' What a noble spectacle this valley must have been in the height of its woody glory! How it would enhance the grandeur of these mountains, when their rugged slopes and precipitous sides were hung with one continuous sheathing of fragrance and verdure! But with ruthless hand the proud honours of '*Sylva Caledonia*' have been laid low; for at this point only a few trees remain to tell of the perished splendour. It is stated as a fact, that in five years' time 80,000 of these hoary veterans of the forest were cut down in this part of the valley.

The *Linn* is spanned by a bridge (finished in 1859), which will doubtless now be looked upon with considerable interest, from the fact that its opening has been described in the recently published volume of Her Majesty the Queen.

Descending the river by the road on the south side, we come upon a small village or clachan. Somewhat less than a mile farther on, we come upon another, considerably larger. These are *Invercy* the little and muckle; between them *Glen Ey* opens into *Strathdee.*

Glen Ey, a narrow valley, stretches southward some eight miles. Looking up the glen, a low rounded hill seems to stand sentinel at its mouth. On each side of this hill a stream comes rushing through rocks, which appear rent as if for the sole purpose of letting it pass. A wooden bridge over each gives all facility for crossing.

One of these bridges—that over the eastmost stream, or *Ey*—is named '*Drochaide-an-leum*,' *i.e.* Bridge of the Leap. About two miles up the glen, in the rocky gorge through which the *Ey* passes, there is a curious place, known as the '*Colonel's Cave*,' or bed.

After visiting the place, I became curious to know the origin of the name; and, having ascertained, give the notes I took on next visiting the cave. 'After a long walk through lovely hills, robed in richest crimson, *i.e.* heather in full bloom, we reached our destination—a romantic spot, where the *Black Colonel*, or Col. John Farquharson of *Inverey*, hid after *Killie-crankie*. Not having made his submission, his castle was burnt, and a price set on his head.

'And now for the place. Apparently there is nothing here. Not yet; but see, there is a narrow path which leads down : for remember it is a hiding-place we seek, and so need expect little external indication of its existence. This path and these steps are artificial: conceive them away, and wouldn't you have a hiding-place?

'But before you descend, look to the stream rushing and tumbling over its rocky bed, as it enters deeper and deeper into the ravine. I suppose we may expect a pretty turmoil when we see it again farther down. And we must be careful in descending. No wonder, reader; for it is a fearful-looking chasm, between high perpendicular cliffs, with the waters which we saw a few minutes before rushing and tumbling over the rocks in such a hurry, now strangely hushed to rest, and looking so black, and deep, and still, that a subtle sort of terror creeps over one; and should we slip!!!

'But our fears magnify the danger: we are down safely, and looking about us for the cave. And having penetrated a little farther among the jutting abutments and ledged recesses, casting occasionally glances somewhat askance to the frowning cliffs overhead, and the deep pool in such close proximity, we reach the cave, and find it to be simply a narrow recess on a ledge of the rock on which we stand, overhung by the rocks above it,—a place, except to the initiated, little likely to be known.'

Leaving the cave, and proceeding a little farther up the valley, we come upon a ruined cottage. Here Dr. M'Gillivray says he sat down and made a survey of the glen. 'Shall I rejoice?' he inquires, 'or take up a lament? Subjects of grief and gladness are before me : a fine green strath, smooth as a well-kept lawn, and covered with herbage of the finest quality, beautiful as that of an English park. Brown hills almost encircle it. A stream glides pleasantly through it. Birch and alder trees fringe its banks. About the middle of the valley a beautiful little birch wood, but not a living creature to be seen—not even a single sheep !'—

' For the stalkers of deer keep their scouts in the glen,
  Which once swarmed with the high-hearted, brave Highland
      men.'

At no very remote date nine families lived in *Glen Ey;* now, not one but a gamekeeper's. I may notice, ere leaving the glen, that a little below where the stream of the *Ey* enters the *Dee,* is a low sandy flat, now covered with young trees, called ' *Sliabh Fear-chair,*' in English *Farquhar's Plain;* and on the hill at the mouth of *Glen Ey,* a spring called ' *Tobar Mhoire,*' or St. Mary's Well (2).

Nearly opposite *Glen Ey,* from the north, *Glen Lui* opens into *Strathdee,* with its tributary, a considerable stream ; so, according to our former figure, they form the first great pair of ribs branching out from, or rather running into, the back-bone of the *Dee.*

Glen Lui (3) is comparatively small, being only some five miles in length, and of no great breadth.

The hills which bound it are pretty lofty, but round, smooth, and covered with grass. The rocky pass, however, by which you enter the glen is fenced with trees.

With all its softness and beauty, *Glen Lui* is extremely lonely ; for, like *Glen Ey*, it is without inhabitant, though once it could boast of families sufficient to put a meal mill in requisition, to supply their wants in that particular department.

About five miles up, a mountain thrusts a spur into the glen, and divides it in two. The valley opening to the left is *Glen Lui Beg*, or *Glen Lui the Little*, through which runs the best and shortest path to the top of *Ben-Macdhui*. The other valley to the right is *Glen Derry*[1] (4), one of the passes towards *Loch Avon* and the basin of the *Spey*. The forest in *Glen Derry*, unlike the others, is quite in a state of nature, as any attempts made to apply the wood to civilised purposes have proved abortive, from the difficulty of removing the trees.

In passing the clachan of *Muckle Inverey*, I must notice the ruins of its old castle (5). Little remains of it but a crumbling wall. Yet straggling heaps of ruins tell effectively the story of former greatness. Near the castle is the churchyard of *Inverey* (6), also in a most desolate condition. No wall environs it, while its swelling mounds have been trodden by the

---

[1] In *Glen Derry* there was until quite lately an interesting forest of dead pines : they are now nearly extinct.

foot of time, or otherwise, into a level with the surrounding plain. Yet interesting, almost extraordinary,
memories linger round the two places ; also an old
pine tree in a wood on the opposite side of the road,
known as the ' *Dark Doom's Pine*' (7).

Still farther down, on the north side of the *Dee*,
is a noble hill range, *Craig Valloch.* It is densely
wooded, and at its base lies *Old Mar Lodge*, a structure in the old baronial style, and somewhat imposing-
looking in the distance. In front, a beautiful lawn
stretches down to the river, which in this place takes
a capricious curve, as if to cool the base of the opposite hills. The road, in consequence, no longer lies
in the depth of the valley, but along the side of the
hill for several miles.

Opposite ' *Old Mar Lodge*,' on the south side of
the river, is ' *Corrymulzie Cottage*,' or ' *New Mar
Lodge*,' at a height of 1250 feet above the level of the
sea, and is said to be the highest gentleman's residence in *Scotland.* It belongs to the Earl of Fife.

A tremendous precipice rises sheer up from the
great plateau on which the cottage stands, and the
great rock would indeed be

' Lonely and bare,'

were not every ledge and crevice hung with trees,
which transform it into an object of wild and singular
beauty. It is named *Craig Fetheach, i.e.* the Raven's

Craig. The torchlight ball described by Her Majesty was held here.

Shortly after passing *Corrymulzie Cottage*, we come upon the '*Falls of Corrymulzie*' (8). In many of the glens the rocks are, as it were, rent asunder to let the streams pass. Some of these crevices are a great depth, and would have a very gloomy appearance, but for the trees which adorn their sides.

One of the most interesting of these places is the '*Fall of Corrymulzie.*' The stream which forms it comes down the hill to the east of *New Mar Lodge.* The ravine in which it runs crosses the road, but a bridge preserves the level ; and did one not previously know of its existence, there is little from the road to make it known, unless indeed the delicious sound of falling water lure you to find out whence it proceeds.

On looking over what appears to be the side of the road, a stream is seen hurling itself down the gorge. There is also a little gate, and narrow zig-zag path leading down the steep banks overlooking the '*Falls*,' evidently for the use of those who wish a better view of the glancing down-come.

Those descending will have to be careful of their steps, as a slip down these precipitous crags would have rather disagreeable consequences. Down a short distance is a small rustic house, where we may have a view of both ; for it is a sort of double fall—height in all, forty feet.

Just below the bridge the stream slips into two, and shoots down, in double file, a steep plain, at the bottom of which it again unites to form a boiling pool. From this it again emerges, and jostles its way over several other falls, linns, whirls, etc. At last it escapes away, moaning most piteously as it hurries through the deep gloom below. By means of a rustic bridge and narrow footpath, those who feel inclined will get to the bottom of the ravine, and along the side of the stream to a considerable distance.

This ravine is, on the whole, very beautiful. Its precipitous sides, blanched and gaunt, do indeed rise up darkly; but they are gorgeously decorated with a rich tapestry of trees and plants, and gracefully festooned with fern and wild-flower. Then, when you descend, all is deeply sunk in shadow; and in the very heart of the delicious gloom, the living water hurling down its liquid mass, forms at all times a scene not only beautiful, but exquisitely enjoyable.

Still farther down, on the opposite or north side of the *Dee, Glen Quoich* (9) opens into *Strathdee.* On the *Quoich Water* is a beautiful linn, quite a region of romance. It very much resembles that on the *Dee*, excepting the steep, wild cliffs which over-hang it.

Through the linn, which is very narrow at its commencement—little more, perhaps, than three feet across — the waters rush with tremendous fury, surging and foaming ; and as they escape into a wider part of the gorge, their dazzling whiteness becomes shaded into a beautifully pellucid green. A delightful place this is ! And what a luxury to sit there in solitary meditation, lulled and solemnized by the voice of the torrent chanting its eternal psalm !

On one side of the linn the cliffs rise sheer up ; on the other side they are so far removed as to admit of a narrow footpath, by which you may descend to a considerable distance. Some little way down this path, a pine tree, torn from its sockets by some wild blast, lies across the stream, forming a fantastic, toy-looking bridge ; and, almost unconsciously, one begins to maze at the fragile crossing near such a dangerous point, and wonder if any one would ever dream of using it. But as you approach, it explains itself : you see it to be but the birth of an accident ; and if it has lured you farther down the path than intended, you will be amply repaid by the fine view from that spot of the linn, and also of a series of rapids stretching up the glen beyond it, as far as the eye can reach.

From that point downwards, the *Quoich* continues to dash its troubled waters, until it reaches the mouth of the glen, where it spreads over the *Strath of Dee*, submerging the ancient lairdship of the *Craggins*, and has done so since the great flood of 1829. In olden times, a fierce battle was here ended by the fall of *Scmus-na-Gruaig, i.e.* James of the flowing locks, Laird of Rothiemurchus (10).

The *Cuiach* or *Quoich, i.e.* Goblet, derives its convivial name from a number of circular cavities hollowed out in the gneiss by the action of the water; one of these cavities in particular being called '*The Earl of Mar's punch-bowl.*'

Somewhat farther down, *Glen Cluny* opens into *Strathdee* from the south, and so may be said to form, with the *Quoich*, the second great pair of ribs entering the *Dee*. At the junction of the *Dee* and *Cluny* stands the *Castle of Braemar*[1] (11), built on the site and from the ruins of one much older. Among some stray papers of a Braemarian, now in a better world, I found the following description of it :—

'One of the most interesting objects in the wide domain which once pertained to the proud and powerful Earl of Mar, is the *Old Castle*. Its situation is beautiful almost beyond description, and curious too, from being built on the top of an isolated knoll in the centre of the great park at the foot of *Kenneth's Craig.*

'It was originally one of the hunting-seats of these 'Earls, and was built at a time when thick and substantial walls had greater charms than airy rooms and large windows. Previous to 1715 it had in a great measure fallen to ruins (it was burnt

---

[1] The appearance of the castle was very much changed soon after the beginning of the present century ; the pepper-box turret, etc., were about that time altered to their present shape.

down towards the end of the sixteenth century). At that date
it was rebuilt, at the expense of Government, for the purpose
of overawing the Farquharson race, as at that time they
were the most powerful chiefs in this part of the Highlands—
peculiarly "their country."

'When it was rebuilt, a rampart enclosing a considerable
portion of ground was added. But neither the rampart nor
the modern portion of the building make any pretensions to
the massive proportions of the early part, though it is supposed
that, so far as outline is concerned, the original plan was pretty
closely followed.'

Turning up *Glen Cluny*, a short distance from
Braemar Castle, we come upon a beautiful village,
or at least a village beautiful for situation. One
half of it, lying on the east bank of the *Cluny*, is
called *Castleton of Braemar ;* the other half, on the
west side, is called *Auchendryne*. A bridge over the
beautiful ravine unites them.

Close by the bridge, on the rocky banks of the
Cluny, are the ruins of the *Ceann-Drochaide Castle* (12)
(*Kindroket*), *i.e.* Bridge Head or End Castle. It was
built by Malcolm Canmore in 1059, and in it he often
lived with Margaret his Queen.

Kindroket Castle stood then in the very centre of
Sylva Caledonia, not a trace of which now remains
in its vicinity. The castle itself is also a mass of
shapeless ruins ; but very interesting they are, from
the memories of the royal Malcolm and his saintly
Queen, which still linger round them like echoes of
the past.

This village—which is, in fact, the capital of the *Braemar Highlands*—is fast becoming a celebrity ; and little wonder : its pure bracing air, magnificent scenery, warm-hearted and intelligent population, have found a fitting climax in being reinvested with that peculiar charm which the presence of Royalty always creates. A native poet has contrived to give expression—though not very elegantly—to a feeling now deeply seated in many a heart :

> ' While Royalty dwells on the banks of the *Dee*,
> The valleys of *Mar* shall be sacred to me.'

CHAPTER III.

EAVING *Castleton* for the present, we proceed up *Glen Cluny*, which runs almost
due south, and separates the *Glen Ey*
range of mountains from that of *Lochnagar*. Some
two miles up, a large rounded hill seems to divide the
glen. On each side a stream comes flowing down,
and unites in front. The one from the west is called
the *Baddoch*, from a small glen of the same name ;
the other is the *Cluny*.

Near the junction of the streams, on the west side
of the *Cluny*, is a small farm-house named the *Coldrach* (13): it was once a lairdship.[1] On the east
bank of the *Cluny* stands a much larger one called
Auchalatar, formerly a lairdship also ; and to the
interesting old lady, once its mistress, I am indebted
for much of my legendary information.

---

[1] Here I may notice that these ancient lairdships consisted very often
of only a few acres of arable land, with a wide range of hill country.
They varied in size, however.

A few yards beyond *Auchalatar, Glen Callatar* opens into *Glen Cluny* from the east, with its tributary, a considerable stream. This glen is remarkable chiefly for its desolate scenery, said to be second in this respect to *Glencoe.* But after passing the lake, some four miles up, it becomes magnificent. Here I may inform my readers, that in whatever direction a glen may stretch towards its mouth or opening, was always spoken of as down, and *vice versa.*   ·

Glen Callatar is narrow, and bounded by lofty hills, very bare, and totally destitute of trees : their only covering is a rough mosaic of stones and heather. The noisy *Callatar,* however, rushing over its stony bed, relieves the monotony not a little. Emphatically may its bed be called stony ; for in some places compact masses present the appearance of paved work, and at other places heap themselves up as if to bar the passage of the stream, so causing it to toil round and over them, and break into miniature falls, cascades, whirlpools, etc., in making its escape. The beauty of this appearance depends, of course, very much upon the size of its stream.

About four miles up the glen we come upon the loch, which is not at all imposing in appearance, as nothing diversifies its shores but a few large stones about the margin. The hills skirting the sides of it are moderately high, and have neither precipice nor torrent-groove to give them a dash of the picturesque.

Loch Callatar, which is only about a mile in length, is formed by some torrents from the outlying ridges of *Lochnagar,* and by two rapid streams from the magnificent hills at the head of the glen, and of which we obtain a glimpse from the northern extremity of the loch.

Like most of its compeers in *Braemar, Glen Callatar* is uninhabited. It possesses only one dwelling, the gamekeeper's, which stands at the lower end of the loch. Near the house the ascent to *Lochnagar* commences, as that ' *Jewel of Mountains* ' is most easily visited from *Castleton* by this glen.

After passing the loch, the mountains along the east side of the glen are connected with *Lochnagar.* The principal are *Cairn Taggart, i.e.* the Priest's Hill ; *Craig-an-Leisdhair,* the Arrowmaker's Hill ; *Craig Pharig,* Peter's Hill ; *Cairn Bannock,* etc. On the opposite or west side are *Cairn Turc* (14), *Cairn Turc beagh,* or *Little Cairn Turc, Cairn-na-Caillich,* etc.

The glen terminates in a sort of oblong plain, most extended from east to west. This plain is bounded by four mountains, *Cairn-a-Claishie, Toliman, Cairn-na-Caillich,* etc. These mountains present a perfect contrast to the rough bleak heights of the lower parts of the glen, as they are covered with a deep green, relieved by the silvery appearance of the rills which

slightly groove their surface. One, on gazing at
them, is forcibly reminded of the lines :

> ‘ Far on the heights the runnels shine,
> In many a noiseless silvery line.’

One of these runnels in particular attracts attention.
One of the huge masses seems to rise almost sheer
up ; and over its green perpendicular face hangs a
single silvery line, like a thread of gossamer waving
in the breeze. That is the celebrated *Break-neck
Waterfall.* Soft and gentle as it now appears, were
we only near enongh, it would startle us with its voice
of thunder, as it pours into the *detritus* at the mountain's base.

About a quarter of a mile from this fall is Professor
Blackie's

> ‘ Lonely, lonely, dark Loch Candor.’

Loch Candor and its corry well repay the trouble
of a visit. The word *corry* is from the Gaelic *corrie*,
signifying a caldron ; and they have generally the
appearance of a scooped-out hollow. They are of all
varieties of size and situation : sometimes they are
found upon the top of a mountain, on its side, or in
the valley at its base.

The corry of *Loch Candor* is therefore simply a
hollow of a large size, scooped out of a mountain near
its top. It looks pretty much as if the mountain had
been split open, with one of the sides, rocky and bare,

rising up almost straight, while the other slopes away more gradually, and is covered with green. In the bottom lies the waters of the loch, dark and deep. They change their inky hue, however, when the sun shines brightly upon them, to a beautiful bluish green. The length of the loch, which is somewhat circular in shape, is not more than half a mile, while the height of the enclosing rock is some 800 feet.

Into some of the precipices about the *Corry* and *Break-neck Fall* the sheep often descend, enticed by the verdure on their broken shelves ; and unable to return, they have to be rescued by letting down a man by a rope, sometimes to the distance of 150 feet.

Sheep, however, have not been the only sufferers on the precipices. There is danger necessarily connected with a visit to these places ; and occasionally there has been a thrilling little episode, one of which is worth relating.

Some seven years ago, Rear-Admiral Jones was pursuing his researches on the precipices near the *Break-neck Fall.* Like the sheep, he got into a position whence he could not return. It was accidentally, however, by the shifting or slipping of some looser portion of the rocks. But his hammer, fortunately, was so wedged in by the stones, that he could hold himself steadily by it. And thus he stood on the face of that tremendous precipice, for part of three days and two nights, with only a few inches of standing room, and holding on by his hammer.

Occasionally, he said, some of the sheep would come to the bottom of the precipice and gaze up a considerable time ; then, as if unable to unravel the mystery, turn and go away. Some people have expressed much surprise that he could hang so long in such a position ; but his hands and arms had so stiffened in that terrible grasp, that they would have never relaxed, even had death ensued.

He had appointed to meet his servant at *Loch Callatar* at two P.M. ; and when night came on, and no appearance of him, all the men of the village set out in search ; but although it was continued, he was not discovered until the third day.

At length one man had his attention providentially directed to the spot where the sufferer stood, and he was speedily rescued. It is said his first act was to kneel down and give God thanks for his deliverance. The grateful man also wished to reward the people who had come in search ; but to their honour it must be stated, not one of them would receive his money. Before leaving the village, however, he arranged that the sum of ten pounds annually should be distributed among the *very poor*.

By the side of *Loch Callatar*, near a large lichen-covered stone, is a spring called the '*Priest's Well.*' The name is said to have originated thus : Frost had been unusually severe one winter, and continued so long, that, when May had come, not a plough had been got into the ground. Famine was feared ; and the people, in great distress, repaired to the priest, beseeching him to pray for a thaw.

People and priest then repaired to this well ; and as he prayed, it thawed sufficiently to supply them with water for mass. After mass he still kept praying, until the thaw fully set in; and the hill on which the blackness first appeared was from that time called *Cairn Taggart*, or the *Priest's Hill*. So the well is also called the *Priest's Well*, in commemoration of the deliverance.

Another version of the story is, that the well in the first place sprung up in answer to his prayers, in order to supply water for mass, and that people and priest then repaired to the hill, where he continued praying until the thaw came. Whichever way, his prayer was looked upon as the procuring cause of the deliverance ; and until some years ago, no Roman Catholic would have passed the well without dropping in a pin. The cause of this singular observance I have not been able to ascertain.

But to return. As before stated, it is through *Glen Callatar* that *Lochnagar* is most easily visited from *Castleton*. As so much has already been written and sung of its glories, it is quite unnecessary to give any elaborate description ; and, in reality, nothing short

of a visit is likely to do it justice ; but being so near,
it may be well to take a cursory glimpse in passing.

The stereotyped route to it begins at the gamekeeper's house, at the lower end of the loch. It is a
toilsome ascent ; but those who have not physical
strength for it may procure a pony, etc., from either
of the inns at the village.

After a pretty long ride, or walk, we begin to ascend
a ridge of *Cairn Taggart.* When its corresponding
descent is crossed, we come upon a noisy brook,
which hurls itself along towards what appears from
this point of view a rather insignificant sheet of water.
Such an estimate of it, however, would be exceedingly
incorrect ; for that is the famous *Duloch, i.e.* Black
Loch, and the little stream is the infant *Muick,* which
has its source near *Cairn Taggart,* and flows through
the deep ravine separating it from *Lochnagar.* This
ravine widening out between the *Craigs of Corbreach*
and those of *Cairn Bannock,* the *Duloch* is formed by
the closing again of their magnificent precipices.

Having crossed the *Muick,* and trudged up-hill in a
north-easterly direction for some two miles, we come
upon the first object of our pursuit—the northern
corry of *Lochnagar.* It is on a large scale. Its great
sides are strewn with huge blocks of granite and
detritus, to such an extent as to give the idea of a
mountain in ruins ; and at the bottom of this great
cavity are three small lakes, the largest of which is

called *Lochan-can*. From these lakes issue several
streams, which, after traversing the *Balloch-bhui Forest*
by different routes, again unite to form the stream of
the *Garrawalt*, on which are some fine falls.

From this corry a stony slope has to be ascended,
and then we stand upon the summit of *Lochnagar ;*
and on moving a little to the south-east, we are fully
in view of the chief of those

> ' Craigs that are wild and majestic,
>   The steep frowning glories of dark *Lochnagar ;*'

or, as one would say in plain prose, its eastern
corry. An immensely large one it is. The depth of
its enclosing rocks has been estimated at 1300 feet.
What a feeling of awe creeps on one while gazing
down the yawning gulf at the deep dark lake, enclosed
by such wondrous battlements ! As a poet says,

> ' We creep stealthily, and catch a trembling glance
> Into the dread abyss. . . .
>   From such a scene,
> So awfully sublime, our senses shrink,
> And fain would shield them at the solid base
> Of the tremendous precipice.'

Great blocks of stone rest on the upper part of the
corry, and appear like so many bastions to the grim
wall formed by its huge precipices. It differs much
in appearance from different points of view ; but the
idea of walls and battlements is peculiarly vivid while
gazing upwards from the loch, to which we can descend
by the slope at the northern corry.

The summit of *Lochnagar* is marked by two large
cairns ; and while passing along to the northern one,
the corry is seen to great advantage. From that
point of view it appears to be divided into several
portions by projecting ridges, which form occasionally
precipitous gorges, which for darkness and depth
might well lead into the bowels of the earth ; and
anything like an active imagination could easily con-
jure up any amount of phantom shapes or mystic
forms. On this spot one can repeat, with new powers
of appreciation, the stanza :

> ' Shades of the dead ! have I not heard your voice
>   Rise on the night-rolling breath of the gale ?
> Surely the soul of the hero rejoices,
>   And rides on the wind o'er his own Highland vale.
> Round *Lochnagar*, while the stormy mist gathers,
>   Winter presides in his cold icy car.
> Clouds there encircle the forms of my fathers ;
>   They dwell in the tempests of dark *Lochnagar*.'

The view from the top of *Lochnagar* is very extensive, but essentially mountainous. To use a phrase
of Royalty, a perfect 'sea of mountains' stretches
round us, 'whose billows,' it has been beautifully remarked, 'are aye at rest, and whose wavy surface no
wind can ever ruffle.' Such are some of the wild sub-
limities of *Lochnagar ;* but they must be *seen* to be
fully understood, for words are weak and cold when
the endeavour is made to picture out its memories.

One other thing I must notice before leaving *Glen*

Callatar and its interesting surroundings. About midway between the *Loch* and *Glen Cluny* we pass a circular hillock, on which Dr. M‘Gillivray remarks, that 'a man yet living had seen the fairies dancing.' A curious fairy legend connected with this hillock I may give in passing, having first remarked that the *Daoine Shith*, or *Shi, i.e.* men of peace, or fairies of the *Highlands*, were supposed to have their abode below such grassy eminences. During moonlight they celebrated their festivities on the outside; at other times they kept within.

One winter evening about Christmas two men were down about this knoll; and one of them coming upon an opening in it, went in, and heard the 'most beautifu' music that ever he heard, and saw a lot o' little fouk dancing—the heartiest fouk that ever he saw.'

After some time he went out for his friend, that he might share his pleasures, and both went in together. But the new-comer knew the danger, and hurried out as fast as possible, after vainly trying to induce his companion to follow.

As the loiterer never made his appearance, the other was taken to task, as having been last seen in his company; and it was like to go hard with him. The poor man could only tell his wonderful story, and plead for time, that he might try and get him back. And accordingly he made many visits to the knoll, but never succeeded in getting in until Christ-

mas came round again. On entering, he found his
friend standing just as he left him ; so he at once
took hold of him, and began to pull him away by
force.

'Hoots, man,' was the angry expostulation of the
spell-bound, 'ye needna be in sic a terrible hurry; I
ha'na been in mony hours yet.'

But the other continued to pull and pull, until he
got him out. Still nothing would convince him that
he had been in so long, until he went home and saw
the difference on his family. Such is a specimen of
the fairy tale, a belief of which still lingers in the
district.

CHAPTER IV.

Glen Cluny—Castleton of Braemar—Auchendryne—Morrone—
Kenneth's Craig—Croy, etc.

S we return to *Castleton*, down *Glen Cluny*, we observe that it widens out very gradually, and at its mouth assumes something like a bell-shape; then, by means of the rounded hills of *Morrone* on the west, and *Craig Choinaich* on the east, gracefully turns itself into *Strathdee*. The *Cluny Water*, which about half a mile up the glen, winds very near the base of *Morrone*, then strikes diagonally across the plain, and enters the Dee in front of *Craig Choinaich*.

In the centre of the triangular plain formed by the widening of *Glen Cluny*, lie the united villages of *Castleton* and *Auchendryne*. *Glen Cluny* separates the *Glen Ey* range of mountains from those of *Lochnagar* range, which terminates in *Craig Choinaich*, while the hill *Morrone* is the most outlying of the *Glen Ey* range; and an immense mass it is, one side of it

running parallel with *Glen Cluny*, while the other
fronts *Strathdee*, so forming a sort of corner-piece.

The base of this hill slopes very gradually; so
much so, that it is cultivated to the height of 1500
feet, the highest cultivated land in Scotland. This
cultivated part of the hill is called *Tomintoul, i. e.*
the Hill of the Two Views, from the fact that it
commands a view of both glens. 'The Highlanders,'
it has been remarked, 'are famous toponimists;' and
they do generally, in the names they give places,
express in the shortest, simplest manner possible,
their principal characteristics.

At the head of the cultivated part of *Tomintoul*
there is a plateau of considerable size, from which
rises *Morrone*, rough and bleak, to the height of
2796 feet. In the hollows and crevices in its sides
the snow lies until midsummer.

It is a stiff climb to the summit; but by the time
you reach it, such is the delightful effect of, I suppose,
the rarefaction of the air, that you begin to imagine
it quite a possible thing to fly, 'if,' as a friend remarked, 'one were only started.'

When at the highest point, you quite lose sight of
the village and glens, but are fully compensated by
the wondrous panorama of hills spread out before
you; while from the position of *Morrone* one has
the idea that it is the great centre-piece round which
they all spread, circular fashion.

If you look to the south, *Lochnagar* presents its scarred front, and seems to frown at you over the heads of its lesser neighbours. If to the north, the noble *Ben-Macdhui* demands your homage, as king of the mountains ; if to the east, the *Glengairn* hills lower themselves a little, that you may catch a distant glimpse of the sylvan palace of our much-loved Queen.

Looking in the same direction, through vistas of the nearer hills, *Invercauld House* appears at this distance pre-eminently beautiful. You have, however, to descend from the highest point ere you see it, and only then from certain positions.

At a still lower point, and looking towards the north-west, you have a view of the whole valley of the *Dee*—a gorgeous mosaic, on which, according to season, there is a perpetual change of beauty. If it is August, the hills are draped in rich crimson, contrasting beautifully with the dark green of the stately pine, or the lighter shades of the graceful birch. And then, in the depths of the valley, amid the deep, rich, almost transparent green which fills up the centre, the *Dee* winds gracefully, flashing back the light like a long wavy line of burnished silver.

If it is autumn, the drapery of the hills is a rich colouring of brown, in all its variety of tints, which, with the green and sparkle beneath, produces a singular effect. If it is winter, they are grand beyond description, as they assume such a defiant appearance. Theirs is then *stern* grandeur; but it is grandeur, and the magnificence of it!

But I must have done with *Morrone*, after stating that, at a point still farther down, the village and many other points of interest come into view. And here, when one has become sufficiently acquainted with the storied legendry of the district, what traditional visions will pass before the mental eye, as you gaze on the places connected with them!

While descending the hill, a large handsome edifice attracts attention: it is the Roman Catholic chapel. Fully one-half of the population are of that persuasion. It stands on one of the angles formed by the junction of the *Dee* and *Cluny.* Behind it is a small height named *Tom-Ghainmhaine* (15), pronounced Geéan, *i.e.* Hill of Peace.

Also on the *Auchendryne* side of the village are the Free Church, manse, and schoolhouse—all within a very tasteful and well-kept enclosure. On the *Castleton* side, close by the banks of the *Cluny*, is the Established Church, a small handsome structure, in a beautiful situation. *Dalvreckachy*, the manse, lies just at the foot of *Tomintoul*, embowered in a beautiful birch wood. The school and schoolhouse are on the *Castleton* side of the *Cluny.*

I must notice, in passing, two points on the *Cluny Water*, close to the Established Church: these are the

' *Cheese Peel*' (16), or Pool, and ' *Putan Sassenich* (17), *i.e.* the Englishman's Butt; I will have occasion to notice them after.

Nearly opposite the Established Church is the *Invercauld Arms*, a large, handsome inn. The *Fife Arms*, also very extensive, is on the *Auchendryne* side of the village, on the Earl of Fife's property.

Behind the *Invercauld Arms*, where its offices now stand, was an old building, formerly known as the *Earl of Mar's Courthouse.* After his defection it was used as an inn, but was accidentally burned down some years ago.

On a knoll (18) in front of the present inn, the standard of rebellion was raised by the Earl of Mar in 1715. The exact spot where the standard was fixed is now occupied by a large bow-window at the east side of the inn.

Passing on the road a little is the churchyard, on the left, a secluded spot : it is surrounded with a large wall and some fine trees. In the centre of the churchyard, formed partly from the ruins of the old church, is the burying-place of the Farquharsons of *Invercauld.* Near the entrance to this enclosure is a grave of some note—that of Peter Grant (19), the last rebel in *Scotland.* He outlived all his compeers at *Culloden*, etc., as he reached the extreme age of a hundred and ten years.

Another thing in this churchyard which strikes

one, is that people of the same name are all laid beside each other, in their own division ; but perhaps this is common in the *Highlands.* This, too, is the place where another local celebrity absolutely refused to rest after he was buried, and obliged his relations to let him have his own way, and bury him, as he wished to be, in the churchyard of *Inverey.*

Passing the churchyard a short distance, we come upon *Braemar Castle,* as already described, at the mouth of the *Cluny,* near its junction with the *Dee.* The road passes along the side of the park in which the castle stands, round the base of *Kenneth's Craig.* This road is modern : conceive it away, and the situation of the old castle is superb.

Craig Choinaich, or *Kenneth's Craig,* is a remarkably beautiful hill. 'Romantic' and 'picturesque' are words commonly used in describing it, and they are not unfittingly applied. It takes its name from Kenneth II., who, it is said, used, when he was old, and no longer able to enjoy the pleasures of the chase, to go up this hill, and view it conducted by others through the strath below.

Near the junction of the rivers there is a ford, a place also called the *Croy* (20), *i.e.* large stones laid at regular distances through the bed of the river. These stones, tradition says, were laid there by the Romans about 185.

CHAPTER V.

BY the north side of the *Dee*, on a very conspicuous little knoll, stands a monumental column, erected to the memory of the late proprietor of *Invercauld*, and near that point is the mouth or opening of *Glen Candlic* (21). Its tributary is called the *Sluggan Water*. In this glen is the stone mentioned by Her Majesty as being the remnant of the shieling built by the first Farquharson.

Scarcely a mile farther down than *Glen Candlic*, we come upon *Invercauld House*, on the north side of the *Dee*. It is an irregular but exceedingly picturesque-looking pile of building, and forms the central figure of a framework of magnificent scenery, where it looks quite as much in place, as if nature had devised all the surroundings on purpose for it.

It stands on a great natural terrace, from which a beautiful lawn studded with trees slopes away down to the river, which here winds about on the beautiful

45

strath in the form of the letter S, or rather of the
figure 8, enclosing two little islands in its sparkling
circles. Behind the house, a magnificent range of
hills, hung with the dark verdure of a pine forest,
forms an admirable background. From the extent of
lawn in front, and also on account of the *Dee*, you
cannot get near enough to break the spell of its
weird-like beauty; so, as a finishing touch to the
exquisite picture,

‘ Distance lends enchantment to the view.’

From this point to the bridge of *Invercauld*, some
miles down the valley, even the public road is exceedingly beautiful, the greater part of it being overhung with splendid specimens of the weeping birch,
graceful larch, and many other trees. In early
summer, a very curious and beautiful effect is produced by the light green tips of the various fir-trees,
contrasting so artistically with the soberer green of
the upper part of the leaves.   .

In addition to these beautiful trees, the southern
side of the road is almost overhung with abrupt rocks
and tremendous precipices, often rising almost perpendicularly to an immense height, and culminating
in a curious kind of overhanging peak. At the base
they are profusely wooded, while upwards trees and
plants shoot from every rift and crevice; while on
the summit trees of exquisite form, arranged like

a coronet, give to the scene a wild and singular beauty.

One of these peculiarly romantic-looking craigs is called the '*Lion's Face.*' Formerly it was known as '*Craig-na-Mhurdaire,*' *i.e.* the Murderer's Craig. This place, independently of its name, is in reality one of the 'lions' of *Braemar.* Not far from the village is a road through the *Duclaish* or black furrow leading to it, which visitors are now permitted to traverse.

Next to the *Lion's Face* is *Craig Cluny.* It is described in the *Deeside Guide* as 'a most stately, and awful rock, rising up nobly from the bottom of the glen, almost straight as an arrow; and as you go along the road at the foot of it, presents a most awful appearance,—its great rocks rising up one above another, almost to the clouds, and hanging gloomily over the road, as if they were to fall and crush you to powder. A more noble rock than this is nowhere to be seen.

'It is sometimes called the "*Charter Chest,*" because there the Laird of *Cluny* in times of danger used to hide his charter chest. After the battle of *Culloden,* Colonel Farquharson of *Cluny* hid himself in a cave far up this rock for the space of ten months; and it is said, when lying there, could hear the sounds of merriment made by the soldiers in his own house.' That is quite possible, as *Cluny House* stood at a very little distance from the rock, on the north side of the road ; only there was no road then. The old house is now demolished, and *Cluny Cottage*, a fanciful little dwelling, stands not far from the old site.

Along the road a small distance, is the *Big Stone of Cluny*. It was a favourite haunt of fairies. A man still living had one night a rather mischancy encounter with them. He was returning home by moonlight, and to his astonishment beheld a number of the tiny creatures dancing on its top. With the extremely agile movements of one he was exceedingly delighted ; but on his giving expression to his feelings, she in a fury flew at him, and had him almost strangled ere he could get '*a prayer said.*' Happily he succeeded in giving it utterance, and was delivered. The fairy race are hardly extinct yet in *Braemar*, as one person yet living says that 'people may say what they like, but she has seen them with her *ain een!*'

A little farther along is the new bridge of *Invercauld*, and not many hundred yards farther down is the old one. Travellers now cross the new bridge, as the public road from this point lies on the north side of the river. There is a road also on the south side, through the *Balloch-bhui Forest*, and past *Balmoral ;* but it is now strictly private, since that place became the residence of the Queen. It is open, however, as far down as the *Falls of the Garrawalt.*

Between the bridges the bed of the river is pretty rugged. And how the swift waters do come on!— rushing and dashing impetuously against the stoical-looking boulders, as if they would drive all the *vis inertiæ* out of them. The view from the old bridge is sublime ; a strange combination there is of quiet loveliness and solemn grandeur. One seems in an amphitheatre of hills, most of them densely wooded, rising higher and higher in the distance, and above them all *Lochnagar* towering pre-eminent.

Dr. MacGillivray, after an animated description of the scene, which he considers a 'perfect specimen of a Highland forest,' adds, 'Beautiful scene ! I almost weep when I look upon thee ; for tears flow from the pure fountain of pure happiness, as well as from the troubled spring of sorrow.'

The *Old Bridge of Invercauld* was built in 1752. A considerable time before that date lived Duncan Calder, 'the Seer of *Glen Lui*.' He had the mis-fortune to be laughed at for many of his predictions, and this one among the rest, 'that a thorn tree was to grow in a deep pool in the *Dee*, where it washed the base of *Craig Cluny*.' The correctness of it was, however, admitted when, after the bridge was built over the place, a thorn tree sprang up by the side of an arch near the middle of the river. There are still several trees in the same position, but they are *fir*, and not thorn.

D

The road over this bridge and along the south side
of the river is open as far as the *Falls of the Garrawalt.* Only this liberty is not to be abused : you are
expected to walk straight through ; only, of course,
taking as long time as you please to see and admire
the fine views as you enter the forest, or the stately
pines which thicken upon you as you enter deeper
and deeper into its shades.

Friendly boards point out the way to the ravine of
the *Garrawalt, i.e.* Rough Brook.   How it riots in its
solitude !—good-humouredly for a time dashing its
waters against the stones in noisy laughter ; but as

> ' It reaches the place
>   Of its steep descent,
>   Great tumult and wrath in
>   The cataract strong, plunges along,
>   Striking and raging, as if a war waging
>   Its caverns and rocks among,
> ' Dizzying and deafening the ear with its sound ;
>   And this never ending, but always descending,
>   Its sounds and motions for ever and ever are blending,
>   All at once, and all o'er, with a mighty uproar.'

A short distance below the bridges is a road leading to the glen of *Aberairder* (22).   This road leads
through a dense wood for some distance ; but when
it is cleared, the bare hills of the glen have a very
desolate appearance.   *Aberairder* runs nearly parallel
with *Strathdee,* and opens into it about two miles
from *Balmoral,* and was the scene, tradition says, of
a very summary administration of justice.

Farther down the valley, and close by the brink of the river, is a considerable heap of smallish stones, surmounted by a flagstaff and vane. This is *Cairn-a-Chuimhue*, or *Quheen*, *i.e.* Cairn of Remembrance, and is of some note as being the only really historical cairn on *Deeside*. It represents the number of *Strathdee* men, or of the Clan Farquharson, that fell in battle from about 1562, when their feuds with the Forbeses began, to at least the end of the wars with Montrose.

It was formed in this manner : As the spot on which it stands was the rendezvous of the clan, when all were assembled, each man brought a stone, and laid it on a clear space of ground, so forming a small cairn or heap. When they returned home, each survivor took a stone from the heap. The remaining stones indicated, of course, the number of the fallen, and were then carefully removed and placed on the original cairn, or *Cairn-a-Quheen.*

Next comes the *Street of Monaltrie*, *i.e.* a few small houses on each side of the road, built for some of the old Highlanders after their return from the American war. On the south side of the road are some stones, supposed to be the remains of a Druidical temple. On the north side of the road, a little farther down, is a farm-house, built on the site of the *Old House of Monaltrie*, which was burned down after the rebellion of ''45.' Donald Oig, or *Domhnull-Og-na-h-Alba, i.e.*

Young Donald of Albion (23), a great celebrity in olden times, had his residence there.

The next and greatest point of interest is *Balmoral*, lying on the south side of the river. So much has been recently made known of this interesting place, by one best fitted to touch on the subject, that room is only left for a few minor details.

The Castle stands on a beautiful level, round which the *Dee* curves with gentle sweep. Behind it *Craig-na-Gowan* rises to a considerable height, with all its harsher features toned down to picturesque beauty by the soft and fragrant foliage of the extensive birch woods which drape its sides.

There are so many interesting points in the district, that it becomes difficult to select or describe satisfactorily. The Castle is, in short, surrounded by *all* the varieties of Highland scenery, so that the eye can turn to *any* of its elements, from the rude to the beautiful, the sternly grand, or where they all unitedly rise into the sublime, while its pure air is invigorating almost to exhilaration.

The estate of *Balmoral* extends from the *Dee* southwards to the summit of *Lochnagar*, where it joins the *Birkhall* and *Abergeldie* properties. The three estates contain upwards of 35,000 imperial acres, and extend along the south bank of the *Dee* for eleven miles.

The new Castle is a magnificent and very extensive

pile of building, built of the finest dressed granite, and presents the clean appearance so characteristic of the stone. In its main features it is of the Scotch baronial style of architecture, which in this modernized condition gives to the castle the appearance of the ancient stronghold blending with the elegances and comforts of a modern mansion.

The large square tower, 100 feet high, is a massive structure, and visible at a great distance, and has a magnificent view from its summit. It has also a fine clock, which regulates the time all over the district, being set twice a-week to that of Greenwich.

The dining, drawing, billiard rooms, and library, are on the ground floor, and above them are the Royal apartments. If an admirable chasteness of design and exquisite workmanship characterize the outside of the castle, simplicity of style and purity of taste prevail within.

The entrance is from the south. Two beautiful statues of 'Fair Ellen' and 'Highland Mary' are, if I remember aright, almost the only ornaments of the entrance hall. The windows of the dining-room are hung with crimson bordered with Stuart tartan, and the walls with paper of green and gold. In the drawing-room the hangings are of Victoria tartan; chairs, couches, etc. etc., are all covered with the same. The carpet is of Stuart tartan, and on the walls a paper of blue and gold.

The Queen's private apartments are more richly furnished than those below, yet still with chastened elegance.   In the different rooms, the paintings, prints, cartes, etc., are exceedingly numerous and interesting.

The grounds are tastefully laid out, and have now two new points of interest, though sad ones.   These are the statue of the lamented Prince Consort, and the obelisk erected by the tenants to give expression to the deep affection and respect in which they held his memory, and their profound sorrow for his loss. A massive cast-iron bridge connects *Balmoral* with the public road on the north side of the valley.

CHAPTER VI.

AFTER passing the bridge connecting *Balmoral* with the north side is the Parish Church of *Crathie*, in a fine situation. Two miles farther down the valley is the *Castle of Abergeldie*, on the south side of the river. It is an ancient-looking castle, in the old baronial style, but now considerably enlarged and modernized. As is well known, it is now part of the Royal demesnes, being held upon a lease of forty years from the family of Gordon—was occupied by the lamented Duchess of Kent, and now by the Prince of Wales. A curious rope-and-cradle bridge connects it with the north side.

Craig-na-ban, i.e. Rock of the Woman, a noble hill, which forms part of its background, gained considerable celebrity when witches were rampant. The last one in the district was burnt there. The date is rather indefinite; but here is the tradition:—

At the time when witches were all over Scotland, and honest people burnt as many of them as they could convict, an old woman who lived by the *Dee* was accused of witchcraft, and condemned to die. An old man of like character, and under the same sentence, was confined with her. One dark night the witch made her escape; the warlock engaged to bring her back, on condition that he would be pardoned.

He had not travelled in search very far, when he saw a hare, which he knew to be her. Transforming himself into a greyhound, he gave chase; and just as he was about to seize her, she transformed herself into a mouse, and ran into the crevice of a dyke. Instantly the greyhound assumed the shape of a weasel, pursued, and brought her out. The two then assumed their proper shape, and the old woman, delivered up to her enemies, was burnt on the top of *Craig-na-ban.*

After passing *Abergeldie*, the road leads through the wood of *Coillie Crich*. But I should notice first a range of hills on the north side of the river, the highest point of which is called *Geallaig*, or White Mountain. About the base of this hill, not far from the road, are some traces of a Roman Catholic chapel, and a large upright standing-stone, said to be the remains of a Druidical temple which existed there before St. Nathalan introduced Christianity into *Braemar*, or according to others, an old French priest.

There are some curious legends about this St. Nathalan, the patron saint of the lower part of *Braemar*. One of them states that he sprang from a noble family near *Ballater;* but that being the case, all the legends make a sad omission in not telling how he himself became acquainted with the Christianity which they say he introduced. Here is one of the legends :—

St. Nathalan belonged to one of the noble families on *Deeside*, near *Ballater*, yet differed from them so much as to prefer the quiet pursuits of agriculture to all the glories of rapine and war. So exceedingly devout was he, that he spent the most of his time in divine contemplation and acts of beneficence.

During a great scarcity he fed his starving neighbours from his own abundant stores. But of course they could not last for ever ; so, when spring-time returned, St. Nathalan was without seed for his ground. But there could be no fear for a saint like him : so he gathered a quantity of the finest sand that could possibly be had, and with it his lands were sown ; and when harvest-time came round, never was such a crop seen as loaded the fields of St. Nathalan.

After the generosity he had shown his neighbours, it was little enough that they should assist him; so they turned out *en masse*, and began to reap in right earnest. While all were thus busily engaged, the heavens grew black, and anon the murky clouds poured forth tremendous torrents. The *Gairn* and *Dee* rose, and rose, until at length their ruthless floods swept the whole of this wonderful crop into their devouring vortex.

The shock was so sudden, that the saint so far forgot himself as to be very angry, and utter some unguarded expressions. Just then the heavens grew serene, and St. Nathalan at the same moment became convinced of his great wickedness in murmuring against God, and resolved also to expiate his great sin by a penance correspondingly severe. So, getting a heavy iron chain, he bound it round his ankle, and fastened it with a padlock; then threw the key into the *Dee* (that particular part being still known as the *Key Pool*), as it was not to be unlocked until he did something at *Rome*—I forget what.

After a weary pilgrimage he reached his destination; and having performed his vow, was walking along the street in quiet meditation. A boy selling fish, however, caught his attention. He bought one, and, strange enough, on opening it there was the identical key he had thrown into the *Dee* among the *Braes of Mar*. Of course he concluded that this was a sure token that his sin was pardoned, and took accordingly all the comfort flowing from such a legitimate source.

After this brilliant affair he remained several years

at *Rome*, edifying it with his wonderful piety. But, as was natural, he began to have a strong desire to revisit his native hills. So, enriched with the Pope's blessing, and invested also with some wonderful gifts of healing, etc., he returned home ; and having built several chapels, spittals, etc., at his own expense (among the others, the chapel at this place), ' he was forthwith hailed as the *patron saint* of the *Braes of Mar.*' He must have been content, however, with a limited diocese, as St. Andrew held that honour in the upper part, or what is now known as *Braemar*.

In passing through the beautiful wood of *Collie Crich*, a curious fact may be noticed. Most of the trees along the side of the road, and in every other situation where exposed to the northern blast, are *minus* branches on that side. The scenery is still magnificent, though the hills are lower than those farther up the river. Near a very beautiful one, named *Craig Youze*, *i.e.* Hill of the Firs, a small stream falls into the *Dee* on the south side. It is the *Girnock*. The glen through which it flows is called *Strathgirnock* (24). A terrible tragedy took place there in olden times. In modern days a much more pleasing association has been linked to it, and lately made known to us by Her Majesty the Queen.

Next comes *Knock Hill*, also on the south side. On it are the ruins of an old castle (25), also connected with the tragedy of *Strathgirnock*. A little below

Knock Hill, Glen Muick opens into *Strathdee* from
the south, and nearly opposite *Glengairn* opens into it
from the north, so forming the third great pair of ribs
branching out from the great back-bone of the *Dee.*

Glen Muick, which contains the finest and most
diversified scenery of all the glens in *Braemar*, commences in the *corry* of the *Duloch*, between *Cairn
Taggart* and *Lochnagar.*   Its upper portion, where
the mountains are entirely granite, is narrow and
elevated, very rugged and bare ; but from the foot of
the loch it is much more open and level.

In this latter portion are the remains of many old
houses.   The only habitable ones, however, are the
gamekeepers' shielings, the shepherds' bothies, and
Ault-na-guisach Cottage.   At the *Linn*, about nine
miles from its head, the glen contracts very much ;
but again expands, and continues to do so until it
reaches its greatest width, between the hill of *Knock*
and the ridge of *Panannich*, where it joins *Strathdee.*
The *Water of Muick* is the largest tributary of the
Dee from the south, and, as before stated, has its
source near *Cairn Taggart.*   After issuing from the
Duloch it forms a succession of noisy cataracts, then
expands into a loch, about two miles in length and
half a mile in breadth.

Loch Muick is surrounded by lofty ranges of steep
hills, deeply furrowed by mountain torrents ; while
in some places the frowning precipices of *Lochnagar*

hang darkly over it.   Its scenery at every point is grand, but towards its head it rises into the sublime.

The *Water of Muick*, while a tributary of the *Dee*, has in turn its own tributaries, the principal of which is the *burn* of the *Glassalt*, on which is a beautiful fall some 160 feet in height.   About nine miles from its source the *Muick* rushes through a linn, in the heart of a beautiful fir wood ; and after clearing the wood, it hurls itself over a high precipice into a foaming pool beneath, and after a course in all of some fifteen miles, it falls into the *Dee*.

In the mouth of *Glen Muick*, about a mile and a half south from *Ballater*, stood the *Castle of Braichley* (26), ' a place of much renown,' as the *Deeside Guide* states, ' on account of a mournful tragedy which took place here, and is recorded in the old ballad, *The Barrone of Braichley*.   The *Castle of Braichley* is now altogether demolished, nothing thereof remaining but one or two small fragments.   A hollow is still pointed out, between two small knolls, where the Farquharsons fell upon the baron, and killed him.'

Glengairn, which is nearly opposite, is the largest on the north side of the *Dee*, being about eighteen miles in length.   It commences in a deep hollow, between *Ben-Aun* and *Craigandal*.   Its upper part, which is very bleak and bare, contains only one habitation—a shepherd's bothie.

About *Corandavon Lodge*, a shooting-box for the

deer forest of *Ben-Aun*, the first traces of cultivation appear. From this point all the way to its mouth, it preserves a pretty uniform character, occasionally contracting or expanding as the hills encroach or recede. Compared to the other glens of *Braemar*, its scenery is tame; yet occasionally there is a dash of the picturesque. Towards its mouth there is a considerable number of farm-houses.

We are now nearing the verge of the *Braemar Highlands*. The only entrance to them formerly was through the *Pass of Ballater*. Now a road, not so direct, but more convenient, winds round the base of *Craig-an-Darroch, i.e.* Hill of the Oaks, to the village of *Ballater*, which is beautifully situated on an extensive plain, formed by a great curve in the river *Dee*.

'The *Pass* (27) *of Ballater*,' it has been said, 'presents scenery in some respects unsurpassed by any in *Scotland*.' The road seems to go right through the heart of the mountain, which looks as if it had been split asunder. The cloven sides, rising up almost perpendicularly, form a gorge of surpassing magnificence, leaving little more than space for a road, and a small stream which runs along its side.

Craig-an-Darroch, on the south side of the *Pass*, is 1400 feet in height. The view from it is exceedingly fine. The village, in particular, appears to great advantage, yet so small as to give the impression of a child's toy lying on a miniature plain,—the railway,

trains, etc., all looking equally diminutive.   The hills
alone look truly great and grand.

A little below the *Pass* is the ancient village of
Tullich.   On the south side of the road, which passes
through it, are the ruins of the '*Auld Kirk of Tullich.*'
Connected with these ruins is a very extraordinary
legend.   I briefly relate what of it I heard from an
old Highlander some time ago :—

'Most people have heard of the *Reel of Tullich.*
The incident which gave rise to it occurred in this,
or rather in an older structure which this ruin superseded.   About 160 or 170 years ago, the minister of
it lived at the *Milton of Tullich*, at some little distance ; and one stormy Sabbath he, not expecting
the people to come out, remained at home.

'The people gathered, however ; and as they had
no such things as heating apparatus, they were very
cold.   While waiting for the minister, they began,
innocently enough, at first, to clap their hands and
stamp their feet, to get a little warmth.   The majority
of the people being young, and their notions of Sabbath sanctity not very rigid, this led to more lively
action still.   It was at length proposed that, as the
minister was not appearing, they should have a "*jine*"
of "*placks*" and "*bodles*"—moneys then current.   Some
"gude ale" was then procured, which produced its
usual effects, even in the kirk, especially when another
and another supply followed.

'While all were thus jumping and stamping about, one suggested that it was quite as well to dance in a regular manner as not, and proposed a reel, which was at once agreed to. A musician was procured; then followed a scene without precedent, I suppose, in any place set apart for God's worship : they set a-dancing. Having thus laid aside all restraint, they grew more and more uproarious in their unhallowed glee. One, after ascending the pulpit, was uttering a lot of gibberish; another, occupying the precentor's desk, was trolling out a bacchanalian song, while the rest were dancing as in a frenzy; and it was during these disgraceful scenes that the "*Reel of Tullich*" was improvised.

'Just judgment,' added my informant, 'followed this terrible desecration of God's day and house ; for, ere that day twelve months, every one then present lay in their graves.' For the truth of this account I am not responsible ; only it was related to me as a thing firmly believed by the old people. And certainly one does not look with less interest on the *Milton of Tullich*, or the ruins of the '*auld kirk*,' after hearing this sombre story.

We are now in the vicinity of Byron's[1] '*Morven* of snow, and the rocks that o'ershadow *Culbleen.*' While

[1] Lately the bedstead on which his lordship slept was accidentally burnt down, to the no small disappointment of the proprietor. Multitudes of visitors annually thronged to see it ; and at one time the owner was offered forty pounds for it, but he preferred keeping it.

a little farther down the river, on the opposite or
south side, is *Ballatrich*, where he lived when a boy,
and spent his holidays when attending the grammar
school in *Aberdeen*.

Next comes the *Moor of Dinnet*, and it is a lone-
some one, lying along there most drearily. Strange
the power by which that gifted one could turn ugli-
ness itself into a thing of poetical beauty, as when he
sang :

'Land of *brown heath* and shaggy wood.'

Not many would think that great stretch of brown
heath there very interesting.

On the north-west corner of the moor lies *Loch
Cannor*, or *Kinnord*. On one of its islands Malcolm
Canmore had a castle, and a prison on the other.
Both islands are artificial. At the side of this moor
is a burn, which is, or was, considered the boundary
between the *Highlands* and the *Lowlands*.

Not far from *Loch Kinnord* is a smaller one, called
Loch Davin. North from it is a hill with a great
cairn on its summit, not conical, as most of them are,
but of an oval shape, and flattened on the top. Its
antiquity may account for its peculiar shape, as it is
said to have been erected in the time of Malcolm
Canmore. According to tradition, a bloody battle
was fought with the Danes near the base of the hill,
while their general, Mulloch, was killed on its summit.
Hence the *cairn*, and name '*Hill of Mulloch*' (28).

E

Aboyne is the next place of interest. It lies on
the north side of the river ; and nearly opposite, *Glen
Tanar* opens into *Strathdee.* This glen at one time
must have been densely wooded, as the quantity of
wood exported has been enormous ; and still it may
be truthfully described as a ' really beautiful and
richly wooded glen.'

On the north side of the river, a few miles farther
down, rises a hill called the '*Red Cap of Mortlach ;*'
so named from the fact, traditional at least, that some
restless spirit took a great fancy to nocturnal rambles
on it. Nor would it walk quietly like a decent spirit,
but when it was about midnight ; spoke loudly, either
to itself or the terrified people, they did not know
which, as it used an 'unknown language.' And those
who had the temerity to look in the direction, saw an
' awful vision, and terrible to behold,' with something
on its head like a red night-cap. This hill is easily
distinguished by a monument on its summit.

On the south side of the river lies the ancient house
and estate of *Fenzean* (29). The proprietors were
originally from *Braemar ;* and the way in which they
are said to have acquired the property forms one of
the most interesting legends.

Still farther down the river is the ancient village
of *Kincardine O'Neil,* built, tradition says, some 700
years ago, by one who figures largely in the early
legends of *Braemar.* Passing many other points of

interest, as I am now beyond the boundaries of *Brae-mar*, I notice only one other place on account of its connection with *Bracmar* history ; that is, the *Hill of Fare*, a long low range north from *Banchory* some four miles. There is in its south side a hollow called *Corrichic*, where a great battle was fought between the Earl of Moray and the Earl of Huntly, the forces of the latter being totally defeated, and himself cruelly slain. Eighteen miles farther down, the *Dee* falls into the sea near *Aberdeen*.

CHAPTER VII.

Braemar *via* Perth—Glenshee—Pass of the Cairnwell—Castleton—The Gathering, etc.

ESIDES the usual route to *Braemar* from the east up *Deeside*, there is another from the south *via Perth* · and *Blairgowrie*, straight through *Glenshee* and *Glen Cluny*, right into the heart of *Braemar*. So, to finish up my previous description of that locality, I give some cursory notes of a visit to *Braemar* by that route some years ago.

My travelling companion (a thorough *Braemarian*) and myself having reached *Blairgowrie*, our first care was to find out some means of transit through the glen ; and soon found that a coach ran daily during the months of August and September.

When fairly on the road, with *Blairgowrie* several miles in the rear, the scene presenting itself was exceedingly striking and impressive. In front, mountain began to rise behind mountain, in apparently endless succession ; their superficial outlines not conical, but rounded and wavy, while all were clothed to their summit in a deep green.

As we drove on, I sat gazing at the interminable maze, wondering where the road could be ; and on inquiry, learned, to my great surprise, that it lay right through the hills ; although every one of them, from our present point of view, seemed to intimate as plainly as possible that there *could* be no passage that way.

As we went on, the dwellings became much more scattered. Among the last of them was a farm-house of considerable size, and once of some importance, named *Feith-nan-Ceann,* a Gaelic name signifying Bog or Burn of the Heads, and is pronounced *Fenny-gang.* The name originated thus :

A race of the name of Campbell were once lords superior of *Glenshee,* and did indeed lord it over their less powerful neighbours, as well as their own immediate retainers. Once a year, it is said, they made the circuit of the glen for the purpose of exacting tribute. Bells were attached to the heads of their horses, so that when the tinkling was heard the oppressed people might bring out their tithes without any trouble to the receivers. By and by their spirit was roused ; and, so the legend goes, James Stewart of *Drumforkit,* with twelve gallant fellows, instead of bringing out their tithes, made a fierce onslaught on the Campbells, and, after getting the mastery, cut off their heads and rolled them into a burn or boggy place, from that time named *Feith-nan-Ceann.*

After passing the *Spittal of Glenshee*, now an inn,
the scenery becomes increasingly grand ; and as we
enter deeper and deeper into this mountain wilderness, not a trace of human habitation is visible.   Life
of every kind except the vegetable, and that only of
the lowest type, has fled the scene : not even a single
sheep browsing in any quiet nook can be detected.
Such a strange sensation of utter loneliness creeps
over one—what a contrast to the strife and din of
the fevered city !

We have been gradually but slowly ascending for
some time.   Now we are come to what is worth the
name of ascent, said to be about 1100 feet.   Up this
our road winds zig-zag fashion.   A peculiarly dangerous part of this road is called the ' *Devil's Elbow*,'
I know not for what reason, except that, while descending, the merest trifle would send the coach with
all its occupants spinning down the precipitous sides
of the *Cairnwell*, which is said to rise 3116 feet above
the level of the sea.   Still, lonely and even dangerous
as this place sometimes is, it has a mysterious loveliness—a terrifying fascination peculiar to itself.   How
cold it is, too, on the bleak summit ! and this the
11th of August.   Yet there is something delightful in
the bracing mountain air :

> ' How one bounds along with the living breeze,
> For here Æolus is always blowing.'

Glen Cluny, through which we next proceed, is a

continuation of the same scenery, except that the hills have assumed purple robes instead of green, *i.e.* the grass has given place to heather ; and as it is now at its best, in full bloom they really look lovely.

There is little to mark in this glen, excepting numerous sites of ruined dwellings. But as it is rich in legendary lore, busy fancy, ever on the alert, will think of this ruin as being the place whence a hapless little fellow was stolen by a wolf, but strangely spared by the female, and brought up with her young ; or of that other ruin as being the dwelling of the *Cam-Ruedh.* Who is the *Cam-Ruedh ?* did you inquire. A famous archer he was, who with his own unaided bow could put a whole host of the Katrin to flight. We have just passed the scene of one of his exploits—' the *Katrin's Howe,*' the scene of the battle of the *Cairnwell,* when the *Cam* by his prowess completely turned the fortunes of the day. With his own bow alone fourteen of them were laid low, while the remainder were soon put to an ignominious flight. The graves of the slain may yet be seen on the opposite or south side of the road ; but more of the *Cam* and his exploits after.

Now we come upon *Auchalatar,* within two miles of the *Castleton* of *Bracmar.* Here we are to reside for some time. It is well for us that we have not to go a lodging-hunting, as we have happened to visit the village at no ordinary time. To-morrow is the great gathering : the Prince and Princess of Wales are expected to be there, and consequently the influx of visitors is tremendous : lodgings of every kind are at fabulous prices ; but more of this anon.

On arriving at *Auchalatar*, as the day was not far spent, after resting a little we went on to see the village. About a mile and a half farther down the glen, at a slight turn of the road, the beautiful little capital of the *Aberdeenshire Highlands* lay in all its loveliness before us.

There it lay, amidst an amphitheatre of hills— mountains I should rather term them—covered to their summit with heather in full blossom, like an un- broken sheet of gorgeous velvet ; the lovely green of the birch trees, and the meadow through which the *Dee* was gliding in quiet loveliness, serving as a foil. And, as if to add the last touch to this scene of beauty, the descending sun was steeping the whole in a perfect flood of purple and gold.

As we neared it, however, the spell was partially broken : not that its loveliness was less—its beauties will bear inspection—but it was far from being the quiet spot we expected. It looked rather like a bee- hive, swarming at every point, and people still pour- ing in to join those already engaged in a vain search after lodgings.

Before midnight set in there was a near approach to the old Highland custom of pulling a sufficient quantity of the bushy heather, and lying down on it in some quiet nook ; as lofts and every available place were spread with hay, and many a weary pedestrian gladly stretched himself thereon.

But to some that was a luxury quite unattainable. One poor fellow, out at every point, was fain to creep into an empty cask at the end of the store. Coaches, etc., were in general requisition as bed-rooms ; and two ladies found out one of still more romantic character, in the little rustic house at the *Falls of Corrymulzie,* one sleeping and the other watching alternately.

It is needless to enter into detail ; so, after sauntering about for some time, we turned our backs on the sweet village, into which, though already so full, others were continually pouring.

Morning dawned most inauspiciously. Fierce gusts of wind swept along the glens, accompanied by all the usual premonitions of rain. For a little space it seemed to relent, as if unwilling to cast a shade over *Braemar's* only gala day. But anon the pitiless storm burst forth, to the great discomfiture of the pleasure-hunting pilgrims.

Before this, surly as the day was, we had started per gig to see some of the 'lions' of *Braemar.* Our road, as already described, lay along the south side of the *Dee,* past *Old Mar Lodge,* in front of which the games were to be held that year, not at the usual place on the *Invercauld* estate, owing to the recent death of the proprietor.

Though it was pretty early, the Highlanders were already astir ; and who could but admire the stalwart fellows in their picturesque dress, with their distinctive tartan, and badge of holly, broom, etc., stuck in the side of their Highland bonnets, so well termed 'the simple covering of a manly head ?'

Before starting, we had no intention of being present at the games ; but as my friend had not seen the Princess, and I had no objection, but rather desire, to see the Highlanders *en masse*, we resolved to gratify our curiosity. The Prince and Princess of Wales soon arrived, with the Earl and Countess of Fife, and many other ladies and gentlemen, and immediately after the games commenced ; and some quarter of an hour after, as the weather continued very unpropitious, we took our homeward route.

Thus far, then, the physical features of *Braemar*, as looked at with the eyes of an ordinary sight-seer. In the following part of this volume it is my intention to record all that I found remaining of traditions, legends, etc., that still loom out with considerable distinctness from the mist-enshrouded past ; not, however, becoming responsible for the absolute truth of these legends, nor for anything further than a correct relation of statements made to me.

PART THE SECOND.

——

EARLIEST TRADITIONS OF BRAEMAR.

'Chronicles of days that were,
And legends that the hoary-headed keep
In Memory's treasure-house.'

CHAPTER I.

N A.D. 81, when Agricola invaded *North Britain*, it was possessed by twenty-one tribes of aboriginal Britons. One people evidently in origin, they spoke the same language and followed the same customs, yet had no political connection.

The *Vacomagi*, one of these tribes, inhabited the southern side of the *Moray Frith*, from the *Dovern* on the east to the *Ness* on the west ; their territory comprehending the shires of *Banff, Elgin, Nairn*, the eastern part of *Inverness*, and *Braemar* in *Aberdeenshire*.

According to Roman historians, these tribes, though little acquainted with the arts of social life, were yet such a brave and hardy people, that, but for the fact of their being divided into clans and tribes, without any political union or amalgamation of interest, they would have proved a formidable enemy even to the Romans.

The next historical notice of *Braemar* is in 138, when Lollius Urbicus extended his arms as far north as the *Varar*, or *Moray Frith*. When roads were formed from the *Solway Frith* to the *Frith of Clyde*, and from thence to the *Burghhead* of *Moray*, and stations were established in the most commanding places, *Iters* were then conducted along the road. One of these, of which there is special mention made, proceeding from *Burghhead* of *Moray*, had its first station at *Forres*, a distance of eight miles. From *Forres* it proceeded to the *Spey* at *Cromdale*, a distance of eighteen miles. It then proceeded southward along *Strathavon*, by *Loch Beauly*, to the junction of the *Dee* and *Cluny*, where historians say they crossed the commodious ford in that vicinity, and took their course southward through *Glenshee*, etc.

Being curious to know if any traces remained of these Roman visits, when in the locality I sought out one likely to possess the desired information. 'Oi aye,' was the hearty response to my queries, 'the Romans *were* up as far as this. Do you mind yonder, whare ye crossed in the boat aside the castle, a lot o' big stanes that mak' a kin' o' a rush in the water—the *Croy* they call it? Well, that's the place where the Romans crossed.'

'But if there was a ford, why put in stones?' I queried.

'It would be much easier for them, as they would

only have to step from the ane to the ither, and so
get over dry. But a gey job they must have had to
get that great stanes put down yonder : ye may ken
that, when a' the floods and floats frae that time to
this hasna moved them oot o' the place : only they
are mostly under water now ; but since I mind they
were quite visible. The way they did was this : they
brought one of the big stanes to the side of the water,
and put it in ; then they brought another, and rowed
it ower the head of the first ; and so on, till they got
to the ither side. And that made a fine passage to
them ; for ye see they had some gey sharp battles,
and were driven back and lost a good many men.'

I know not if my old informer be correct or not,
but we do read of the Romans losing 30,000 men in
one of their northern campaigns, through fatigue, the
severity of the climate, and the incessant and harass-
ing warfare kept up by the Caledonians. And one
old historian quaintly remarks of a general, that
'having the good fortune to carry his arms farther
than any of his predecessors, he yet had the modera-
tion not to go *much* farther, as they met with nothing
but *blows, cold,* and *hunger.*'

From 446, when the Romans finally quitted their
possessions in *North Britain*, to 843, is known in
history as the *Pictish* period. During that time forty
kings reigned, and Christianity was introduced by
St. Columba. It was doubtless a considerable time

ere it penetrated to the *Braes of Mar.* The only traditional account I can find of its introduction is the following legend, which emanates from the Roman Catholic part of the population :—

Long, long ago, an old man wearing strange apparel, and speaking a strange language, came journeying up the water of *Dee.* He went from door to door begging a crust of bread and the hospitality of the owner ; but his emaciated appearance, weary gait, and sad countenance, showed that the supplies he received were scant, and the sympathy little.

The old man toiled on, however ; and at length, footsore and weary, he entered the clachan of *Inverey.* Weary as he was, he began to speak to them of a new religion, explaining it as he best could ; for he had but a mere smattering of the Celtic, which he had picked up on the way. But here he had less sympathy than ever, for they refused him even a cup of water to quench his thirst.

So again he went on, and crossing the *Ey,* he climbed up the hill on the other side. Here he found a spring of the most pellucid water in a hollow near the top, and, seating himself on the grass, he drank copiously of the living stream. Feeling himself invigorated in no ordinary degree, in gratitude he devoted the well to the blessed Virgin ; and seating himself beside it, became so fully engrossed in meditation, that he did not observe the approach of another person.'

'Curse the fountain which gave thee the life-continuing draught!' cried the new-comer.

'Curse it not,' replied the stranger, 'for I have blessed it, and blessed it shall be.'

'But I do curse it, and insult it, and the blessing thou hast given it.' And then, bending down, he took a handful of mud and dashed it into the eye of the fountain. For a moment the eye seemed to sparkle with anger, clear and pure through the muddy water, and anon it bubbled up no more.

'Friend,' said the weary stranger, 'the fountain did thee no harm, and I have done thee no wrong: why dost thou curse and insult us?'

'I do it because I am a Druid priest, and because thou tellest the people of a new religion.'

'And I tell thee,' said the stranger, rising up and speaking with authority, 'that as this fountain shall again spring up through the dark mass of earth that covers it, so shall the truth which I speak as a servant shine with primal lustre on your heart, and to the whole world.' And as he spoke, the fountain again sent out its stream in a new place, purer and sweeter than before.

'Master, master!' cried the Druid, 'the power of the Great Spirit is with thee, and I am thy servant.' From that time the French priest prospered, and the Druid became one of the most active in propagating the truth. Druidical superstitions vanished, and little chapels arose in every rugged glen, for Christianity had now assumed its beneficent sway.

Respecting this legend, it would be difficult to decide as to whether it is a coincidence of invention, or merely an imitation of the legend of the *Sludach*, a spring in the parish of *Cromarty ;* in which legend not a Druid and Catholic priest, but two farmers, bearing a not very good will to each other, were the actors in the scene ; and the only other difference is, that the insulted spring withdrew its waters for a considerable time, and still only presents them occasionally, and always at a time when they are not much needed.

The spring on the banks of the *Ey* has shown, however, a much better spirit, as its waters not only continued to flow permanently, but in many instances gave out a healing virtue, no doubt owing to its being taken under the patronage of ' Mary.' ' *Tober Mhoire*,' St. Mary's Well, was long a celebrated spot, to which those who had any special favour to ask of her resorted, some instances of which I may notice as I pass along.

In more modern times it was known better as the ' *Well of the Prins*,' *i.e.* pins, from the fact that every devotee, as at the ' *Priest Well*' at *Glen Callater*, dropped in one. By the cutting of a new road ' *Tobar Mhoire*' was interfered with seriously, as it went right over it, of course filling it up ; but the spring made an opening for itself a little farther down the hill, where it still remains, but quite devoid of all its wonderful qualities.

Before proceeding further, I must notice some traditions belonging to an age still more remote than even the Druids or Romans. It has been remarked that the oldest of all the traditions of *Britain* is that which represents it as peopled by giants, which one Brutus, an Italian, succeeded in extirpating. He had not penetrated so far as *Braemar* evidently, as they have a different manner of accounting for their extinction there. However these legends may have originated, they run thus :—

At one time there was a people inhabiting *Braemar*, so tall that they could step from hill-top to hill-top, without taking the trouble of descending. They could even slake their thirst from wells at their base, by bending down and using their long arms, etc.

They spent their time chiefly in hunting wild boars, which at that time were of a size quite worthy their gigantic prowess. These boars must have been peculiarly dangerous creatures, for they were covered with vast bristles or spines, hollow, and full of a substance so poisonous, that if it pierced their skin so as to draw blood, it was death most sure and certain.

Their mode of hunting was peculiar. Those engaged in the chase took their place on each hill-top : some of the giants then uttered a sound that roused the animal from his lair, who at once made for the place whence the sound proceeded. But ere he had time to reach that hunter, another giant emitted a similar sound, on hearing which the boar immediately turned and made for him, and so on, until the creature was quite wearied out, when he fell an easy prey to his captors.

It so happened that a sort of rivalry broke out among these mighty men. One of them was not only more handsome than the others, but was also, according to their views of things, endowed with many good qualities. But, above all, he had succeeded in winning the heart of one of their fairest maidens—a prize for which the competition had been very keen.

On all these accounts, therefore, there was a secret grudge, and some plan was wanted by which they might get rid of him. Where the will is, there will soon be a way; so they speedily discovered that, if they were only to forbear turning the boar when he had to shout, they would soon get rid of him.

Next hunting expedition, it so happened that he took his stand on the hill, now called *Cairn Turc*, all unsuspicious of the misfortunes awaiting him. The boar was roused, as usual, and passed from one to another several times. At length the plan was put in operation, but the gallant giant came off victorious; and when the others came up to him, the monster lay dead at his feet.

Many excuses were made for their negligence, and great admiration expressed for his bravery ; but, as a further test of it, he was asked by the chief giant to measure the boar, which he did, and yet escaped unscathed. 'Now, when you have done so well in measuring the length, measure it round now, that we may know the breadth of it,' said the chief. The poor giant again obeyed, but was so unfortunate as to pierce his hand with one of the bristles, and he was soon no more. The mountain on which the tragedy took place was, from that circumstance, called *Cairn Turc*, Hill of the Boar.

From that time a blight fell on the race of the giants, and they dwindled away, until only one of them and his wife remained. I suppose the wild boars had dwindled away too, or the giant's tastes had altered strangely, for he descended so low as to become a pilferer. And a sad pest he was to the poor people ; for, no sooner was their grain ready for use, than he came by night and took it away, etc.

Many plans were made to rid themselves of him, but all were unsuccessful, until a second Judith offered, on condition that they gave her what she required, soon to rid them of the giant. Her requirements were few : only a large fire in a barn well supplied with grain ; a very large pot full of water, and sids, *i.e.* the outside of the grain ; a large 'cog,' similar in shape to that used in milking. So the fire was kindled, the pot was put on, and boiling bravely, and the woman sat down to her stocking.

Soon after midnight the giant made his appearance. After crawling into the barn, and seeing things so comfortable, he coiled himself up before the fire, to have the benefit of it fully ; and when comfortably laired, the woman came in for a full share of his attention. At length he asked her name. 'Mysel' and Mysel',' was her tart reply.

The giant, after remarking what a brave fire she had, wished to know what was in the pot. 'I'll let you see,' was the reply. And taking off the lid, and filling her cog with the boiling sids, she dashed them about the giant's feet and legs ; and filling it again as fast as possible, repeated the application until the huge giant was bellowing with pain. And as his dimensions prevented him getting quickly out of his untoward position, the woman made her escape.

It was a considerable time ere the giant could take his departure—*minus* grain, of course. His wife had been waiting for him on a neighbouring hill ; and seeing his deplorable condition, wished to know who had been the cause of it, that she might be revenged. 'Mysel' and Mysel',' was all that the poor giant was able to say. 'Weel, weel,' responded his spouse, ' if it was yoursel' and yoursel', it cannot be helped ; but had it been any other body, I would have made them suffer.' Thus died the last of the giant race among the *Bracs of Mar !*

I need scarcely say that this legend, though still existing in the memories of many, is *not believed.* They seldom give it but in mere fragments. I had no little difficulty in getting the whole, fearing lest I would suppose they attached *any* degree of credit to it.

CHAPTER II.

Kenneth the Hardy—Malcolm Canmore—Origin of the Gatherings, etc.

THE Pictish period (from 446 to 843) was not only marked by the introduction of Christianity by St. Columba, but also by the arrival and settlement of the Dalriads, or Scoto-Irish, on the shores of *Argyle.* Hence ensued a series of conflicts, which issued in the complete downfall of the Pictish monarchy, when in 843 Chionaisith Chruaidh, *i.e.* Kenneth the Hardy, placed the crown of both kingdoms on his head.

This Chionaisith Chruaidh had a residence at *Braemar*, though all traces of it have now disappeared; the only memorial of him in the locality being that beautiful hill called *Kenneth's Craig*, which took its name from him.

Passing over a period of somewhat more than 200 years, we come upon the nineteenth king of the united kingdom of the Picts and Scots — Malcolm Canmore. And now the mist of antiquity clears away a little, and he appears before us a sort of central figure round which many of the *Braemar* traditions culminate. In this and the next few chapters I intend to notice some of his doings, as they are still in *traditional* existence.

Most people have heard of the great annual gatherings of the clans at *Braemar*, under the auspices of the Highland Society, as they have a kind of celebrity, especially since Her Majesty the Queen has been pleased to honour them so often with her presence. According to tradition, these gatherings, races, etc., date their origin as far back as Malcolm Canmore. The first of them is said to have taken place in the following manner :—

Having a mind to establish a sort of post system by means of foot-runners, Malcolm summoned his subjects to meet him in the plain where the present *Castle of Braemar* now stands. When assembled, a purse of gold, with a full suit of dress and arms, were then offered to the man who first reached the summit of *Craig Chionaisith, i.e.* Kenneth's Craig, as seen from the place where the king and people were assembled.

Many competitors at once entered the lists, and were placed in readiness for starting. Judges were appointed. All being thus arranged, the king gave the signal, and at once they bounded across the plain towards the hill. They had almost reached its foot, when another competitor, breathless with haste, came, pleading for leave to run also.

'You are too late, my brave man,' said the king.

'No, no! only let me run,' he cried imploringly, throwing aside his arms and upper garments as he spoke.

'Go, if you wish,' was the king's answer; 'but you are too late.' But the youth had almost cleared the plain while the words hung on his lips.

'Who is the stripling?' inquired Malcolm, charmed with his eagerness.

'Macgregor of *Balloch-bhui's* youngest son,' was the answer. 'His two brothers are already up the hill before him.'

The foremost of the competitors were indeed far up the hill in advance, but young Macgregor seemed as much at home on the hill as a frolicsome goat.

'That springal will beat them all,' said Malcolm, as he saw him, now climbing on all-fours, and anon seizing the long heather and swinging himself forward.

'More power to him!' cried Allen Durward, of whom we will hear more presently.

Thus the race became more and more exciting. Many had given up, yet numbers were pressing forward. Foremost of these were the two eldest Macgregors, while Macgregor the younger was still springing forward with unabated energy. Passing the others one by one, he reached one of his brothers.

'Halves, brother,' he cried, 'and I'll stop!'

'Gain what you can, and keep what you get ; I'll do the same,' was the answer of one, while the other was too breathless to speak. Up and up the springal bounded, until within a few paces of the foremost.

'Halves again, brother, and I'll yield.'

'Never !' replied the other. 'Keep what you get.'

Now they were in sight of the goal, but every muscle and nerve was already tightened to breaking. Terribly pressed was the eldest brother ; but, determined to gain, he put out his hand to impede the progress of the younger. Feeling nothing, he looked round, expecting to see his brother on the ground, while at that moment the youngest leaped forward below the outstretched arm. Furious, the eldest brother bounded on after him, and fell just as his hand clutched with maddened grasp the kilt of his rival. Encouraged by this accident, those in the rear came pressing forward, when, quick as thought, the youngest Macgregor unbuckled his kilt, saying as he did so, 'I have yielded all to you hitherto : take that also.' Then springing forward, he seized the signal-staff, and throwing it up in the air, sank down on the earth beside it.

A loud shout rose from the spectators below ; but the victor and his vanquished brother heeded it not, as they lay on the ground in a state of complete prostration. Nor could it be otherwise, if what the legend says be true, that the youngest reached the top in three minutes.

Now, assuming that this legend possesses just the slightest possible degree of veracity, how interesting to read in connection with it (after a lapse of 800 years, fraught with change and countless blessings to our country), an account from the pen of Royalty of similar races over the same ground, and as witnessed from the same point of view :—

'*September* 12, 1850.

' We lunched early, and then went at half-past two o'clock with the children and all our party, excepting Lady Douro, to the gathering at the *Castle of Braemar*. . . . The Duffs, Farquharsons, Leedses, and those staying with them, and Captain Forbes, with forty of his men, who had come over from *Strathdon*, were there also. There were the usual games of "putting the stone," "throwing the hammer and caber," and racing up the hill *Craig Chionaisith*, which was accomplished in less than six minutes and a half ; and we were all much pleased to see our gillie Duncan, who is an active, good-looking young man, win. He was far before the others the whole way. It is a fearful exertion. . . . Eighteen or nineteen started ; and it looked very pretty to see them run off in their different coloured kilts, with their white shirts .(the jackets, or doublets, had been taken off for all the games), and scramble up through the wood, emerging gradually at the edge of it, and climbing the hill.'

Soon after the gathering thus described, to the great joy, not so much of the runners themselves as those connected with them, the racing *up the hill* was discontinued. Some had died in former years from the effects of the exertion, and many had been injured : the victors especially had won their prize dear.

In 1850, as in former years, it was the same. 'One of our keepers (the victor in the race), like many others, spit blood after running up that steep hill in this short space of time, and has never been so well since. The running up the hill has consequently been discontinued,' says Her Majesty in her footnote to the account of this gathering. Thus we have the traditional account of the first of these races, and an authentic one of the last.

CHAPTER III.

ORIGIN OF BRAEMAR SURNAMES.

Durward—Lumsden—Mulloch—Coutts—M'Hardy—Stewart, etc.

HE origin and derivation of surnames,' says one, 'is always a curious subject ; and while replete with philological interest, is sure to produce something to excite amusement. The study of surnames, moreover, often supplies some curious contributions to moral philosophy. It does at least exhibit frail humanity in curious aspects, by making known the shifts whereby possessors of plebeian-sounding names endeavour to escape the literal and grammatical sense of their patronymics.'

The origin and derivation of the surnames peculiar to *Braemar* well exemplify the first of these remarks : they are curious and amusing. The second is not at all applicable, either to the Braemarians or to Highlanders in general : their tendencies are all in the opposite direction. So much so, that not only do they pride themselves in their distinctive patronymics, whatever their sound may be, but also in any phrase, or as it is called, ' *tcc-name*,' which from any peculiar circumstance may attach itself to them, and by which they are distinguished. Several legends, therefore, bearing on this curious and interesting subject, *Bracmar* surnames, will form the subject of this chapter.

One of the most ancient in *Braemar* was that of Durward. According to tradition, it originated thus. During the first stay of Malcolm Canmore in *Braemar* after he ascended the throne, some of his great men conspired against him, and, but for the faithfulness of one of his body-guard, would have succeeded in their purpose of assassination. When the turbulent thanes came in a body to Malcolm's chamber, the faithful man shut the door, and kept it closed against the united strength of them all, until Malcolm had time to give the alarm from a window, after which he was speedily rescued from his perilous position.

He was rewarded with the lands of *Coull* and *Migvie*, and was henceforth known as Allen Door-ward, contracted afterwards to Durward ; and from him sprang the Durward family, once possessed of considerable property in the *Braes of Mar*.

The ancient village of *Kincardine O'Neil* is said to have been built by him, a bridge also over the *Dee*, and a *spittal* in its close vicinity—both very impor-tant things in those days ; but no trace now remains

of either. Allen seems to have been an amiable
character, as all traces remaining of him are in connection with some kindly or noble deed.

Another legend gives the origin of a trio of names
—Lumsden, Mulloch, and Coutts. It runs thus : On
one occasion the Danes were terribly incensed against
Malcolm Canmore, and came against him with an
army of 30,000 men, under the command of General
Mulloch. The Scottish king could only raise 7000
men, whom he marched through *Athole, Glen Tilt,*
and *Braemar* to *Culblean,* where the Danes were encamped. Twelve men were sent to him from the
Thane of Argyle ; but Malcolm was so enraged at the
smallness of the number, that he ordered them home.
Anxious, however, to see the fight, the men hid themselves among those in the rear.

The Scots occupied the moor stretching from *Loch
Dawin* eastward ; the Danes, the heights sloping from
these hills to *Mill of Dinnet.* On a Monday morning
the battle began. The Argyle men, anxious to get a
good view of the fight, went up to a hill overlooking
the plain. It happened to be the one from which the
Danish general superintended the fight ; and all his
men being off with orders, they killed him at once.
A cairn was afterwards raised upon the spot, and the
hill is still called by his name.

Up to this time the Danes had been driving everything before them ; but as they were receiving no

orders, they stood still a breathing space. Just at
that time the Argyle men showed themselves on the
top of the hill, cheering loudly. The Danes began to
waver ; the Scots pushed on, led by Allen Durward.
Malcolm also left his station, and pushed forward with
his nobles. The heights were taken, and the Danes
fled.

At the *Hill of Mortlach* they made a stand, but
were so cut down that a brook running past it is still
called the '*Bleedy Burn.*' The pursuit continued
almost to the seaside, and by that time the Danes
were all but exterminated.

One of them, however, managed to get unobserved
into one of the old Picts' houses, and hid himself in
the opening in the roof for the egress of smoke, called
the '*Lum.*' Here he continued until the fury of the
people had passed away. Then he ventured to creep
out, and meeting with a kindly reception he settled
in the country, and was known always as the '*Lum's
Dane,*'—a name which, in the contracted form of
'Lumsden,' has been perpetuated in his descendants.

After the battle was over, Malcolm, much fatigued,
retired to his castle on *Loch Kinoird,* and, so the
legend goes, on lying down to sleep was sadly annoyed with a continued howling which assailed his
ears. Calling the captain of his guard, Allen Durward, he instructed him to go and '*coutts,*' *i.e.* still,
these dogs, as he could get no sleep for them.

G

The captain and some of his men proceeded forthwith to still the dogs, but found, to their great amusement, that the howling did not proceed from dogs,
but from some babies which had recently made their
appearance. As they knew his Majesty would fully
appreciate the joke, they returned to tell him of their
non-success, and to suggest that the only way they
could carry his orders into effect was by naming them
Coutts.

To this comical mode of *couttsing* Malcolm gave
his sanction, and the children were afterwards taken
under the royal patronage. On growing up, they
were put into possession of a great part of *Cromar*,
and kept themselves a distinct clan. This Clan
Coutts, during one of its feuds with the Clan Allen of
Corgarff, were cut off to one man near the *Vannich
Hill.*

While residing for a short time near the place in
Corgarff, I found that the local tradition of the battle
ran thus :—

Near a hill in *Corgarff* called *Diedhsoider* a smart
battle took place between the Clan Coutts and Clan
Allen of that place, about the year 1508 ; and some
miles farther up *Corgarff*, where the *Vannich Hill*
rises, near a hunting-shiel belonging to Sir Charles
Forbes, is a large stone known as the '*Clach Couttsich*,'
where the captain of the party was killed, the rest
having all been cut off save one. This one surviving

Coutts had three sons, from whom sprang three distinct families of Couttses, whose distinctive appellations, or *tee-names*, being none of the most refined, I may as well leave them unrecorded.

Another and still more curious origin of a name very common in Braemar, is found in the following legend. Before giving it, I may remark that Malcolm Canmore's forest-laws seem to have resembled those made by the Norman conqueror in severity, which made it death for any one to kill a stag, and a felony punishable with loss of limb to be found trespassing in a forest.

A young man named M'Leod had been hunting one day in the Royal Forest. A favourite hound of the king's having attacked M'Leod, was killed by him. The king soon heard of the slaughter of his favourite, and was exceedingly angry—so much so, that M'Leod was condemned to death.

The gibbet was erected on *Craig Choinnich, i.e.* Kenneth's Craig. As there was less of justice than revenge in the sentence, little time was permitted ere it was carried into execution. The prisoner was led out by the north gate of the castle. The king, in great state, surrounded by a crowd of his nobles, followed in procession. Sorrowing crowds of the people came after, in wondering amazement. As they moved slowly on, an incident occurred which arrested universal attention. A young woman with a child in her arms came rushing through the crowd, and, throwing herself before the king, pleaded with him to spare her husband's life, though it should be at the expense of all they possessed.

Her impassioned entreaties were met with silence. Malcolm was not to be moved from his purpose of death. Seeing that her efforts to move the king were useless, she made her way to her husband, and throwing her arms round him, declared that she would not leave him—she *would* go and die with him.

Malcolm was somewhat moved by the touching scene. Allen Durward noticing the favourable moment, ventured to put in the suggestion that it was a pity to hang such a splendid archer.

'A splendid archer, is he?' replied the king; 'then he shall have his skill tried.'

So he ordered that M'Leod's wife and child should be placed on the opposite side of the river; something to serve as a mark was to be placed on the child's head. If M'Leod succeeded in hitting the mark, without injuring his wife or child, his life was to be spared, otherwise the sentence was to be carried into immediate execution. Accordingly (so the legend goes) the young wife and her child were put across the river, and placed on *Tom-ghainmheine;* according to some, a little farther down the river, near where a boat-house once stood. The width of the *Dee* was to be the distance separating M'Leod from his mark.

He asked for a bow and *two* arrows; and having examined each with the greatest care, he took his position. The eventful moment come, the people gathered round him, and stood in profound silence. On the opposite side of the river his wife stood, the central figure of a crowd of eager bystanders, tears glistening on her cheeks as she gazed alternately at her husband and child in dumb emotion.

M'Leod took aim; but his body shook like an aspen leaf in the evening breeze. This was a trial for him far harder than death. Again he placed himself in position; but he trembled to such a degree that he could not shoot, and, turning to the king, who stood near, he said in a voice scarcely articulate in its suppressed agony, 'This is hard.'

But the king relented not: so the third time he fell into the attitude; and as he did so, almost roared, 'This is hard!' Then, as if all his nervousness and unsteadiness had escaped through the cry, he let the arrow fly. It struck the mark. The mother seized her child, and in a transport of joy seemed to devour it with kisses; while the pent-up emotion of the crowd found vent through a loud cry of wonder and triumph, which repeated itself again and again as the echoes rolled slowly away among the neighbouring hills.

The king now approached M'Leod, and, after confirming his pardon, inquired why he, so sure of hand and keen of sight, had asked *two* arrows?

'Because,' replied M'Leod, 'had I missed the mark, or hurt my wife or child, I was determined *not to miss you.*'

The king grew pale, and turned away as if undecided what to do. His better nature prevailed; so he again approached M'Leod, and with kindly voice and manner told him that he would receive him into his body-guard, and that he would be well provided for.

'Never!' answered the undaunted Celt. 'After the painful proof to which you have just put my heart, I could never love you enough to serve you faithfully.'

The king in amazement cried out, 'Thou art a Hardy! and as Hardy thou *art*, so Hardy thou *shalt* be.' From that time M'Leod went under the appellation of Hardy, while his descendants were termed the M'Hardys, Mac being the Gaelic word for son.

'Why, that is a corruption of the story of William Tell,' I rather uncourteously remarked, on hearing for the first time this M'Hardy legend.

The old lady who had just related it, retorted with considerable warmth, and ended by asking *when* the story of William Tell took place.

'About the year 1307,' I replied.

'There,' she said, with such an air of triumph, 'I thought that: the William Tell story happened in 1307, and ours in 1060 or thereabouts, more than 200 years before. Na, na! our story is nae a corrup-

tion of William Tell, though William Tell's may weel
be a corruption of ours.'

I ought to state, in regard to this story, that there
is a different rendering as to M'Leod's offence.   The
various reading is this : Malcolm Canmore had some
monstrous animal which he kept on a small island
on the *Dee*, near *Braemar Castle*, known to some of
the old people as '*Ille na Tadd*,' *i.e.* Island of the
Monster ; it is now called '*Ille na Meann*,' Island of
the Young Roe.

The inhabitants of *Braemar* were taxed for its
support.   They had to give in turn a cow, etc., to
satisfy its rather voracious appetite ; for it was of the
crocodile order.

When it came to the turn of M'Leod's mother to
supply the wants of the *Tadd*, she felt the imposition
to be very hard indeed, as she had only one cow ; and
in her bitterness she fully roused the spirit of her son,
by saying tauntingly in his presence, that it was a
pity there was none of the race of the M'Leod left,
or they would have had spirit enough to rid the
country of such a nuisance.

In the course of the following night young M'Leod
managed to despatch the monster ; and as his crime
was soon discovered, he was sentenced to death for
his temerity.   His house stood on the bank of the
Dee, near where the boat crosses to *Allen More*, *Craig
Choinnich* behind it, on which the king in his rage

immediately ordered the gibbet to be erected. In all the rest of the details the stories are coincident.

There is, however, a more likely origin for the name, which goes thus :—

In the fourteenth century the lands of *Corgarff* were held by the 'valiant Hardie,' who was of French origin, and obtained the name of Hardie or Hardy, while in attendance upon John King of *France*, who was a prisoner in *England* at the same time as David King of *Scotland*.

The two kings were confined together; and during a visit which Edward of *England* made his prisoners one day, he ordered his cup-bearer to fill up a glass of wine and give it to the most worthy. The cup-bearer filled up the wine and handed it to the Scotch monarch, on which the Frenchman gave him a hearty box on the ear.

'Tout, Hardy,' was King David's laconic reproof.

The exactness with which this appellation (which had the force of hardy or fearless one) answered to his character, fixed it from that moment on the French gentleman, who was ever afterwards known as 'Hardy.' He came over to *Scotland* with King David, who gave him the lands of *Corgarff* by charter and letters patent under the Royal seal in 1388 ; and his descendants, who still reside there, call themselves the M'Hardys, *i.e.* Sons of Hardy, the motto on their coat of arms being 'Tout, Hardie.'

Stuart is another name very common in *Braemar*. From an old record belonging to one of the residents, I noted down the following account of its origin:—

Duncan King of the Scots had two principal men whom he employed on all matters of importance— Macbeth and Banquho. They, travelling together in a wood one day, met three fairies : the first, after making her obeisance, saluted Mabeth as Thane of *Glamis;* the second, Thane of *Cawdor;* the third, King of *Scotland.*

When Banquho complained loudly of their unequal dealing in giving all the honours to Macbeth, one of them thus addressed him : ' Be content, Banquho ; for though you will never be King of *Scotland*, a race of kings will proceed from you that will rule it for ever.'

Macbeth was scarce warm in his seat as king ere he thought of the prediction given to Banquho ; and to prevent its fulfilment, caused him to be killed, and all his posterity. But by some means Fleance, one of his sons, escaped, and fled to *Wales*, where he prospered greatly, and was married to the prince's daughter of that court.

Fleance had a son named Walter, who returned to *Scotland* in the time of Edgar, Malcolm Canmore's son. And Edgar not only restored Walter to all Banquho's estates and honours, but made him steward over all his house,—the name and office of Stewart becoming hereditary in his posterity.

'From this Walter the steward descended Robert Stuart, who succeeded David Bruce in the kingdom of *Scotland.* For this Robert II., surnamed Stuart, became King of *Scotland* by descent from the eldest sister of David Bruce, and was also extracted from the ancient princes of *Wales*, by Fleance, as before said ; thus restoring British blood to the throne of *Scotland.*'

Thus the name of Stuart originated ; and in early times it was one of the predominant names in *Braemar.*

Two other surnames are the noble ones of Mar and Duff. The following account of their origin, which also I have picked up in the district, have more of a matter-of-fact appearance than some of the others. To that of Mar, as being earliest connected with *Braemar* history, I give the precedence.

Many years before the Christian era, a great warrior named Martach settled on the lands afterwards known as Mar. His descendants continued to hold possession until about the year 982, when Graeme, the Scots king, raised one of them to the dignity of Thane. At the time when Malcolm Canmore ascended the throne, Marticus, son of Gilchrist the first Thane, held the honour, and rendered Malcolm great assistance in quelling the intestine discords of his kingdom ; and, in particular, by bribing the captains of a strong body of men, who had encamped at *Kildrummy* on their way to join the rebels' camp at *Monymusk*, to leave the country quietly, etc.

After Malcolm's campaign on the banks of the *Spey* had terminated successfully, he repaired to *Forfar*, where in 1057 he convoked a great meeting of all the estates in his kingdom ; at which meeting a great many of the thanes were raised to the dignity of Earl. Among them were the Thanes of Mar, Fife, Angus, etc.

Another act which Malcolm passed, with consent of this Parliament, was that the peers were, for more distinction, to take surnames, which should descend to their families in succession. Mar was adopted by the newly appointed Earl Marticus. His lands had for a long time, from his great ancestor Martach, been called Mar ; but independently of the title he derived from them, his descendants from henceforth, in all their branches, were to bear the name of Mar.

In like manner, Duff, or M'Duff, was confirmed to the family of the newly appointed Earl of Fife, from their great ancestor Prince Fifus, who had also the additional one of Duffus, or Duff. As the family of Mar is intimately connected with *Braemar* history down to the year 1715, a brief sketch of it will be given at the conclusion of the earlier legends ; while the Duffs' connection with it, which only begins at that period, comes in more appropriately after.

CHAPTER IV.

SURNAMES CONTINUED.

M'Gregor—M'Donald—M'Intosh—Cumming, etc.—Destruction of Kindroket Castle.

BESIDES the fore-mentioned surnames, which may be looked upon in the light of local antiquities, there is another class or order of names which fixed themselves in *Braemar* under peculiar circumstances.

Foremost amongst these names is ' *Groig-airich-na-smuide* '—M'Gregors of the Smoke—so called from the circumstance that a fugitive M'Gregor, whose history will be briefly related, built a little shieling in a wood, the smoke proceeding from which was the first visible for a long stretch of road before reaching *Castleton.* This circumstance gave rise to the phrase ' *na-smuide.*'

The history of the M'Gregors' *entrée* to *Braemar* was related to me as follows :—

Sir Alexander M'Gregor, chief of his clan, had a feud with Sir John Colquhoun, which one time issued in a great battle. One M'Murrich, *i.e.* M'Pherson, was standard-bearer to Sir A. M'Gregor, and, by the way, had a secret grudge at his chief on account of neglect shown him on some public occasion. There was a school at *Dumbarton* attended by the sons of many great men ; and Sir Alexander was very anxious that these young men should be kept from the scene of battle, lest, taking part in the fray, there should be any fresh cause for bloodshed. So he set M'Murrich to watch at the school, to prevent any one for a time having egress. M'Murrich kept watch, but it was a black one ; for when the young men appeared he cut them down, and threw their bodies behind a gate or wall, I forget which. Sir A. M'Gregor and his people were the victors ; and his great anxiety after the battle was to know how M'Murrich had managed, and if all the young men were safe. At the earliest opportunity he questioned M'Murrich, who answered that he could pledge his word that not one of them had seen the battle, as his sword had done for every one that attempted to pass the gate. ' Waes me,' said Sir Alexander ; ' I was a prood man that I had gained the battle, but it's the blackest day for my puir clan that ever the sun shone on.' And so it was : the country was raised against the M'Gregors ; the whole clan was outlawed, and had to flee, followed by fire and sword. Thus M'Murrich had his revenge.

A son of Sir Alexander's escaped by the way of *Athole*, a poor fugitive, and took refuge in the hills and woods between *Crathie* and *Kindroket*. From skulking in the wood he got the length of building a shieling, the smoke of which being visible from the road, gave rise to the cognomination, M'Gregor of the Smoke.

There was another race of M'Gregors in *Braemar*, the *Gillean-ruadh*, or red loons, who were a terrible pest to the people. About *Culblean* and *Easter Morven* were their haunts for a time ; the ' *Vat Cave* ' is still pointed out as an occasional retreat of the famous Rob Roy M'Gregor, their leader. An extensive forest at *Culblean* is said to have been burned by them, and the inhabitants harried without mercy. At length one of them, getting a little more civilised, settled down, and from him sprang the second race of M'Gregors, still found in *Braemar*.

There are also two races of M'Donalds in *Braemar*, each with their own distinctive legend. One of them states that a little boy of the name of M'Donald was carried away by a wolf—wolves being at that time very plentiful. After carrying him off, the wolf did not destroy him, but treated him instead as one of her own cubs. So he grew up a veritable wild man of the woods, and not unfrequently joined the wolves in their predatory expeditions.

With such companionship and designs, he often

visited the house of his mother, and was hounded off by the dogs. By some means it was discovered who he was; and his relations, having traced him out to his lair, succeeded in communicating the circumstances of his birth and abduction. They prevailed on him also to leave his sylvan life, and settle down in a somewhat tamer manner.

He never would return to his mother, however, being apparently unable to get over the fact that she had hounded him off with dogs; and he often reproached her, it is said, in some Gaelic rhyme, which is a little too coarse for translation or insertion here. He married at length, and from him proceeded the race known as the '*Sliochd a' Mhadaidh Alluidh*,' *i.e.* the Race of the Wolf.

'The first thing that drew my attention to this story,' said the old man who related the legend, 'was being at the marriage of a relation of mine to one of the "*Wolf M'Donalds*." I mind weel, though I was but a laddie, o' hearing my uncle say to the bridegroom, "Weel, but ye hae gotten a bonnie wifie, though she be come o' the race o' the wolf." That raised my boyish curiosity, and I didna rest till I had a' the story of the wolf, just as you've gotten't the day.'

The other race are called the '*Gruthais*,' or Fir M'Donalds. The legend respecting them is, that a man of the name of M'Donald having killed another of the name of Grant, had to flee from his own country, *Strathspey*. The chief of the Grants and several men followed in pursuit. It was continued for a considerable time with no success; so the chief and his men, wearied out, lay down on the heather one day and fell asleep. M'Donald, who had seen them, crept up to the chief stealthily, and laid his sword across his throat. Then he retired to a height at some distance, and cried loud enough to be heard. All started to their feet, and were amazed to see the fugitive at a little distance. The chief, charmed at the forbearance of his foe, called on him to approach, shook hands with him, and so the pursuit ended. M'Donald did not, however, return to *Strathspey*, but settled down in *Braemar;* and from having skulked so long among the woods, he was called *Seumas Ghiuthais*, James of the Fir, and his descendants the *Giuthas*, or Fir M'Donalds.

There are also two races of M'Intoshes: the *Tir Igny* and the *Mariech*. The legend of the *Tir Igny* M'Intoshes accounts also for the name of Cumming being found in *Braemar*. I give it briefly; but before doing so, let me notice the origin of the name M'Intosh itself:—

Many hundreds of years ago, when strife and discord were the rule of the day in the *Highlands*, the Clan Chattan split themselves into various families, or septs, each assuming a distinctive patronymic, and acknowledging a separate head, or chieftain,—the result of which was a continued series of struggles for the supremacy.

In order, if possible, to remove the cause of this continual strife, the Scottish Government enacted that one special chief, or captain, should be appointed by warrant of the king to the supreme headship of the confederacy, and that all branches of the clan should acknowledge him as their chief, and be bound to obey and be led by him in the day of battle.

This dignity was conferred upon Shaw M'Duff, brother of Duncan third Earl of Fife. Shaw had married Eva, only daughter and heiress of Donald Dale, who had previously been considered as the hereditary chief. Shaw having thus obtained the leadership of the Clan Chattan, assumed the name of *Toiseach*, or First Man.

About the fourteenth century the *Tir Igny* M'Intoshes held an estate of that name near *Blair-Athole*. The Cummings, who ruled with a rod of iron, were lords superior. One of them is said to have killed sixteen lairds in one day, who lived on the stream of the *Tarf*, in order to get possession of their lands. But he was himself killed that same day by a fall from his horse as he rode through *Glen Tilt*. Cruelty was not the only ugly trait of the

H

Cumming character; another one is perpetuated by the Gaelic couplet :

> ' While in the wood there is a tree,
>   A Cumming will deceitful be.'

The 'Big Cumming,' son of the laird who was killed, on going, according to the usual custom, the round of his retainers at Christmas for the annual gift, got on one occasion from M'Intosh of *Tir Igny* the unusually large one of a bull and several cows. This only excited the cupidity of Cumming; and with a body of his retainers he returned that night, and put all the M'Intoshes to death, in order to add the lands of *Tir Igny* to his estate of *Blair.*

The nurse, however, escaped with the youngest child, and made her way to its mother's relations. On growing up to manhood, young *Tir Igny* and a party of his relations attacked the Cummings unexpectedly, who, being defeated, fled with their leader up *Glen Tilt.* Many of them fell during the pursuit ; and at last the Big Cumming escaped alone by the way of *Loch Lochin,* while young *Tir Igny* followed hard, determined to revenge the death of his family. As they were on different sides of the loch, Cumming sat down on a stone to rest for a moment ; and as he wiped the perspiration from his brow, an arrow from the bow of *Tir Igny* pierced his temples, and he fell dead. A cairn is said still to mark the spot. Some of the vanquished Cummings found their way into

Bracmar, and from them are descended the Cummings still found there.

Tir Igny again settled in his father's lands ; but he had not enjoyed them long ere he fell again into the hands of the Cummings, and was killed. His friends then fled to *Bracmar*, and having settled there, are still known as the *Tir Igny* M'Intoshes.

The other race of the M'Intoshes claim descent from Shaw, laird of *Glen Markie, Invermarkie,* and *Glen Feshie*, who having during a feud killed a M'Pherson of some note, the whole clan turned out to revenge it. Shaw with his people fled by the way of *Rothiemurchus* and *Abernethy*. At the head of the river *Nethy* they made a stand, but were defeated. Shaw escaped alone, and entered *Braemar* by the way of the *Larig Ru*, and assumed the name of M'Intosh to avoid detection. The descendants of Shaw are still known as the *Mariech* M'Intoshes. They were a poetical race, as they became afterwards the bards of the Farquharsons of *Inverey*.

A fitting sequel to these legends will be found in one still more quaint, respecting the destruction of the old castle of *Kindrocket*. At a period somewhat indefinite, the 'Galar Mor,' or Great Disease, ravaged Scotland. *Braemar*, despite all the purity and strength of its mountain air, was not exempted ; on the contrary, it seemed to rage there with intense virulence. Not only were its terrible effects felt, but the destroyer assumed a visible appearance, and hovered in the air like a blue 'haesp,' ever and anon lowering itself on some particular spot, bringing with it certain destruction. They adopted a very summary mode of dealing with it, on the principle, I suppose, that desperate diseases require desperate remedies. No sooner was it known that the ' Galar Mor ' had broken out in any house, than it was battered down, and all the inmates, infected or otherwise, buried in the ruins.

Unfortunately it broke out in the castle ; and as there was no respect of persons with the disease, so there could be none made in their mode of dealing with it. The doom of the castle was therefore sealed. A company of artillery was ordered from *Blair Castle;* they came up through *Athole.* Roads had to be cut in some places for their cannon (the cuttings, it is even said, are still visible in *Glen Fernat,* and at the *Coldrach,* etc., but I have not seen them). They went on to *Corrimulzic,* and turned down *Cornammuc,* a hollow in the side of *Morrone,* and were placed in position for operation on a small ridge on *Tomintoul,* called *Scra-vechty,* which fully commands the castle and plain.

When the work of destruction began, a lady stood at the castle door combing her hair. 'Aye,' said my informant, ' it was a *gowden came*' (golden comb). The first round brought a part of the walls down about her. Not one within escaped; and thus the castle of *Ceann Drochaide* was levelled to the ground.

Several extravagant stories are also extant about the old ruins. For example: many ages after the destruction of the castle, when the soldiers were stationed at *Braemar*, one of them was prevailed upon for a sum of money to explore the vaults. There was one hole open like a flue; its mouth is still to be seen, into which when a stone was thrown, it could be heard descending a flight of steps for a very long way. Down this hole he was lowered by a rope to the first steps, whence he proceeded, torch in hand, on his adventure.

In a short time the signal was given, and pale and trembling he was brought to the upper surface. On recovering a little, he declared that nothing would ever induce him to go back, he had seen such dreadful things. For instance, he had come upon one room or vault, in which was a ghastly company sitting round it in life-like position, dressed in a strange costume, but silent, motionless, and dead.

Here is another story, in which there is also a touch of the supernatural: About the end of the eighteenth century, the Watsons, a family who had the inn at *Castleton*, began to clear out the ruins, and found numbers of old coins, broken vessels, iron doors, smashed gratings, etc., with immense quantities of deers' horns, and bones of other animals. But a little old man with a red cap appeared, and bade them desist, if they valued their own welfare, etc.

The amount of truth in this story I was able to ascertain correctly, as an old man, William Gruer, still lives in the village who was at the clearing out of the ruins.   He has no recollection of the 'iron doors' or 'gratings,' etc., but he found a rusty old sword, very large, with two edges ; and a large silver brooch, such as are used in fastening the plaids. There was also an enormous quantity of deers' horns of great size ; while everything they came upon seemed to have undergone the action of fire.   Some eighty-two cart-loads of rubbish were at the time taken from the ruins, but no little old man with a red cap interfered ; only the carting was stopped by the laird of *Invercauld's* orders.

Subterranean passages are supposed really to exist.   One stair there was, also leading down to a considerable depth ; and as boys, he said, they used to amuse themselves by throwing down stones, to hear the noise they made in rattling over the steps.

About twenty years ago or more, an old woman had a cottage close to the ruins, built over one of these subterranean passages, and through some crevice about her fireplace the wind used to come rushing with great force, and on windy nights especially it would make her fire burn very brightly ; and the young people gathered round used to remark jocularly, that ' Malcolm was blowing his bellows.'

That cottage, by the command of the late proprietor, was taken down, as it marred the picturesque appearance of the ruins. From that time they remained intact, until the erection of two prosaic shops has greatly interfered with them.

This part of the legends may now be fitly concluded by a brief sketch of the Earls of Mar, into whose hands the castle of *Kindrocket* fell when it ceased to be a Royal residence.

CHAPTER V.

N 1096, when a great crusade of 30,000 Christians set out for the *Holy Land*, Marticus first Earl of Mar took the command of a party of Scotch devotees. In 1099 he was present at the taking of *Jerusalem*, and in returning home, died in 1100. He was succeeded by his son Gratanach, or Graitney, as second Earl of Mar. In 1118 his son Morgund succeeded as third Earl, and died in 1160. His son Gilchrist only lived until 1166, and was succeeded by his son Morgund, the fifth Earl, who served King William in many wars. In 1174 the battle of Morwick was fought, where His Majesty was taken prisoner, and continued in confinement until December 1175, when Morgund paid a ransom of £300,000, collected throughout the kingdom; and as a reward for his fidelity, he received from King William the lands of *Drumlanrig*. After a donation of many lands to the *Priory of St. An-*

drews for the salvation of his own soul and that of his wife Agnes Countess of Mar, he died in 1177, and was succeeded by his son Gilbert.

This Gilbert, sixth Earl of Mar, laid the foundation of *Kildrummy Castle* in *Mar*, 'which,' in the language of my informant, 'when entire, was the greatest object of national splendour and antiquity in the kingdom.' Gilbert died in 1181, and was succeeded by his brother Gilchrist, who built a priory for the Culdee canons regular of *St. Andrews*, in 1213. In 1215 he died, and was succeeded by his brother Duncan, who in the year after made the following donation : 'We, Duncan Earl of Mar, for the glory of God, and for the salvation of the souls of His Majesty King William, Morgund Earl of Mar, and Margret his Countess, and for all the souls of the faithful, and for prosperity to His Majesty Alexander II., freely grant the lands and tythings of the Church of *Leochel* to the Culdee brethren of *Monymusk Priory*, dedicated to the Virgin Mary.'

He was succeeded by his son William as ninth Earl of Mar, who by His Majesty Alexander III. was created Great Chamberlain of *Scotland* in 1264. He died in 1268, and was succeeded by Donald, his son, as tenth Earl of Mar, who again in 1294 was succeeded by his son Graitney, whose sister Isabella married Robert Bruce, afterwards King of *Scotland*. Graitney was a steady supporter of Bruce, and was rewarded with the hand of Christina, daughter of Robert Bruce, Earl of Carrick. He also received the lordship of *Garioch* by charter from His Majesty.

In 1313 his son Donald succeeded, although in confinement, as he had been taken prisoner by the English at the battle of *Methven*, and kept until the battle of *Bannockburn*, when he and Isabella, wife of Robert Bruce, were given in exchange for the Earl of Hertford. He was called Donald Bain, or White Donald, and was a person of great honour and integrity, a steady friend also of Robert Bruce, and was rewarded with charters of the Thanage of *Alveth* in *Angus*, *Selene* in *Fife*, and *Mount Blairly* in *Banffshire*. Through his daughter Helen, the Earldom of Mar afterwards descended to the Erskine family. In 1330 he was elected Regent of *Scotland*, but fell soon after in an engagement with Baliol, and was succeeded by Duncan, his son, as thirteenth Earl of Mar.

In 1342 Duncan was succeeded by Thomas, who, having offended his Royal master, was attainted, and in 1361 went into exile. In 1371 he returned home, and was restored to all his honours, and more than the former degree of Royal favour. On his death in 1377, Sir James Douglas, the husband of his sister Margaret Mar, succeeded in right of his wife as fifteenth Earl. This Earl of Douglas and Mar committed great ravages in *England*, but fell at length with his son at *Otterburn*, when the Earldom of

Mar devolved on Isabella Mar, daughter of Thomas the fourteenth Earl. Malcolm Drummond of *Drummond*, her first husband, became sixteenth, and Alexander Stuart, her second husband, seventeenth Earl of Mar. On Isabella's death, as she had no family, the earldom was claimed by Robert seventh Lord Erskine, he being descended from Helen, daughter of Graitney the twelfth Earl of Mar. In 1435 he was succeeded by his son Robert as eighth Lord Erskine and nineteenth Earl of Mar ; and on being served heir to Lady Isabella Douglas, Countess of Mar, before the Sheriff of *Aberdeen*, April 22, 1438, he afterwards, viz. in 1465, received a charter on the Earldom of Mar, comprehending *Strathdon*, *Strathdee*, *Cargarff*, *Braemar*, *Cromar*, and the lordship of *Garioch*.

When James III. ascended the throne, his brother John was made twentieth Earl of Mar, and in 1480 he was bled to death by command of the king his brother, on the charges of conspiracy and witchcraft. Immediately after his death, Robert Cochrane, a favourite of James III., was made by him Earl of Mar. After the death of Cochrane, who was hanged on the *Bridge of Lauder* by a number of Scottish noblemen, John Stuart, illegitimate son of James III., was made Earl ; to whom succeeded Thomas Erskine ; and again, when James IV. ascended the throne, he presented the Earldom to John Stuart by

the Countess of Boulogne.   This twenty-fifth Earl of
Mar died at *Edinburgh* in 1508, and was succeeded
by Alexander Erskine as twenty-sixth Earl of Mar.
Alexander, son of John Lord Elphinston, was
twenty-seventh, while Alexander, his son, who fell
at the battle of *Pinkie*, was twenty-eighth Earl of
Mar ; and again, Robert, his son, the twenty-ninth.

In 1541 George Gordon, Earl of Huntly, was
created thirtieth Earl of Mar, and in 1542 was
appointed administrator, collector, and trustee for
Mar, the lordship of the *Garioch*, the lands and
bailiwicks of *Braemar* and *Cromar*, all of which the
last Earl had forfeited.   Changes were, however, the
order of the times ; for in 1561 James Stuart, illegitimate son of James V., was made thirty-first Earl.
To him succeeded Robert Erskine as thirty-second
Earl, and his son Robert as thirty-third.

June 4, 1563, John Erskine took his seat in
Parliament as thirty-fourth Earl of Mar.   He was
governor of *Stirling*, and while Regent, founded in
1572 the building at the head of the *High Street* of
that city, known as '*Mar's Work.*'   Before his death
he appointed his brother Alexander to be governor
of *Stirling*, until his own son came of age ; and also
recommended to him and Lady Mar, his wife, the
charge of the young king, now about seven years of age.

The Regent was succeeded by his son John as
fourteenth Lord Erskine and thirty-fifth Earl of

Mar. The young Earl received his education with the king, whom the Estates of the kingdom had committed to the care of the Dowager Countess of Mar. For the part this Earl took, when grown up, in the raid of *Ruthven* and subsequent events, he was sent into exile, and his estates forfeited to the Crown ; but on sending a very contrite letter to His Majesty he was pardoned, and soon after returned home. Not only was he restored to all his lands and honours, but to such a degree of Royal favour and confidence, that on the 9th of October 1595 King James gave his son Henry in charge to the Earl, by the following letter, written by his own hand :—

'MY LORD OF MAR,—Because on the security of my son, I have concredited to you the charge of his keeping, upon the trust I have in your honesty. This I command out of my own mouth, being in the company of those I like. Otherwise than from any charge that comes from me, you shall not deliver him ; and in case God calls me at any time, see that neither for the Queen, Estates, their pleasure, you deliver him till he be eighteen years of age, and then he can command himself.

'Given at *Stirling*, July 24, 1595.'

In January 1603, the mother of this Earl, the Dowager Countess of Mar, died. The fashions in those days had not been so evanescent as they are now, or her last legacy had not been of much value. I give one or two of the items :—

'I, Dame Amabelle Murray, Countess of Mar, relict of John umquhile Erl of Mar, Regent of *Scotland,* lavis in legacie to Marie Erskyne, my oy (grand-child), my goun of black damas, with the black grogram taftie, to be ain new goun.'

'*Item,* I laive to Annie Erskyne, my oy, my goun of damask taftie round taillet, the foir breists thairof lynit with plush, and to her twelf elas of whyte gro-gram taftie of my auin making.

'*Item,* To my sister, the Lady Abercairney, my goun of chamlet of silk, pastmentit wt bred velvet pastments, the brestis thairof lynit with plush, wt my doublet and skirt of plain black velvet.

'*Item,* To the Parson of *Innernauhtie* (*Inver-nochtie*) and Agnes Bruce his spouse, by attour my former legacie, aught bolls of meale.

'*Item,* To William Brogg, chirurgeon, four bolls eat meale.

'AMABELLE MURRAY C. MAR.'

On the 1st of April James took his journey for *England* with the Earl of Mar and a great retinue. Before, however, they had gone as far as *York*, the Earl of Mar was compelled to return to *Scotland* to

appease Queen Anne, who had demanded from Lady
Mar, Henry, Charles, and Elizabeth, her children ;
which Lady Mar could not grant, as the Earl had
left her with instructions not to resign them into the
hands of *any* person without an order under his own
hand.

Having accommodated matters with the Queen, he
prepared to return to *England ;* but considering his
having to turn back as an omen of evil—of death,
in short—he believed it necessary to make his will.
This will is curious, but too long for insertion here.
Happily his fears were not verified : he continued to
live and enjoy the king's favour, and not a little
degree of his confidence too, as the following copy
of an autograph letter from James shows. It was
written in September 1607, when Prince Joinville,
brother to the Duke of Guise, came over to *England*,
and with the French ambassador made a visit to
His Majesty in *Edinburgh :*—

'DEAR JOCK,—As I'm gaing to gie an audience
this morning to the French ambassador, I desier you
to be sae gude to send me a pair of yeir best silken
hose, with the goud clocks at them.—Your affectionat
cusine,   ' JAMES R.'

The Earl died at a very advanced age, in the year
1634, and was succeeded by his son John as fifteenth

Lord Erskine and thirty-sixth Earl of Mar. On the breaking out of the rebellion he joined the Covenanters, but soon left them for the Royal party, with whom for the remainder of his life he acted steadily. He was succeeded by his son John, who was also attached to the king's interest. For this adherence he was sentenced to pay a fine of 24,000 merks. After other fines, his whole estate was sequestrated, and during Cromwell's time he lived in a small cottage at the gate of *Alloa House.* His estates were restored by Charles II. He died in 1664, and was succeeded by his son Charles as seventeenth Lord Erskine and thirty-eighth Earl of Mar. He was also attached to the interests of Charles II., and was made a member of his Privy Council in 1682. He raised, at his own charge, a regiment of foot, and continued colonel of it until his death. The regiment is still known as 'The Royal Scots Fusiliers' —the 21st.

After his death, in 1689, his son John succeeded as eighteenth Lord Erskine and thirty-ninth Earl of Mar. Shortly after his accession he was appointed one of the Privy Council for *Scotland;* and among many other honours and offices, was one of the sixteen Scots Peers in the first British Parliament. He continued in favour until the death of Queen Anne, when, being deprived of all his offices, he went north to the *Castle of Kildrummy,* and soon after, unfortunately for himself and country, went to *Glenlivet*, and proclaimed the Chevalier de St. George under the title of James VIII.; the sequel of which event belongs to another part of this volume.

PART THE THIRD.

———•———

THE RISE OF THE FARQUHARSONS.

'Those mighty chiefs who once had sway,
But vanished now like mist away.'

CHAPTER I.

Finla, the first Chief of the Farquharsons.

THE origin of the Farquharson family is thus given in Buchanan's *Rise of the Clans*: 'The Farquharsons, a numerous clan on the banks of the *Dee*, trace their origin from the German *Catti*, or Clan Chattan. Macduff Thane of Fife, their Phylarch, had an ancestor named Sheagh or Shaw Macduff, second son to Constantine third Earl of Fife, and great-grandchild to Duncan Macduff, last Thane and first Earl of Fife.

'This Sheagh was captain under Malcolm IV., in the expeditions against the Murrays of the province of *Murray*, in A.D. 1163. For his valour Malcolm made him governor of *Inverness Castle*, and gave him the lands of *Peaty*, *Brachly*, with the forest of *Stratherin*, which belonged to the rebels. The country people gave him the name of M'Intosh, or Thane's son, which continued to his progeny; yet some of them claimed the name of Shaw.

'One of them was Shaw of *Rothiemurchus*, whose offspring settled in *Strathdee*, and were named Farquharson. From Ferquard Shaw, the eldest son of this family, are the Farquharsons of *Invercauld, Inverey, Monaltrie*, etc., descended.'

With this aristocratic mode of tracing the Farquharson descent, the *Braemar* legends, though somewhat plebeian, tally strangely, and are not a little interesting.

About the beginning of the fourteenth century, a poor man came from *Speyside* to *Braemar*. His name was Fearchar Shaw, *alias* a Gaelic phrase, signifying *gleyed*, or one-eyed Fearchar. He was a basket-maker, or rather wicker-worker,—a trade of no small importance in those days, as reins, currachs, harness, and even houses, were made of wicker-work.

While cutting twigs near the *Linn of Dee* one day, he unfortunately lost his footing, fell in, and was swept away by the relentless torrent. Search was made for his body, but it was unavailing, until his wife bethought herself of soliciting the aid of Mary. So she repaired to the *Virgin's Well* at *Glen Ey*, and spent the night there, praying Mary to intercede with her Son to discover the body of her husband.

Her importunity (so the legend goes) was not un-rewarded; for, as she passed along the side of the river on her way home in the morning, she saw the body of her husband, rolled in his plaid, lying on a sandy flat near the *Dee*, which was henceforth called *Sliabh Fhearchair, i.e.* Fearchar's Plain. The body was soon after buried in the churchyard of *Invercy.*

The widow, with her son Donald, continued to live at *Cnoc Mucan* in *Glen Cluny;* and when the boy grew up he entered the service of Stuart, who was then laird of the estate now called *Invercauld.*

The laird, Stuart, had only one child, a daughter, and very beautiful. One can scarcely admire the young lady's taste in fancying Donald, Fearchar's son, yet she did so ; and the clandestine attachment ended in an elopement. And as Donald had taken the precaution to build a shieling beforehand in *Glen Candlic*, they took up their residence there, Donald supporting his young wife by hunting. A stone of that shieling is still to be seen, and is that mentioned by Her Majesty the Queen.

One furious winter evening, a considerable time after the elopement, Mrs. Farquharson requiring medical aid, Donald set out to procure it for her. At no great distance from the shieling he met a woman dressed in green. I forget what passed between them, but Donald held on his way ; and shortly after the woman entered the hut, and 'rendered Mrs. Farquharson all necessary aid. The woman, after having dressed the child, handed him to his mother, told her it was a son, and that if she would take care not to touch or look at him until her return, she would give him a weird which would make him the greatest man in the kingdom.

After the woman's departure, the young mother, naturally desirous to see her son, gratified her curiosity to the full, and had scarcely put the child back into the same position when the woman returned, looking much displeased, and said :

' Now, I know you have been looking at him, though I have not been here to see, so I can do little for him now to what I would have done ; but he and his posterity will prosper, and be great to the tenth generation.' This child was Fhionladh Mor, *i.e.* Finla the Great, founder of the Clan Farquharson.

Shortly after the birth of Finla, the Laird Stuart was reconciled to the young couple, and they returned to his house. When the old gentleman died, Donald, his son-in-law, succeeded as laird ; and as from his father he was called Mac Ferquhair, *i.e.* in English, Farquhar's son, the name was continued to his descendants.

Donald, the new laird, was not permitted to take possession quietly ; but finally he succeeded in putting down all who opposed his claims, and held for a time undisturbed possession. After his death Finla was duly installed laird in his stead, and his brother Fearchar got the little lairdship of the *Coldrach* in *Glen Cluny.* But the laird of *Rothiemurchus* being related to the old laird Stuart, again laid claim to his estate, believing that he had a better right to it than the Farquharsons.

Might was right in those days; so the two rival parties met on the banks of a small stream north from *Invercauld.* After a severe conflict, victory declared for Finla Mor. The stream was henceforth named *The Burn of the Defeat;* hence originated the name *Inverchalla, i.e.* The Mouth of the Burn of the Defeat; in English it is *Invercauld.* The *Rothiemurchus* men were pursued up the *Dee;* and the laird, poor *Seumas-na-Gruaig, i.e.* James of the Flowing Locks, fell at the *Craggius,* and the feud ended.

Finla's troubles were not yet over, however. The *Glen of Aberairder* was full of small lairdships. Most of these proprietors being related to the laird Stuart, looked upon the Farquharsons as usurpers, and so were very envious of their prosperity. From this source arose innumerable strifes and battles, until the country was becoming desolated. But on Finla being appointed Bailie for *Strathdee* by the Earl of Mar, he resolved to bring this state of matters to a summary close—all the more readily when he had found out that these lairds had much to do with raising the *Rothiemurchus* feud.

Finla Mor accordingly summoned them to meet him in *Aberairder.* A large barn served for court-house; nineteen of them promptly attended at the appointed time. The Farquharsons came in great strength to enforce obedience to their mandates.

The trial commenced, and the guilt of all as implicated in some foul deed, being clearly proven, sentence was passed accordingly. The mode of administering justice was summary: they were called in singly; and no sooner was sentence passed than it was carried into execution, by hanging them up on the rafters of a part of the barn partitioned off from the rest, and that to the number of eighteen. The last and nineteenth, seeing none of his companions reappear, began to suspect something was wrong, and succeeded in making his escape.

These executions made a tremendous stir among the relations of the culprit, and the Farquharsons were cited to appear before a court sitting in *Aberdeen.* As those executed really deserved their doom, they could not make out a charge of assassination against them; so a charge of private administration of justice and secret execution was agreed upon. But the force of this charge, equal in guilt to that of murder, was evaded by the defenders stating that the place in which the execution took place had more windows in it than there were days in the year. This statement in a sense was actually correct, as the barn, like many of the houses in *Aberdeenshire* at the time, was made of wicker-work, and of course had openings innumerable.

This cunning defence procured the Farquharsons' discharge; and the Earl of Mar was so pleased with his deputy's vigorous measures, that he gave him all the vacant lairdships. The good did not end there; for the rest of his turbulent neighbours were so over-awed, that the internal peace of *Braemar* was not again infringed during the life of Finla Mor.

Though Finla had thus made peace at home, his prowess was yet sufficiently tried from another quarter. The wealth of the Highlanders in those days consisted principally in flocks and herds; so predatory expeditions into their neighbours' lands were but too common, as then

> 'The good old rule, the simple plan
> Obtained, that they should take who have the power,
> And they should keep who can.'

It was generally, however, the cattle of hostile clans and rival tribes that these ancient heroes plundered. Only when at feud with each other did they plunder, or 'harry,' as they phrased it, those of their own race. On the other hand, the cattle of the lowland farmers were considered lawful property, and the Saxons themselves usurpers, by whom they had been unlawfully dispossessed.

Finla Mor, therefore, had still work enough, and that sometimes of a dark enough nature, to prevent the *Rannoch*, *Speyside*, or *Lochaber Katrin* from en-riching themselves at the expense of the Braemarians.

One or two incidents, displaying the best side of his Katrin surveillance, may be noticed.

One evening some of his shepherds brought the information that they had observed a party of Katrin skulking among the hills. The laird went out alone to reconnoitre, and soon discovered five young men. With his usual good fortune, he succeeded in coming upon them unawares, and, snatching their arms from them ere they had time to use them, drove them home before him prisoners.

Having reached home, he observed to them that he saw no reason why they should not at once be justiced, *i.e.* hanged. They pleaded in self-defence that they had done no harm.

'Only for want of opportunity,' retorted Finla. 'Armed men do not prowl about my place for nothing.'

'That is quite true, chief,' said one of them : 'it was our design to carry off some cattle, as we were in great straits at home ; but as we have taken nothing, have pity upon us. Let us go, and we will never come back.' On that condition he allowed them to depart.

To this system of cattle-lifting no idea of moral turpitude was attached ; so far from it, that they were scarcely considered *men* until they had successfully accomplished something of that nature : hence the couplet :

> 'To toom a fauld, and sweep a glen,
> Are just the deeds of pretty men.'

A curious incident, illustrative of this, happened to Finla after his successful rencounter with the five men in the *Balloch-bhuie* forest.

While out hunting one day, he went down into a hollow to quench his thirst at a spring. As he stooped down to drink, a man of gigantic proportions leaped upon him from among the heather. Finla jerked himself round and seized the man, who muttered, 'Grip hard, for you will find now that you have a man.'

'Not a man, but a cowardly dog,' replied Finla, 'who steals behind to attack his foe.'

'An advantage that Finla Mor did not despise when he attacked boys,' retorted the stranger.

'I understand,' said Finla, 'and one of these boys wishes now to repay me.' So the two tightened their grasp of each other, the Kern above and Finla below. Thus they struggled and twisted, until, entirely exhausted, it seemed as if the duel must end through sheer fatigue. But the wondrous power of endurance and activity of Finla prevailed against the almost gigantic strength of his antagonist; and he held him pinned to the ground, exhausted and breathless.

'Do your pleasure,' at length cried the stranger, 'I am at your mercy.'

'Do you yield yourself my prisoner?' demanded Finla.

'Yes, since I can do no better.' So the two bent their steps to *Invercauld*. Finla, curious to know the cause of the surprise at the fountain, made inquiry. So the stranger, by way of explanation, told him that he was the eldest son of a chief, and was also about to marry the daughter of another chief, but had never done anything to prove himself a man.

'When,' continued he, 'the five young men returned whom you made prisoners, I was surprised at the account they gave : one to five was no ordinary feat. Here is a chance now, I thought, as hitherto I had not met my equal. And I imagined that if I could only contrive a private meeting with Finla Mor, take him prisoner, and exact a ransom, I would then have done something to prove myself worthy of my bride. So, after announcing my purpose to my future father-in-law, I set out for *Braemar ;* and you know the rest.'

'Your failure will be punishment enough then,' said Finla, 'but I'll not promise any more adventurers the same lenity.'

'You need not,' replied the stranger ; 'for when people hear that I have lost with you, there are not many more in the *Highlands* likely to seek the same trial.' So the young chief was hospitably entertained, and allowed to go on his way in the morning.

Before relating the sequel to this affair, I may notice another piece of good fortune which tradition says happened to Finla. One evening, in the gloaming, a stranger came to claim the hospitality of *Invercauld*. A very suspicious-looking character he was, being wrapped in a great cloak, with a slouched kind of hat over his face, and seemed altogether very desirous of concealing his person as much as possible.

Notwithstanding all these drawbacks, a claim of the kind could not be refused in the *Highlands*. So the lady, with no very good grace, went about the preparation of supper. Soon after, Finla returned home, and hearing of the suspicious-looking stranger, went in to make his personal observations. After a brief inspection of his guest's physiognomy, he gave his wife to understand that she must mend her manners. So the best cheer that *Invercauld* could produce was set before the hungry stranger, who did ample justice to all, and then retired to rest, apparently much pleased with his entertainment.

Next morning Finla accompanied him a considerable distance, showing him how to get to *Strathavon* by the *Bealach Dearg* and *Inch Rory* route, discoursing as they went on of Finla's present standing and future prospects, of the Rothiemurchus clams to the estate, etc.; and at length they parted with mutual expressions of good-will.

Not long after, a letter was forwarded to *Invercauld* bearing the Royal seal. On opening it, Finla, my informant stated, found himself promoted to some great honour—' she wasna richt sure what it was, but she thoucht it was to be Royal Standard-bearer of *Scotland;*' then confirmed in the possession of all his property ; and lastly, that all that remained of Crown rights in *Braemar* were made over to him, in consideration of the hospitality shown to His Majesty, for no less a personage had been the suspicious-looking stranger.

It was not, however, until after the death of the king, when the Regent called out the Scots to resist the English king, and thwart his purpose of marrying his son to the Princess Mary, that Finla, with the flower of *Strathdee,* joined the army as Royal Standard-bearer of *Scotland ;* and while Finla and his men lay in *Edinburgh,* waiting for the assembling of the troops, an incident occurred which forms a fitting sequel to the rencounter at the fountain.

He was one evening promenading the streets at a pretty late hour. Some one, coming in an opposite direction, wished to 'crop the causey.'[1] To this Finla would not yield, unless the aggressor could prove his right to it by superior prowess ; so the two drew their swords. Finla was alone, but this unknown had a

---

[1] Of the expression, 'crop the causey,' the following passage gives a satisfactory explanation :—

'Glance, now, at a Scottish town in those days. It is girdled with a fortified wall. It contains one or more residences of the nobility. . . . A cantle of the causey, or single row of stones, runs along the middle of the narrow street. This "cantle" is appropriated to foot-

suite. Nothing daunted, Finla planted himself firmly
on the contested spot, and, drawing his claymore, he
made it describe a circle round him, within which no
one had the temerity to venture, while every weapon
put forth to parry was either splintered to pieces or
sent whirling into the air.

A private signal, however, was increasing the number of assailants to an alarming extent, while Finla's
shout of 'Braemar!' brought no response. About
thirty or forty men were now assembled, and there
seemed nothing for him but to succumb. But as he
once more raised his cry, 'Braemar!' the door of a
neighbouring hostelry opened, and a tall, strong man,
after a moment's reconnoitre, rushed forward and
placed himself by the side of the chivalrous Farquharson, raising, as he did so, his own war-cry.

It brought a whole swarm of Highlanders to the
rescue, and the enemy at once retired, when his
unknown friends *en masse* conducted him to his
lodgings. When he wished to know to whom he had
been so greatly indebted, one of them said jocularly,
'Oh, we have seen Finla Mor before this.' In that
voice he recognised the young chief who surprised

passengers, while horses bearing their loads on panniers plod along the
muddy strand on either side. A broad-bonneted burgher steps along
the cantle; but, meeting a monk in the robes of his order, he yields it
with an abject air, and steps off into the dirt. The armed retainer of
some neighbouring laird swaggers along the cantle; but he, too, humbly
yields to his superior.'

K

him at the fountain ; and among the others were the five men whom he had once made prisoners in the *Balloch-bhuie* forest.

A few days after, the gallant Finla was slain at the battle of *Pinkie*, and was buried at *Musselburgh*.

CHAPTER II.

Donald Farquharson of *Castleton*, and collateral Traditions.

AVING traced the successful career of Finla Mor, and noted the solid foundation laid by him for the future aggrandizement of his clan, I may notice next the traditions respecting the history of his family. They were not by any means slow to avail themselves of the advantages their chivalrous father had procured for them, or to strike out new paths for themselves. William, the eldest son, married a daughter of Lord Sutherland, and probably left *Braemar*, as he does not again figure in the traditions. James, the second son, bought the *Castleton* from Cluny Gordon, and settled there. A third son, Alexander, took up his residence in *Glen Tilt*. John, the fourth son, left *Braemar*, and settled in *Craigniety*. From him sprang the Farquharsons of that name.

A second family, of five sons and a daughter, were disposed of in the following manner. Donald, the eldest, succeeded his half-brother James in the *Castleton*; Robert, the second, succeeded to *Invercauld*; Lauchlin obtained with his wife the property of *Broughdearg*; George got *Deskry* and *Glen Conry*; while Finla, the fifth son, bought with his wife's dowry *Achreachan*, in *Glenlivet*. From one of his sons sprang the *Allergue* family of Farquharsons.

Beatrix, his daughter, though remarkable for her beauty, was not so fortunate in her settlement. She had herself to blame, however: although she had a large choice of partners of suitable rank, with a perversity by no means uncommon, her preference fell upon her father's shepherd, a poor but handsome youth.

Though poor, Kenneth M'Kenzie was in one respect equal to Miss Farquharson, as he claimed descent from Kenneth II. Be that as it may, Finla was very angry when he came to understand the state of matters. But as the maiden was inflexible in her purpose of marrying the shepherd, Finla gave in with a good grace. He had not quite forgotten the result of a like unequal match in the case of his own father.

The shepherd, when consulted as to where he would like to reside, replied in Gaelic, '*Air an Dail Mhor goram*,' etc., *i.e.* on that big haugh far west, etc. Thus originated the name and family of *Dalmor*. The place is now called *Mar Lodge*.

As the first family of Finla left only daughters, the genealogy of the Farquharsons is continued through the second. The traditional account of Donald, the eldest, will form the subject of this chapter, as he succeeded to the chieftainship of the clan.

About the year 1541, Donald Farquharson, on succeeding to the property of his half-brother James of the *Castleton*, was appointed bailie of *Strathdee* by George the fourth Earl of Huntly, who had lately been by special commission made Lieutenant-General of all the *Highlands*.

This office of bailie was a great accession of power to Donald. It has been thus explained : The Lords of Regality, with the great barons and chiefs, had jurisdiction conferred on them by the Crown. This power they sometimes exercised in person, and sometimes by deputy. The persons to whom they delegated their authority were called ' bailies.'

The office could be no sinecure, however ; for every part of the *Highlands* was the scene of a constant petty warfare between the different clans, and often between families of the same clan. Feuds were considered family property—a sort of sacred heirloom ; while all the rancorous feelings engendered by them were cherished carefully until an ample revenge was secured.

In illustration of these remarks, I may notice a feud between James of the *Castleton* and Donald of the *Coldrach*. I mentioned in a former chapter that Fearchar, brother of Finla Mor, obtained the lairdship

of the *Coldrach* in *Glen Cluny*, and when Fearchar
died his son Donald succeeded. His cousin James
having settled on the opposite side of the river, the
two quarrelled about marches; and as might was the
only right then, James killed Donald, and that for a
season settled the matter.

Donald of *Coldrach* left a son called Fearchar.
When he grew up, he married a daughter of the laird
of *Abergeldie;* and when he had obtained this increase
of power, the 'troubles' broke out afresh. It was
not long until he also lost his life in the quarrel; for
while crossing the *Dee* in a corrach (a small framework of wicker-work covered with skin) to labour
a piece of the controverted land, the weight of his
arms and implements upset the corrach, and he was
drowned.

The contest even then was not given up, but continued by his son William Buidhie, *i.e.* Yellow-haired
William, until he lost his life also, on which the feud
ended. The *Coldrach* family left *Braemar*, and the
lairdship was sold for a trifle to William Buidhie's
sister, who, despite all the quarrelling, had married
Donald of the *Castleton's* son, her cousin William,
who acted as fiscal to his father.

Before touching on Donald's more public character
as bailie of *Strathdee*, I may slightly notice his domestic history, alliances, and settlements of his family.
Milton's description of the celebrated banyan tree I

have often thought very applicable to the Farquharsons. He says :

> ' The fig-tree, not that kind for fruit renowned,
>   But such as at this day to *India* known,
>   In *Malabar* or *Deccan* spreads her arms,
>   Branching so broad and long, that in the ground
>   The bended twigs take root, and daughters grow
>   About the mother tree.'

Donald of *Castleton*, like his father Finla, had two
families. The first consisted of seven sons and a
daughter; the second, of three sons and a daughter. A
third wife he repudiated, on account of a feud with
her clan. She was the mother of William of *Coldrach.*

His eldest son and namesake succeeded him in
Castleton; his history comes in anon. The second
son, Robert, became the progenitor of the *Fenzean*
Farquharsons. As we do not again come across him,
I give his history now.

From some disagreement which took place at
home, Robert left his father's house. As a curious
illustration of the customs of the times, it is said
that on finally quitting it he shut his eyes, and,
turning round three times, threw his staff into the
air : the direction in which it fell indicated, of course,
the route it was best for him to follow. It happened
to fall so, that going straight before him he arrived
at *Dundee;* and when there, though at first doubtless
not a little galling to his Highland pride, he became
first a plodding, but ultimately an expert carpenter.

Fortune, however, had no intention of dealing harshly with Robert. It so happened that a great man and his daughter, a young widow, came to *Dundee* to visit some relations. It also happened that, in going to and returning from his work, having to pass the young lady's window, the handsome carpenter made, all unconsciously, an impression which nothing would eradicate.

The lady became ill, and pined away; and though several doctors were called in, none of them had skill enough to reach the seat of her disease. But by some means her father began to suspect the real cause; and on his very peremptory demand to be made acquainted with it, she made a full confession.

'Pretty work,' said the chief, 'but just let me know the first time you see him passing.'

Next morning, to Robert's great surprise, he was accosted by a fine-looking old gentleman, who asked him to go into his house. On going in, he was informed what mischief he had been doing; but Robert had not the least compunction, for the old gentleman's proposal for a family alliance met with a flat denial.

The old man took it very quietly, merely saying, 'Very well; only you must see Maggie, and give her the denial yourself.' He then ordered his daughter to make her appearance. No sooner did the really beautiful Maggie make her *entrée*, than the father stepped out ; but somehow or other Robert never gave her the denial. Instead of that, he soon after made her Mrs. Farquharson, and received a very handsome dower on his marriage-day.

Soon after these events he returned to his native place, and set up as a miller at *Crathie*. But, not prospering there as he expected, he went farther down the *Dee*, and erected a mill in *Birse* on the Fenzean estate. The laird of *Fenzean* lived far too fast, and, being often in want of money, had to borrow from his tenants. The repayment was often rather uncertain.

Mrs. Farquharson was a pretty good tactician ; so she resolved to take advantage of that circumstance, and as a first step sent her husband with an overflow-ing purse on the rent-day. The laird did not fail to notice that, and, as Mrs. Farquharson expected, soon applied for a loan. It was given with the greatest alacrity, on the security of the mill and adjoining farm. Shortly after another loan was required, and given on the same conditions, the mortgage of another farm. This was so often repeated, that Robert, who was not in the secret, got alarmed at the rapid de-crease of his gold. His wife's explanation, however, relieved him not a little.

At last there came a time when no more farms remained to mortgage, and Mrs. Farquharson at the same time found that she had no more money to lend—that, in fact, she would require to have some of

the former sums repaid.   That could not be done ; so
the laird had to take his departure from the castle,
while the miller and herself entered into possession of
the estate of *Fenzean.*

To return to Donald of *Castleton.*   Alexander, his
third son, became laird of *Allen-cuiach ;* James, the
fourth son, got *Inverey ;* the fifth, John, became the
founder of the *Tullycairn* Farquharsons.   The history
of these settlements comes out fully in connection
with their father's public life.

As the Earl of Huntly, from his confidence in the
bravery and prudence of Donald, had appointed him
to the difficult office of bailie, so it was accepted in
good faith ; and whatever may be said of the justice
of Donald's measures, they were vigorous enough, as
the following instances will show.

Two brothers, of the name of Lamont, had come
from *Perthshire* and settled in *Braemar.*   One of the
brothers had the property of *Inverey,* the other that
of *Allen-cuiach.*   A wealthy drover, of the name of
Rory, was in the habit of lodging with *Allen-cuiach* on
his way to and from the south markets.   One evening,
after drawing an unusually large some of money,
he arrived at *Allen-cuiach,* and was, as on former
occasions, hospitably entertained.   Next morning he
departed, accompanied by the laird's son, young
Lamont, who was to show him a nearer cut by the
Bealeachdearg and *Strathaven* route.

A few days after, the drover's body was found by two shepherds, with a deep cut in the back of his head. Rory had been murdered without doubt, and the great matter was to find out who had done it. As the young laird of *Allen-cuiach* was the last person known to be in the drover's company, Donald of *Castleton* summoned him to appear.

The Lamonts and Farquharsons had long been on very indifferent terms. Jealous of the growing power of the Farquharsons, and doubtful as to the justice of some of the measures taken to increase it, a spirit of distrust had taken possession of the Lamonts; and now that the young laird was summoned to appear before Donald, fearing that he would not get fair play, he refused to do so.

The unfortunate lad, aware that his people could never withstand their powerful neighbours, and knowing also that William of *Coldrach*, the indefatigable fiscal, would soon be in search of him, fled to the hills. It was not consciousness of guilt which led to this course (his innocence was afterwards fully proved), but dread of the Farquharsons' arbitrary measures.

Just as he expected, a party of Farquharsons, led by the fiscal, were speedily in pursuit; and as their knowledge of the district equalled Lamont's, they soon ferreted him out, and at last succeeded in hemming him in beside a deep pool formed by the

Dee, a little to the east of *Cairn-a-quheen*. Driven to desperation, he leaped into the pool with the intention of swimming to the other side ; but he never reached it : the poor lad was drowned. His old father died of grief, and the confiscated lairdship was given to Alexander Farquharson, Donald's third son.

Many years after, a number of Katrin were apprehended in *Moray* for cattle - lifting. Among them was the gillie who accompanied the murdered drover. Before his execution he confessed to the murder of Rory. After Lamont had left them, tempted by the large sum of money in his master's sporran, he, while walking behind him, drew his sword, and with a single blow felled him to the ground. He then took the money and went and joined a band of Katrin. Although the innocence of Allen - cuiach was thus fully proved, the Farquharsons retained possession of the property until towards the close of the last century, when it was sold by them to the Earl of Fife.

It has been said that the greatest insult which could be offered to a clan, collectively or individually, was to speak disrespectfully of its chief, each considering it a personal insult which they were bound to resent and revenge. If this was the general rule, Donald of *Castleton* made no exception to it. One instance of this, given at the expense of personal feeling, brings it out pretty clearly.

In 1562, a great battle was fought between the Earls of Moray and Huntly (Donald's master) at *Corrichie*. Huntly's army was defeated, and himself slain by some of the Forbeses, who were in the opposing party.

On hearing of this, Donald immediately put away his wife, as she was a niece of the Lord Forbes, which of course led to deadly feud with her tribe, or clan ; and it was during the wars which ensued that the war-cry of *Cairn-a-quheen* was adopted, though the cairn itself had been in existence earlier, as from the time of Finla Mor it was the spot where the *Strath-dee* men assembled for war.

Shortly after the repudiation of his wife, Donald and his men assembled at *Cairn-a-quheen*, and proceeded to *Lonach* on *Donside*, where a fierce battle was fought, the Farquharsons claiming the victory. The results of it certainly favoured their interest. After this battle the feud was suppressed for a time, but it broke out again with great virulence ; Arthur, brother of Lord Forbes, and the laird of *Strath-girnock*, being the aggressors.

Donald, as before, took the side of the Gordons ; and when a fierce battle took place at the *Crabstanes* between the Forbeses and Adam Gordon of *Auchindoun*, deputy to his brother the Earl of Huntly, Donald rendered the latter essential service. At this onset one of the Gordons took Alexander Forbes,

laird of *Strathgirnock*, prisoner ; and as he had been
a principal means of stirring up the strife, he was
sentenced to death.   The sentence, however, was not
carried into execution.   Adam Gordon, in virtue of
his power as deputy, after a short confinement at
Auchindoun, set him at liberty.

Instead of being grateful for his deliverance, Forbes
treasured up the injury of being taken prisoner in his
heart, and only waited his time to take a terrible
revenge.   To wipe out the stigma of a defeat, or revenge the death of a relation, were considered sacred
and paramount duties ; and the working out of these
perverted ideas gave full scope to the wildest passions
of the human heart.   And perhaps one of the ugliest
traits of the Highland character, was the patience
with which they could wait for the fitting opportunity
of revenging themselves, and at the same time conceal
their vengeful intentions under a guise of friendship.
Thus waited Forbes of *Strathgirnock* for his opportunity.   At length it presented itself.

The lands and castle of *Knock* adjoined *Strathgirnock ;* and on the death of the laird, Henry Gordon,
his brother, the capturer of Forbes, succeeded to the
estate.   The new laird had seven sons ; and as it was
not then considered below young gentlemen to engage
in what is now considered menial employments, they
went out one day to cast divots or sods, and all un-
wittingly set to work on Strathgirnock's land.

Here, then, was the long-looked-for opportunity of an ample revenge. Forbes, calling out a number of his people, surrounded the lads. Unarmed, of course they could make little resistance ; and with his own sword he cut off the heads of all the seven, then ordered them to be attached to the top of the spades they had been using, and set in a row along the side of the hill.

Such was the fearful spectacle presenting itself when a servant arrived with their dinner. The sudden return of the servant, and his terrible state of excitement, brought the laird out of his chamber to inquire what was wrong. On hearing the dreadful fate of his sons, Gordon, completely overcome, fell over the banister of the stair on which he was leaning, and was killed. Thus Forbes was revenged.

Gordon of *Abergeldie*, a near relation of Knock's, hanged Forbes in his own house, to avenge in turn the death of his relations, and then took possession of the lands both of *Knock* and *Strathgirnock*. This he did with some show of justice, as Donald of *Castleton* being now old and infirm, Abergeldie had been appointed bailie in his room.

With some account of the raid of the Clan Chattan into *Strathdee* and *Glen Muick*, I will conclude this legendary account of Donald of *Castleton*, as it accounts for the acquisition of *Inverey* by his son James. The great power conferred on the Earl of

Huntly as Lieutenant-General of the north of *Scotland*, the promptitude and severity with which he put down the insurrections of the chiefs, etc., raised him up many enemies.   Among them was M'Intosh, chief of the Clan Chattan ; and he being convicted of heading a conspiracy against Huntly, was beheaded by him in 1550.   From that time the clan watched for a favourable opportunity of revenging his death.

Huntly having retired for a time to his possessions in the north, resolved on erecting a castle at *Ruthven*, in the neighbourhood of the forest of *Badenoch*. This gave great offence to the Clan Chattan, as they believed his intention in erecting it was to overawe them ; and from being at first somewhat dilatory, they at last positively refused to render the service required of them as vassals of Huntly in building it. This led to an open feud, in which they persuaded the Earls of Athole and Moray to assist them.   This feud, which cost the Earl of Moray his life, ended in the defeat of the Clan Chattan ; but so far were they from being subdued, that, as soon as they had recovered a little strength, under the command of Angus Donald M'William, they invaded *Strathdee* and *Glen Muick*, because they were the friends and allies of Huntly.

Lamont of *Invercy*, considering this a fitting time to avenge the treatment which his relations of *Allen-*

Quoich had met with from Donald of *Castleton*, joined the M'Intoshes; and having swept *Braemar*, they descended the *Dee* through *Crathie*, to visit on a similar errand *Glen Muick, Glengairn*, and *Tullich.* They took, however, the precaution to send spies before them. There is a legend connected with these spies which will be best told here :

A son of Adam Gordon of *Auchindoun* had committed some misdemeanour, for which he was for ever banished from his father's presence. Young Gordon, who from that time led a very unsettled life, came one night upon the old castle of *Braichley.* As was customary in the Highlands, he was hospitably entertained ; and so agreeable did Gordon make himself to the baron, that he would not allow him to depart in the morning.

The baron, an old man, had lately married a young wife, and to this lady Gordon succeeded also in making himself equally agreeable. In consequence of this, some dark ideas were forming themselves in his mind. These incipient plans were suddenly brought to maturity by the following circumstance : One evening, while about the *Milton of Tullich*, he observed two men wandering about ; he made up to them, and after some talk brought them into the hostelry and treated them liberally.

These two men were the spies of the Clan Chattan, and Gordon succeeded in bribing them to murder

L

the old baron.   After committing the deed they returned to Gordon, who, instead of rewarding them as he had promised, pretended the greatest horror at their crime, and with the help of the baron's servants put the two men to death.   A short time after, Gordon married the young widow, and so became laird of *Braichley*.   His share in the death of the old baron at length became known, and being henceforth shunned and detested both by his wife and tenantry, he died miserably.

To return to the Clan Chattan.   In revenge for the death of their spies, many of the proprietors of *Glen Muick* were killed, their castles and houses burnt to the ground.   *Braichley* alone escaped, as it was well fortified, and garrisoned also by the tenantry.

About the time of this raid Donald of *Castleton* died ; and it fell, therefore, upon Abergeldie, now Bailie of *Strathdee, Strathaven*, and *Badenoch*, to see that the Clan Chattan and their accomplices were punished for this outrage.   The better to secure the aid of the Farquharsons, Abergeldie offered his daughter Catherine in marriage to James the fourth son of Donald of *Castleton*.   The proposal was at once accepted ; for, besides the match being in other respects eligible, the Farquharsons had suffered in the raid along with the rest of the *Strathdee* people. So the whole clan turned out in its strength.

The first offender to be dealt with was Lamont of

Invercy. With the force now assembled, there was little difficulty in seizing him. No proof was needed of Lamont's guilt ; his part in the raid had been too conspicuous for that : so his punishment was summary. He was led out to a pine tree, not far from his own dwelling, and hanged on one of its branches. The tree still stands, with the branch on which poor Lamont was hanged stretching out sternly beyond the others ; and from the tragical circumstance just related, and another which took place at the execution, it has been named the '*Dark Doom's Pine.*'

Lamont was the only son of his widowed mother ; and when the party marched him off to execution, she followed them, pleading, as only mother in such circumstances could plead, to spare his life, and take all they had in place of it. Seeing all her entreaties to be unavailing, and believing that the Farquharsons were the principal agents in the whole affair, she cursed them in the bitterness of her spirit, and also, in a sort of Gaelic rhyme, predicted the downfall of the clan. The substance of the rhyme was, that the tree would be green and flourishing when not one of the Farquharson tribe would be found on the banks of the *Dee.*

This prophecy is regarded by many of the people as accomplished, as of the Farquharsons of *Monaltrie, Invercy, Auchendryne, Balmoral, Allen-Quoich, Tullochcoy,* etc., not one remain, and even *Invercauld* has become

extinct in the male line.   Captain Ross, who married
the daughter and only child of the last laird of
Invercauld, assumed the name of Farquharson.   The
Fenzean Farquharsons, however, are of the old stock ;
and as they had nothing to do with this affair at
Inverey, they are supposed to have escaped the ban.

After the summary proceedings with Lamont,
Abergeldie and the Farquharsons, joined also by the
M'Donalds, continued the avenging march, and laid
waste all the lands of the M'Intoshes or Clan Chattan
in *Badenoch*, the Grants also in *Strathspey*.   Then,
joined by the Earl of Huntly, they devastated all
Pettie ; after which they returned home laden with
plunder, or, as they termed it, ' spulzie.'   James Farquharson, as beforehand arranged, married Catherine
Gordon, and received with her, as a portion, the confiscated lairdship of *Inverey*.   Besides being the first
laird of *Inverey*, he was also the ancestor of the Farquharsons of *Auchendryne* and *Tullochcoy*.

Another and very different version of this raid is
given, which is indignantly repudiated by the Braemar
people as a total misrepresentation of the whole
matter ; and it must be admitted that local traditions
and historical notices of it bear them out in that.

CHAPTER III.

Donald Oig.

OF the second Donald of *Castleton* little is known, except that he exchanged *Castleton* with the Earl of Mar for *Monaltric* about the end of the reign of Queen Mary. His son, however, Donald Oig, was much more celebrated; and round his quaint name not a few vague and mysterious legends still linger. These cannot be received as true, yet probably there existed some foundation for them. Others of them, being more historical in their nature, afford almost an epitome of his life and times. In the following chapter I give a specimen of both.

The first public appearance of Donald after being appointed bailie for the lands of *Strathaven* was in 1630, in connection with the burning of the *Tower of Frendraught.* The history of that 'dolorous tower' is as follows :—

James Crichton of *Frendraught* and George Gordon

of *Rothiemay* were near neighbours, part of their lands marching with each other. A dispute occurred about a very trifling matter, which led to an irre-concilable difference. They had recourse to law. Crichton prevailed, and succeeded in getting Gordon pronounced outlaw. Gordon, feeling that he had been very harshly treated, resolved to set the law at defiance, and, gathering a number of restless spirits, he exceedingly annoyed Frendraught. He in turn collecting men, a fierce onslaught took place, in which Rothiemay and another Gordon of some importance were killed.

Young Gordon of *Rothiemay* collected in turn a number of men to revenge his father's death. With this collection Donald Oig had something to do. An arrangement at length took place ; but in a short time the quarrel broke out anew, when one of the parties who assisted Frendraught, not thinking himself sufficiently rewarded, wished a new arrangement for himself, instead of which they came to blows, and one of his party was shot. Frendraught, afraid of the conse-quences of this fresh quarrel, went to the Marquis of Huntly to beg of him to try and get matters settled. The Marquis undertook the mediation, but did not succeed. He procured a meeting, but Leslie would listen to no terms : he *would* be revenged, and rode off in great wrath. Huntly, afraid that they might waylay Frendraught, kept him some days, and then sent his son John Viscount of Aboyne, and the laird of *Rothiemay*, home with him to protect and defend him if necessary.

Frendraught persuaded the gentlemen to remain with him all night in his castle. The sleeping apartments of the Viscount and three other gentlemen, with their servants, were in the old tower. About midnight the whole of it instantaneously took fire, and the Viscount, with five others, perished in the flames. The Marquis suspected Frendraught to be the author of the fire; but though a special commission[1] was appointed to search out the cause, it completely failed, as torture, and even the death of some of the suspected parties, failed to extort any confession.

From this circumstance Frendraught's property was considered fair game. The Gordons and their friends were particularly active in annoying him.[2] At length they were cited to appear in *Edinburgh* to answer for their conduct, Donald Farquharson among

---

[1] 'The Marquis of Huntly, resolved to prosecute Frendraught, went to *Edinburgh*, anno 1631, accompanied by many of his friends, and gave in his petition to the Council. . . . They granted commission to the Bishops of *Aberdeen* and *Murray*, the Lord Carnegy, and Colonel Bruce, to go to the House of *Frendraught*, and then ingenuously to try how the tower took fire,' etc.

[2] 'After this, several companies of Highlanders fell down upon Frendraught, and spoilt and destroyed his whole lands, driving away all the horse, nolt, and sheep they could find to *Briack* fair, and there sold them, a cow for a dollar, and a sheep for a groat.'—*History of the Illustrious Family of Gordon.*

the rest. 'But having set caution for a thousand pounds, Donald fled, and left his brother James, a writer in *Edinburgh*, to be warded until he paid the fine, which he did, and was set at liberty.'

Donald Oig acted thus by Huntly's request, whose interests in the north would have suffered too much by the bailie's absence to permit a few pounds to stand in the way. 'The Marquis and Mr. James Farquharson, it is said, settled that matter quietly between themselves, the wadset of Whitehouse of *Cromar* being his recompense.'

When 'the troubles' broke out, Huntly furnished his trusty servants with arms, provided by the king; and about that time, the early part of March 1639, it is stated :—

'Donald Farquharson of *Tilliegarmouth*, bailie of the Marquis' lands of *Strathaven*, having got some muskets, pikes, and other armour fra him while he was dwelling in *Aberdeen*, and his servants bringing home their armour to him out of *Aberdeen* at his direction, Alexander Strachan of *Glenkindie*, a great covenanter, masterfully took them by the way, whereat the said Donald took great offence.' And about the end of April, it is again stated, 'Donald Farquharson and some Highlandmen of the *Braes of Mar* came down to the *Mearns* and plundered the Earl of Marischal's bounds of *Strathauchen*, whereat the Earl was highly offended.' This by way of reprisals, as

Donald believed the Earl had much to do with the *Glenkindie* affair.

After the 'trott of *Turriff,*' where the first blood was shed in the civil war, on the 16th of May 1639, he and the laird of *Abergeldie* joined the barons in the *Mearns* with 'a thousand footmen, all fyrelockes and archers, brought from the neirest of the Marquiesse his Highlanderes of the country of *Straithaven, Strathdye, Glen Muick*, and *Glen Taner.*' He accompanied his friends the barons in their visits to *Durris, Echt, Skene,* and *Monymusk;* and he made it a special point not to forget Alexander Strachan of *Glenkindie,* and, as it is humorously stated, 'lessened wonderfully his cares for the mamon of iniquity by taking all the valuables of the place under his own especial charge.'

'After the pacification between the king and Covenanters, Donald Farquharson of *Tilliegarmouth,* the Lord Ogilvie,' and a number of their friends, took ship for *England* on Monday, 19th October 1640. After arriving in *England,* Donald, according to traditional accounts, must have performed wonderful exploits. One or two of them I subjoin, though credulity itself would have some difficulty in receiving them.

Shortly after reaching *London,* Lord Ogilvie entered a gambling-house, and in a short time not only lost his money, but had to make over a bond on his lands to cover this debt of honour. Seeking out

his friends, Ogilvie acquainted them with his mis-
fortune.

'Show me the house!' cried the indignant Monaltrie. Soon after entering it he agreed to a game of
piquet, and they retired to a room which Donald had
previously had prepared. There were three gamblers,
and it was agreed the winner was to play successively
with the remaining two, and double the stakes at
every game. Of course Donald was made to gain the
first two.

'You have such luck, Farquharson,' said the third,
dealing out the last card, 'I suppose you won't object
to match this.' And he threw down Lord Ogilvie's
bond.

Donald glanced over his cards without affording
the vanquished players, who stood behind him, an
opportunity of affording intelligence to his antagonist.

The *jetté* and *reprise* ended, Monaltrie rang the bell,
the signal for Gilbert Menzies and Lord Ogilvie to
appear. 'The game's mine ; cards tabled !' cried he.

'Impossible !' murmured his opponent.

Donald's friends entered, and pushing away the
gamblers, took their place behind them.

'Look here, then : eight cards, and all following
each other, count twenty-six ; four aces make a hundred ; playing adds thirteen ; and forty for *capio, i.e.*
all the tricks—in all, one hundred and fifty-three : the
game at one hundred and fifty. Take your bond,

Ogilvie.' Then Donald's own gold, and what he had gained from the blacklegs, showered into his sporran ; and the 'bonnie Scots laddies' marched away, none daring to meddle with them. He had contrived, as the story says, to have a mirror placed behind the chair which the blacklegs had in turn occupied : to the intelligence it had afforded him he was obliged for his success.

The next exploit suited Donald Oig's tastes better. 'An Italian champion came to *London.* A wonderful man he was, combining in himself the extraordinary qualities of wizard, magician, and necromancer. Though a stranger, "he cropped the causey," and none dared to impede, as he had not only challenged the bravest cavalier in the kingdom to combat, but slain also all that came to meet him.

'And what was still worse, this stranger lived magnificently, like a prince, and that at the expense of the city. This grieved them greatly, as the laws of chivalry were such that he might so live until vanquished by a champion of the challenged city. So the citizens offered a measure of gold to the man who would successfully do its battle ; but none such could be found.

'The king also was annoyed exceedingly, not only for the burden falling upon his good subjects, but also by the proud stranger passing before his palace daily, preceded by a drummer, challenging gallant knight to the combat, while the poor fellows could only "hang their heads, and the ladies, clothed in black, shudder at the dolorous sound."

'One day, while this stranger knight was the subject of conversation, the queen lifted up her proud head, and looking round on the assemblage of goodly knights before her, said, "And is there none in all our realms, for love of king and country, for love of lady fair, or yet for love of *me*, would draw his sword against this stranger knight of Italy?"

'"There is none," replied an eldren lord, "but a certain Scot, newly come up to *London*, Donald Oig of *Monaltrie*." So immediately a messenger was despatched to summon Donald to the Royal presence.

'As the king's messenger was returning, accompanied by a tall Highlander, they met the procession. The challenge was given, and the drummer about to beat again before repeating it, when Donald, drawing his sword, thrust it through and through the drum. "There," said he, "hae deen wi' yer din."

'The Italian, stepping up before his drummer, demanded who he was who had dared to offer such an insult.

'"Sir stranger, I am Donald Farquharson of *Monaltrie* and *Tilliegarmont*, the chief of the Clan Fearchair, and ready and willing to meet thee in such wise and when and where it listeth thee." So the engagement was set for an early hour next day. Meanwhile

Donald went on with the king's messenger, and was not a little surprised and pleased to hear that he had anticipated the wish of the queen and the king's request.

'That evening Donald made the acquaintance of the Italian champion's servant, and from him obtained the secret that his master's life was a charmed one, as he was in compact with his dark majesty: the compact being, that no man bearing iron on his person could hurt him, nor man walking in leather shoes prevail against him; no sword that iron ever touched or leather ever received pierce him; and if by any means he was pierced, when the sword was withdrawn from the wound he was to revive again; and finally, while fighting, he was to have a shade on each side, which would lead his opponent to suppose that he had three to contend with.

'Donald having possessed himself of all this information, turned it to his own advantage; and he with several others had a busy night of it. And in the morning, when many people came to accompany him to the place of meeting, the peculiarity of his costume struck them not a little.

'When they reached the rendezvous the Italian was waiting; and if Donald's friends had been surprised at the strangeness of his garb, he seemed still more so. They at once engaged, and three opponents, as he had been led to expect, appeared before Monaltrie ; but he, profiting by the servant's information, heeded only the middle one.

'It was a desperate fight. The Italian with his two shadows made dreadful downward plunges, while the Celt kept parrying and thrusting undauntedly ; and so the combat went on. The spectators, fascinated by the terrible struggle, gazed in breathless silence. Again and again came the dread downward thrust, met by the quick, sure parry. At last the Scot's sword glittered through the Italian's side.

'"Withdraw thy sword, Scot," roared the Italian.

'" Let the spit go with the roast," replied Donald, still mindful of the servant's information. So the champion, groaning out, "The devil has kept ill faith with me ! " fell back and expired.

'While the air was yet ringing with shouts of applause, the gold was brought forward and presented to Donald ; and while he was taking possession, some one in the crowd shouted, " See how the Scots beggar pockets our English gold !" Donald, on hearing this, immediately sent it whirling among the crowd. There was a regular scramble, while Donald in turn shouted, " See how the English dogs gather up the gold which they could not win themselves, but a Scot won for them !" From this brilliant exploit the chief of the Clan Farquharson was styled " *Domhnull Og na h-Alba*," *i.e.* Young Donald of Albion.'

According to tradition, Donald's adventures at Court did not end with this affair. He is said to be the hero of the tale in the *Legend of Montrose*, relative to the superiority of Scotch to English candlesticks. The story at least is said to have been current in *Braemar* before the novel was written; and that it took place in *London*, some recruits from *Aberdeenshire* to the ' Garde Ecossaise ' officiating as the candlesticks,—Donald having both made the bet and fallen on the scheme to win it.

The only other notice of Donald during the pacification is in 1643, when he, with Gordon of *Craigie*, and Gordon younger of *Arradoul*, brought into *Aberdeen* a party of soldiers, who were shipped for *France* to recruit the ' Garde Ecossaise,' in which his eldest son held a command, and who died in *France*.

After the renewal of the war he joined Huntly, who was then storming *Dundee*, 20th of April 1644. On the 16th of September, it is again stated, that when Montrose was about to leave *Aberdeen*, there came to him Gordon of *Abergeldie* and Donald Farquharson of *Tulligarmouth*, with divers other friends and followers: all gentlemen distressed for the favouring of the House of Huntly. The next notice of him is given by Patrick Gordon, relating to the part he took in the battle of *Fyvie*. After several other notices of his doings, Donald's death is thus recorded :—

'To reconnoitre and watch the motions of the enemy, Montrose had on the 12th of March sent Sir Nathaniel Gordon, along with Donald Farquharson, Captain Mortimer, and other well-mounted cavaliers, to the number of eighty, to *Aberdeen*. This party, perceiving no enemy in the neighbourhood of *Aberdeen*, utterly neglected to place any sentinels at the gates of the town, and spent their time at their lodgings in entertainments and amusements. This carelessness did not pass unobserved by some of the Covenanters in *Aberdeen*, who, it is said, sent notice to General Baillie, who was lying at the *North Water Bridge* with Lord Balcarras' and other foot regiments. Hurry put himself at the head of an hundred and fifty horse and foot, and rode off to *Aberdeen* in great haste, where he arrived on the 15th March, at eight o'clock in the evening.'

Hurry posted sentinels at the gates to prevent any of Montrose's party escaping, and entered the town at an hour when they were all dispersed through it, carelessly enjoying themselves without apprehension. The noise in the streets occasioned by the tramping of horses was the first indication they had of the presence of the enemy ; but it was too late for them to defend themselves. Donald Farquharson was killed on the street opposite the *Guardhouse.* ' A brave gentleman,' says Spalding, ' and one of the noblest captains among all the Highlanders of *Scot-*

land, and the king's man for life and death.' I give Spalding's account of his death :—

'Hurry having done this exploit in *Aberdeen,* the gentlemen were sorry, but could not mend it. They returned back to Montrose, some on horse and some on foot, ashamed of this accident. Montrose was highly offended for the loss of Donald Farquharson more than the rest, through too great carelessness. Upon the morn, being Saturday, the said Donald Farquharson's corps was found in the street, stripped naked, for they tirred from off his body a rich stand of apparel put on the samen day. His corps was taken up and put in a close chest, and carried to the chapel, there to ly in the *Castle Hill.* The other dead corps were put into their chests, and carried to the samen chapel on the *Castle Hill,* while they should all be buried. . . .

'Upon the morn, being Sunday, this gentleman, with the three other corps, was lifted out of the castle aforesaid, and conveyed to their burial. Donald was buried in the Laird of *Drum's* aisle, with many woe hearts and doleful shots.'

The following eulogistic account of Donald's death and character is something of a curiosity, being given in a peculiar old Scotch dialect :—

'Some of the cawalyres, while they stayed there, went to *Aberdeene* with Collonell Gordonne and Collonell Farquharson, who out of *Strathawin* (where he

M

was balzie to *Huntly*), *Aboyne,* and *Diesyd,* had always
a standeing regiment.   This mane's affable, naturall,
and weel-composed condition had so much oblidged
all men .that ever he was acquainted with, as gene-
rallie he was beloved of all sortes of people, and could
not be otherwayes, for he was of such a harmlesse
and innocent carriage, as there was non alyve whom
he could hate: he was never seen to be angrie,
nor knew he what that unrulie passion meaned, and
yet he gawe proofe of alse much true curraige as any
man could hawe : he was so farre from pryd and
waineglorie as he was all men's companion, not out
of a sillie simplicity, but out of a gentle and myld
freedome, in a nature which did alvise dispose him
to a jowial alacritee ; for his conwersation, even in
the saddest and most desperat tyme, was ever jocund
and ˉcheireful. . . . . All his actions were obledge-
ments.   He spent his patrimony, not laushly, for he
was no prodigall, but with such freedome, and such
a kynd of naturall bountie, as one that knew
that money was coyned for men, and not men for
money. . . .

'He was upon a sax monthes' stay at Court, so
became so weel lyked of his Soueraine Lord as he
ever after called him "*his man.*"   And at the Parliament in *Edinburgh,* His Majestie heareing of a fray,
and how he by some malitious Covenanters was
threatened in it, became suddenly inflamed, and

cried out, "Who dars be so bold as to touch my man Donald Farquharson?" . . . In fine, neither is my judgment nor my experience able to give a true charectore to the lyfe of this gentleman's singular and most commendable parts; only this I can say, that as he never procured ane enemy through his owne procurement. . . . Sir John Hurry, who was sent for, leiving the Covenanting armie, conveyes himselfe with a chosen troope of horse to *Aberdein* under night. Collonelle Gordone, and som that feared the worst, conveyed themselves away; som keipt their lodgings, and wer not sein upon the streats. Only Collonelle Farquharson stayed: wherefore, upon the allarum in the streat, he comes boldly forth, with som of his freinds and servands; and seeing a band of armed men, who at his approach inquyres his name, lest they should mistake, he who hatted no man, and therefore looked for hattred of no man, teles them plainly, becaus he had not yet learned to lie; upon which they incompasse him and his small train on all syds. They wer wnarmed, and had no weapones but swords, which when they drew, this neuer-enough-praised gentleman is shot dead with a pistole, a neir cussing of his greviously wounded and taken prisoner: the rest they let go, having gotten him whom they sought. . . .

'When this newes cam to the camp, their was non that was not struck with sadness, sorrow, and extreim greif for the losse of so brave a caveleire, so reall a freind, and so solatious a commreade. The Generall himselfe and my Lord Gordone wer both very sensible of this loss. The Majore Collquitto procured order for himselfe to tak a strong partie and goe for *Aberdein,* wher iff he could not overtake the murderers, he might sie him honourably interred. Hurrie, forseing the danger, made no stay in the towne, but reteired back, who was followed, but could not be overtaken. The majore gave to this weell-deserving gentleman the interment of a soldger, with the trailing of pickes and thundering vollie of muskets.' 'Montrose mourned for him the same length of time as he did for his son Lord Grahame, a youth of sixteen, who died at *Gordon Castle* a very short time before.'

Donald Oig was succeeded by his second son Charles, as his eldest son Donald died in *France.* From the sacrifices made by his father in the Royal cause, Charles was obliged to sell *Monaltrie* in 1702 to Alexander Farquharson, younger brother of Invercauld ; and so the first chiefs of the ' Clan Fearchair ' became extinct.

The Farquharsons of *Inverey* then assumed the chieftainship ; consequently their history comes next under notice. But it may be well to give, ere entering upon it, some of the traditions collateral with those of Donald Oig. As the Legend of the *Camruadh, i.e.* one-eyed, red-haired man (contemporary of Donald, and fellow-soldier also, though principally employed in battles·at home), will give a pretty good idea of the employments of the people while their bailie was from home, his history will furnish matter for the next chapter.

CHAPTER IV.

The Cam-ruadh.

THE fact sometimes forces itself upon our attention, that there is a constant repetition in .nature of the same object and form. In reading history, a similar tendency to repetition is observed. Characters are produced successively, agreeing in so many particulars, that but for local and chronological differences, we would conclude them to be identical. Thus I found lately, while reading a small volume, *Highland Legends of Glenmore*, that *Strathspey* had its legend of a famous archer, 'Littlejohn M'Andrew,' whose appearance, character, and exploits agree in most points with that of John Grant, *alias* The Cam-ruadh, a famous archer in *Braemar*.

From all that I can gather, the personal appearance of the Cam was anything but prepossessing. His stature did not exceed five feet, the various parts of his limbs being many removes from symmetry or correct proportion. I shall not attempt a more minute description.

He had only one eye, but it had wonderful capabilities. As a proof of that, it could discern 'a bluebottle on a grey stone at a distance of twenty yards.' He could also send an arrow twice as far as an ordinary person, and with accuracy sufficient to 'hit a midge;' and then, though his feet were flat, and his legs not exactly straight, none could beat him at a long race, and but few at a short one.

In character, the Cam was a man of deeds, not words; in disposition not over pleasant, for it was a combination of the mule and wasp, with a double portion of Reynard. Such was the Cam-ruadh, who lived and died also, it is said, at *Aldmhaidh* in *Glen Cluny.*

During the troublous times of 1644, a number of *Argyle* men, called 'Cleansers' from the fact that they left nothing behind them, ravaged the *Aberdeenshire Highlands.* They did not often dare to show themselves above *Crathie,* yet wandering parties occasionally pounced upon the cattle and flocks of the lower parts of *Braemar,* while raids on a large scale were made into *Glenshee* and *Glen Isla,* etc.

Among these foraging expeditions the Cam, with his wonderful powers of archery, did great execution; so much so, that, sick of the sights that met him on every hand, he vowed that, except in self-defence, he would not lift his hand against cleanser or kern for one whole day; and unfortunately that very night a party of cleansers from *Cromar* broke into *Glen Isla* and *Glenshee*, cleansing, as was wont, right before them.

The men of both glens rose, and after consultation, resolved to march from different directions; so that, coming upon the enemy from different points, it would be easy to surround and destroy them. To make sure of success, word was sent to '*M'Coinnich Mor na Dalach,*' *i.e.* Big M'Kenzie, laird of *Dalmore*, to come with his *Braemar* men to their assistance.

By early dawn both parties were in march; but by an unfortunate oversight no leader was chosen or rendezvous appointed. The brave *Glenshee* men, too impatient for delay, pushed forward in small parties, and were despatched at once by the cleansers, with little loss to themselves. The *Glen Isla* men were more prudent; and seeing their inferiority to the cleansers, took their station on a neighbouring hill, the *Moal Odhar*, and did not attempt to assist their brave neighbours of *Glenshee*. The Cam, who had received early intelligence of the raid, hung about the vicinity of the cleansers, sorely repenting of the oath he had sworn, and measuring impatiently the distance the sun had yet to go ere he would be free.

The miller of *Glenshee*, with his seven sons, had come up in a body, and were doing prodigies of valour ; and while they cursed the cowards of *Glen Isla*, often turned their longing eyes in the direction of *Bracmar*. One after another of the seven sons fell ; and so death after death was made known to their father : he only replied, ' We must fight the day, and lament the morn.' And when all were gone, he repeated the cry standing over the body of the last one. Poor man, he saw no to-morrow ! Sorely wounded, and unable to stand, he was fighting upon his knees. A stout cleanser with whom he had been engaged now stept back, for he saw that the miller had but a few minutes to live, and he did not care to expose himself to the last nervous efforts of so dangerous a foe.

The miller during that breathing space turned his fast dimming eyes once more in the direction of *Braemar ;* still no help was visible. But some object nearer hand caused his eye to brighten, and for a moment his vigour seemed restored. The cleanser returned ; but while in the act of lifting his sword to despatch the miller, a sharp twang was heard, and an arrow from some invisible archer pierced the cleanser, and with a shriek he leaped convulsively from the ground. The miller also sprang to his feet ; and the two, clasped in each other's arms, and their daggers driven to the hilt in each other's backs, fell together in that dread embrace of death.

To the great consternation of the cleansers, arrow

after arrow came, dealing death most surely to some one in their ranks. Not one missed its mark, and yet they saw not whence they came. The remains of the *Glenshee* men doing what they could to distract their attention, the cleansers yelled in fury; but the avenging hand smote them still. Fourteen of them, some say eighteen, lay stretched upon the ground, when a blast of wind sweeping across the heather caught the Cam-ruadh plaid and whirled it up in the air.

The cleansers saw it, and the whole band ran yelling to the place. The Cam adjusted his last arrow, but it snapped, and started uselessly aside. So, throwing the bow after the broken arrow, he leapt from his hiding-place and fled down the hill-side like a mountain roe, distancing his pursuers at every step. One of them seeing this, bent his bow, and discharged an arrow with unerring aim. It hit the Cam, but not in any mortal part, for he never abated his speed. A whole shower of arrows were then sent after him, but all fell short of the mark ; so, completely nonplussed, they turned back to finish with the *Glenshee* men.

But a shout echoing and re-echoing among the hills greeted their ears ; while the *Glenshee* men shouted in hearty response, 'Hurrah! *M'Coinnich Mor na Dalach* and the *Braemar* men !' So the cleansers fled amain, leaving the flocks and herds for which they had dared so much, and the bodies of their slaughtered companions, behind them.

Thus far the battle of the *Cairnwell*. It took place near the top of the hill, at a short distance from the road which the coach passes; and often, especially if it be desired, time is allowed for the passengers to visit the '*Katern's Howe*.' On the opposite side of the haugh the cleansers were buried; and the old man to whom I am indebted for this legend, told me that often he and his herding companions used to visit the spot. He remembers only fourteen graves. One of them they used to call the '*Chief's Grave*,' from its great length—upwards of seven feet. He assured me also, that for a long time, on account of their cowardly conduct on that day, the feeling towards the *Glen Isla* men was that of the greatest bitterness and contempt; and that, though now softened down by time, it still exists.

Among the cleansers shot by the Cam-ruadh at the battle of the *Cairnwell* was the Baron M'Diarmid, chief of a sept of Clan Campbell, who left a family of seven sons to avenge his death. Before leaving *Aberdeenshire,* they found out who the terrible archer was, and left with the firm purpose of returning to make the Cam suffer for their father's death.

One very rainy day not long after, the Cam was herding the united flocks and herds of his neighbours; and no doubt they considered them safe under his protection. He was not very particular as to his personal appearance; and with an old plaid hung round him, all dripping wet, he was not at all formidable-looking. He had also, when alone, a habit of muttering to himself, which did not strengthen a stranger's idea of his wisdom.

On this day to which I refer he was, as usual, busily engaged in conference with himself, when he felt a tap on his shoulder, and turning round saw to his astonishment ten or twelve of the cleansers; and he, poor man, without the means of escape or defence. He was quick enough to observe, however, that they considered him a fool; and he resolved to act in character.

Though it was considered of little use by the others, the captain of the party asked if he could tell them where the 'Cam-ruadh' lived.

'Perhaps I can.'

'Is it far from this?'

'Perhaps it is.' But though thus indifferent to their questions, he took such an extraordinary interest in their bows and arrows, as set their risible faculties fully in operation. So the captain, hoping to get some information out of him as to the Cam, put one into his hand.

His wonder at the new-fashioned walking-stick was extreme, and his admiration no less so. Seeing this, the captain said coaxingly, 'Now, if you will tell me where the Cam lives, I will give you one of these pretty things to yourself.'

'Which of them?'

'Whichever you please, and a quiver full of arrows too, if you find out for us the Cam-ruadh.'

'Oui ay, but what's their use?'

'A sensible question, captain,' said one of the party laughingly; 'you'll better teach him.'

The Cam was all attention, while the captain adjusted his bow and sent an arrow to the other side of a stream near them. Then he set to work in the most awkward manner possible; so much so, that he was in danger, they thought, of shooting himself.

The captain then proposed a large stone as a mark, yet arrow after arrow went hissing in every direction but the mark.

When he had sent the whole quiverful to the other side of the stream, a bird happened to alight on the stone. The Cam let fly, and the bird fell. 'A splendid shot!' exclaimed he in ecstasy; and darted across the stream to take up his victim and collect his arrows. Still the cleansers, believing it a mere chance shot, suspected nothing, and were still amusing themselves at his expense; he doing all he could to carry on the deception.

At length, all his arrows gathered, he stepped behind the stone, and adjusting his bow, with a menacing arrow in the one hand, he held up the bird in the other; then made the startling announcement that he was the Cam-ruadh: then, bending behind the stone, bent his bow against them.

'Have mercy on us,' cried the chief, 'and we will go without harming any one.'

'If you don't,' replied the Cam, drawing his bow to its fullest stretch—

They did not need more, but set off at their swiftest; the Cam, in the rear, every now and then hastening their speed with a loud shout. And thus he drove them beyond the confines of *Braemar*.

This last exploit enraged the cleansers exceedingly, especially the seven brothers; and they set out determined not only to revenge their father's death, but this defeat also. It was in winter, and it is no joke when a storm overtakes one in the hills, as one happened to do these cleansers. The Cam and his wife, sheltered from the storm, sat by the fireside blessing themselves that it was so. Their home was humble enough: a shieling, with small holes serving as windows, stuffed with turf instead of glass; one end of the shieling serving as kitchen, bed-room, etc., the other end as barn and byre.

By a strange sort of sympathy, his wife asked what he would do 'if the cleansers were coming the night.'

'Give them meat,' replied the Cam.

'And then?'

'Let them sleep.'

'And what then?'

'Let them be off,' he cried, provoked at her persistence.

'Be as good as your word, then,' said a gruff voice from the outside; 'we sorely want what you promise.'

After surrendering their arms, they were admitted to share the comforts of the Cam's dwelling; and during the evening not only was the peace made up, but an alliance offensive and defensive was entered into, and they parted sworn friends.

As a sequel to this story, I may mention one other instance of his prowess. The sept to which these brothers belonged had a rupture with another tribe; and on the Cam being informed of this, in terms of the late alliance, he set off to assist them.

When he arrived at their dwelling, they were gone; so the Cam anxiously asked their mother to show him the road they had taken.

'Are *you* going to help them?' she asked, evidently not seeing much of the warrior in the strange being before her.

'Yes.'

'Then, if they'll do *with* you, they'll do *without* you.'

'That may be,' he replied dryly, 'but I'll go and see.'

With manifest indifference she pointed out the way. So pushing on, he arrived at the right time: the Campbells were in flight. Crouching himself down in a hollow, his unerring shafts began to fly, dealing certain death in every direction among the antagonists of his friends. The Campbells seeing this, resumed the fight, and by the aid of the Cam-ruadh came off victorious.

When their mother was informed, on their return, how deeply indebted they were to the Cam, she knew not what apologies to make, nor by what acts of kindness and attention to compensate for her former indifference ; and again and again declared she would never judge by appearances any more, since she had found the Cam's appearance and his prowess so widely at variance.

Many other stories are told of the Cam and his adventures, and might be here related ; but it is neither pleasing nor instructive to heap up these tales of blood. So I merely mention, in conclusion, that having served under Donald Oig, and William of *Inverey*, his successor, the Cam was gathered to his kindred dust. And thoughts, which sometimes intrude themselves, as to where such a spirit will spend its eternity, are checked by the certainty that the Judge of all the earth will do right.

CHAPTER V.

The Inverey Farquharsons—William the first Chief, and
John the Black Colonel.

THE traditional account of the *Inverey* branch
of the Farquharsons, who claimed the chieftainship of the clan after Donald Oig's
death, may be fitly introduced by an extract from a
very interesting letter, which I have by me, from one
of their descendants :—

'In the time of Montrose, Donald Farquharson of
Monaltric, called by the country people '"Donald
Oig," raised the *Mar* men, and joined Montrose at
Crathes Castle. Next day, Montrose marched all the
army within two miles of *Aberdeen*. Farquharson of
Monaltrie and other officers slipped from the camp,
and were drinking in a public-house. Some others
went to the Covenanters' camp, on the other side of
the *Dee*, who immediately sent out a party and surrounded the house. Farquharson rushed out, and
was killed in the street. He was a brave man, and
greatly lamented by Montrose. Next morning,

N

Montrose called out in front of the Highland army, "Who is to take up the sword of Donald Oig?" William Farquharson of *Inverey* made answer, and said he would, and it belonged to him by kindred rights. Montrose immediately engaged the Covenanters, and cut them to pieces. William Farquharson of *Inverey* behaved so well at the head of his *Mar* men, that Montrose that very evening cried him round the *Cross of Aberdeen* "the first Colonel in *Scotland*." He afterwards fought with Montrose at *Alford*, *Altearn*, *Inverlochie*, etc. He afterwards died an old man, and was interred in the burying-ground beside the castle.

'The next that was buried there was his son Col. John Farquharson, who was at the killing of the Baron of *Brachlie*, and, as you heard yourself, would not rest until he was taken up from the churchyard at *Castleton of Braemar*, and interred at the burying-ground of *Inverey*. Afterwards his son, Colonel Peter Farquharson, was interred at *Inverey*; and the last that I know was a brother of theirs, a barrister-at-law in *Edinburgh*, who died there, and was taken to the burying-ground of *Inverey*. Thus I have given you all my mother's traditions about our friends. May their souls rest in peace!'

This William, first chief of the Invereys, was the eldest son of James Farquharson, who obtained possession of *Inverey* after the sad death of poor

Lamont. The new laird seems to have settled down pretty quietly, as there seems little remembered of him but an amusing little incident in connection with his second marriage to Agnes Ferguson, the minister of *Crathie's* daughter.

He was sixty when he paid his court to that young lady of sixteen; and imagining, I suppose, that he would succeed best by proxy, sent his eldest son William on the important mission. William was not so honest as the friend of 'Miles Standish,' and perhaps, as a punishment, the results were equally different. The old man was the successful suitor, and the young one went to the wars, and, as we have heard, was with Montrose at the time of Donald Oig's death.

William got over his disappointment, however, and married a daughter of Invercauld's. She was the mother of John the Black Colonel. By a second marriage to a daughter of Abergeldie's, William had another son, Charles of *Balmoral.*

After the Restoration, William went to *London* to the king, and got an order to be refunded of all his losses and expenses during the civil war; but by some quibble neither he nor his family reaped any advantage from it. He lived, as before stated, to a good old age, and was buried at *Inverey.* The sword of Donald Oig, which had been claimed so willingly and wielded so vigorously by him, was carried on

his coffin to the grave, and on that of all the succes-
sive chiefs until the race became extinct.

I come now to the most celebrated of all the
Invereys—John the Black Colonel. Some time before the death of his father, and consequent succession to the estate, he joined Viscount Dundee,
and was with him both at *Drumclog* and *Bothwell
Bridge*, etc.

The Black Colonel was the very *beau ideal* of a
rough cavalier : tall, of commanding presence, dark
complexion, a set of features faultless in form and
expression, and an impetuosity of character that
carried everything before it.

In 1690, when Dundee summoned out the Jacobites, he sent a letter to John, appointing him Colonel
of the *Mar* men. This letter was by no means
unwelcome ; and as in those days letters were not
sent but on important occasions, it created a little
sensation.

'What news, laird ?' said his henchman Alastair
M'Dougal, as he was yet deeply engaged in decipher-
ing his missive.

'Good news ! good news !' replied the Colonel with
his usual impetuosity, 'for we are going down to the
lowlands to harry the Sassenach !'

The fiery cross was immediately hurried through
Braemar. The rendezvous appointed was the
Colonel's own castle. The fiery cross, as is perhaps

sufficiently known, consisted of two pieces of wood in the form of a cross, one end of the horizontal piece being either burning or burnt. To the other end was suspended a piece of white cloth smeared with blood. Two men, each with a cross in his hand, were despatched by the chief in different directions; and while they ran at their greatest speed, kept shouting the war-cry of the clan, and the place of rendezvous, if different from the usual place of meeting. The cross was given from hand to hand; and as each fresh bearer ran at full speed, the Highlanders assembled with wondrous celerity.

Thus was the fiery cross hurried through all the glens of *Braemar*. No time was lost. Major Charles of *Balmoral* at once obeyed the summons. The captains of *Auchendryne* and *Coldrach* were equally ready; and every glen poured out its bravest men, ready to face danger and death at the bidding of their superior. The highest honour to which they aspired was to be the slaughterers of hundreds—thousands if possible!

Everything contributed to make this rising like a gala day. From the top of the castle streamed the Colonel's standard, while pipers almost innumerable played with 'might and main.' The men thus collected were in time for the battle of *Killiecrankie*. The loss they sustained was trifling, but Major Charles Farquharson of *Balmoral* was so severely wounded as to be unfitted ever after for active service.

Though this rising was suppressed, the Black Colonel was not a man of peace ; and when he had no quarrels of his own or his Royal master's, he was ready to aid by his prowess any one who needed his assistance.   And just at this time an instance of this occurred, which led to most tragical consequences.

The Earl of Aboyne and the Baron of Braichley though both Gordons and neighbours, did not live on good terms, nor did they scruple to annoy each other as much as possible. The two differed very much both in person and character : the Baron was a tall, portly man ; the Earl thin, and rather diminutive in stature, poetical also in his tendencies, which was considered in those days anything but a manly accomplishment.

The Baron, to vex Aboyne, prided himself in fishing in that part of the river which belonged to his lordship. Aboyne, on being informed of this, was very angry, and ordered his water-bailie, on the next occasion of his doing so, to say that he would not allow it. Braichley's answer was very impertinent.

' Tell your white-faced lairdie that I'll fish where it likes me ; and tell him also, that if he only dared to come here himself, it would give me great pleasure to pitch him into the river to be a feast for the gads.'

This insult was too glaring to remain unrevenged ;

so the Earl applied to Inverey for assistance. But the Earl, pawky as usual, did not speak of his own grievances until he had informed Inverey of Braichley's very bad treatment of his own tenants of *Tullich*, and impertinent speeches regarding the veritable Black Colonel himself. Then, having done that, he proposed that if Colonel Farquharson would drive away the Baron's cattle, and give the Gordons in that quarter a good poinding, his tenants of *Tullich*, who were very poorly off for fuel, should have the moss of *Easter Morven;* and as the Colonel had a special regard for his *Tullich* tenants, he agreed to the proposition.

On his way home the Colonel called at *Tullich* to learn the truth of the Earl's report, and found that the Baron's alleged ill-treatment of his tenants, and malicious sayings regarding himself, had been exaggerated to such a degree as to make it very evident that he desired only the spulzie of the Baron's lands, and that by nothing else would the right to *Easter Morven* moss be acquired.

The Colonel was not easily outdone in cunning; and he resolved that he would possess himself of the much-needed moss without injuring Braichley. So he communicated with the Baron, explained the whole matter, and arranged that he and twelve of his men were to drive away all the cattle of *Glen Muick*. No resistance was to be made, as all was to be restored in the course of a week.

This was all arranged before the summons came to join Dundee; and on his return with his men from *Killiccrankie*, he proposed to them, as they were together, that he and a few of them should drive away the *Glen Muick* cattle, and that the rest of them were to remain where they were, and settle with the red-coats who were coming up the river to pay them a visit. The Colonel not having made his submission like the the other Highland chiefs, a thousand men under Colonel Cunningham were on their way to burn his castle, and take himself, if possible.

His men being perfectly willing, the arrangements were soon made. From the assembled clan he chose twelve of the best men to accompany himself to *Glen Muick;* and Lewis Farquharson of *Auchendryne*, who had been elected major in place of Charles of *Balmoral*, marched away to oppose the 'red-coats,' while the Black Colonel went on his mission of 'spulzie.'

Inverey drove away all the cattle of *Glen Muick;* and from his arrangement with the Baron, expected that he would remain unmolested. To his astonishment, therefore, Braichley, with a party of the Gordons, came upon the Farquharsons 'at the head of *Etnich.*'

The Colonel repeated his former explanation, and again assured him that all would be returned in a week. But the Gordons, not trusting the Colonel, grew clamorous; and one of them, mad with passion, fired on the *Inverey* men. This altered the whole state of matters, and both parties, with drawn swords, rushed at each other like tigers.

While passion thus raged, the Baron and Inverey met. After a little, as the Black Colonel gave back a few steps, the wind, it is said, caught his plaid, and whirling it from his shoulders twisted it round his feet. At that moment the Baron pressed hard upon him : his peril was imminent, as he could not move without falling, and to fall was death.

One of the men seeing his danger, shouted 'Help the chief !' So Alastair M'Dougal, his henchman, having cut down one of the Gordons, seized the fallen man's gun and shot the Baron, on which the Gordons fled. The Colonel did not pursue them, but went on with the 'her'ship;' and having disposed of them safely, returned with his followers through *Glen Muick.* When passing *Braichley*, the Baron's lady invited him and his men to pass the night, and it was one of extraordinary revelry.

I well remember the bitter invective into which the old lady—one of the Black Colonel's descendants—broke on reaching this part of her narrative. The substance of it was that the vile Kate M'Intosh, the Baron's wife, had been at the bottom of it all ; only the Colonel, it was admitted, 'was no good man mair than she. There was nae denying that he was at the killing of the Baron.'

There is an old ballad commemorative of the event ; but it does not keep to the simple facts of this case, but mixes up with it the incidents of the murder of a former Baron by the spies of the Clan Chattan in the time of Donald of *Castleton*, some hundred years before. The Baron who was slain by the Black Colonel's party was descended from the usurper, who took the old Baron's place by marrying his young widow, she being ignorant that he had procured the death of her husband.

While the revelry was going on at *Braichley*, Colonel Cunningham and his men were quietly and quickly moving up the *Dee*, and early in the morning surprised the Farquharsons at *Culblean*—dancing, it is said, the famous Race or Reel of *Tullich*—and cut them to pieces. The Gordons, on the other side of the water, justly incensed at the conduct of the Baron's lady, and smarting under their defeat, hastened across the river to inform the soldiers of Colonel Farquharson's whereabouts. The result was, that by the time the Colonel was rising, Cunningham and his men were at the castle gates.

The alarm was given. The lady had one of the fleetest steeds saddled. The Colonel mounted and fled, the besiegers following hard in pursuit. Never was wilder chase. Through *Glen Taner* and *Birse* he directed his course, then struck across the *Dee*. Over the *Moor of Dinnet* his foaming steed flew, through *Tullich*, and entered the *Pass of Ballater.* Now there seemed no hope of escape. The whole country was raised behind him. Precipices almost perpendicular rose at every side. The party who had defeated the Farquharsons in the morning were rushing to meet him from the other end of the *Pass.* But just as the two companies were to close, with the Colonel in their midst, he shot aside, up the precipitous sides of the *Pass.*

The company below stood amazed, and every moment expected to see horse and rider dashed to the bottom. But no; up, up, up they went, and anon the Black Colonel and his black steed had reached the summit, and stood beyond all danger of pursuit.

The pursuers stood looking at each other in silence. At length one of the officers, addressing another who had barred the upper end of the *Pass*, said, 'If they had told us that he could *fly* as well as *ride*, we might have spared ourselves the roughest ride I ever had.' It was also sagely concluded, that without help of a very doubtful character no man could have ever accomplished such a feat. Colonel Cunningham, contented with his success at *Culbleen*, did not penetrate farther into *Braemar;* so Farquharson for a time escaped without further molestation.

CHAPTER VI.

The Black Colonel—*continued.*

NOBODY should tak' in strangers, unless they ken weel about them. Na, they shouldna dee that ; for when the Colonel went to the West Countrie, a gentleman took him in, and he carried off one of his daughters. It was said he married her ; but what syne ! He had his ain wife living at *Inverey.* That cam' o' takin' in strangers.'

As this quondam wife, or Annie Ban, *i.e.* Fair-haired Annie, is intimately connected with the Colonel's future history, I have permitted an old lady, descended of the Farquharson race, to introduce her, before I proceed further with it.

As the Colonel still refused to make his submission, the purpose of burning his castle was resolved to be carried out. The Colonel, ignorant of this fact, was going on in his usual course of every-day life ; and reckless enough it was, if we may take the day before the burning of the castle as a fair specimen. Here is the traditional account of it.

Alastair M'Dougal, the Colonel's henchman, was possessed of extraordinary strength. As a proof of it, it is said that, when in want of fuel, he would go to the woods and lay hold of a birch tree, pull it up by the roots, and drag it home after him. This day Alastair was in extra spirits; and as he stepped up and down the stair, kept singing, in a voice not over gentle :

'A good soldier never wanted a weapon,' etc.

A pistol fired at a shield hung on the wall was the Colonel's mode of summoning his servants. And when Alastair, thus summoned, entered the room, the Colonel sprang at him with his drawn sword; his terrier also rushed forward to join in the *melee.* Alastair, with the greatest nonchalance, seized the terrier by the fur of his neck, and rammed it right on the point of the sword. The Colonel, to avoid hurting his favourite, dropped the weapon; and M'Dougal, picking it up, swung it round his head, and sang as before :

'A good soldier never wanted a weapon,' etc.

Such were the home pleasures of the Black Colonel, and thus did he occasionally test the valour of his followers.

The same day on which these incidents occurred, the laird of *Daldownie,* his brother-in-law and friend, came to pay him a visit. After dinner the two were unusually jolly together, so much so as to lead to the remark that it was surely before something. So it was : a squadron of dragoons had already left *Aberdeen*, and were on their way to accomplish the oft-repeated threat of burning the castle.

Wild, reckless, and daring as the Colonel was, he still held a place in the affections of his people ; and one of the lowest of them was at this time the means of saving his life, at least his liberty. A beggar woman was about *Aboyne* when the dragoons rode up. As beggars then were the great newsmongers, and welcomed according to the budget they carried, she hung about them until she learned the mission on which they came.

On hearing also that the officer in command intended to stay where he was until night, she formed her purpose. So, getting away as quietly as possible, she relieved herself of her wallet, some say her 'hose and shoon' also, and set out with all her might for *Invercy*, determined that the Colonel should not remain ignorant of the danger that threatened him.

The faithful creature was just in time ; for when she reached the castle she could hear the clanging of the troopers' horses on the rough bed of the *Dee*, as they crossed the ford a little to the east of the castle. She succeeded in giving the alarm. Immediately the Colonel and Captain Shaw sprang from their beds and fled, just as they were : not an instant was to be lost.

The two made for the *Ey*. It was unfordable from a recent storm ; but the Colonel cleared it with one bound, at a spot still pointed out, and called in consequence '*Drochaide-an-Leum*,' *i.e.* The Bridge of the Leap. Shaw, an immensely powerful man, with the desperate energy of one fleeing for life, pushed through the stream, and but a few minutes after stood beside the Black Colonel on the top of *Creagan Chait.*

Ignorant of this escape, the soldiers drew near very cautiously. A great reward was set on the Colonel's head, and this they hoped to win : so the castle was quietly surrounded, then the gates were stormed ; anon they yield, and shortly the castle was swarming with soldiers. But though every crevice and nook was searched, it was all in vain—there was no Colonel there.

Fire was then set to the castle, and a guard set to the door to prevent the Colonel's escape, for they believed he still lay hid within. To the guard's great joy, he saw a tall person, sparingly dressed, a bundle of clothes under arm, trying to escape from the flames.

'Yield or die!' cried the guard, seizing the person by the arm. The arm was disengaged with a twitch ; and a retort not over delicate was accompanied with such a smack on the face, that the dragoon lost his balance and rolled down the steps. His assailant fol-

lowed leisurely, and jumped lightly over his prostrate
person.   This intrepid heroine was no other than
Annie Ban.

The dragoon was terribly enraged, and to wipe
out his disgrace would have taken condign punishment on Annie, but was prevented by the others.
This exploit of hers had so conciliated their good-
will, that they allowed her to depart in peace, bundle
and all.   This was important, as it contained the
Colonel's clothes, and those also of his friend Captain
Shaw.   Their exposed situation on the top of *Creagan
Chait* made the want of them sorely felt.

By and by the party on the top of the hill was
attracted by the red light gleaming from the castle
windows.   They could but too easily divine its cause.
Both looked sadly on, Shaw not daring a word of
sympathy, when suddenly the Colonel burst out a
laughing in the most extravagant manner.

'Are you mad?' inquired Daldownie.

'Wait a minute,' was the reply, accompanied with
another frantic burst of laughter.

And as Shaw still expostulated as to this untimely
mirth, the Colonel informed him, by way of explanation, that the charter-room was full of powder.

'The last thing in the world to laugh at; it will
blow your castle to pieces.'

'Yes, and blow them to pieces at the same time.'
And as they spoke the hills were lighted up with lurid

blaze. The heavens seemed rent asunder, and for a moment the earth shook to its very centre. The dreadful noise repeated itself again and again, as the more distant hills gave back their echoes ; then all was still—the work of desolation and death was accomplished. Still, to the Colonel's great disappointment, there were not so many of the soldiers killed as he anticipated, as the powder, instead of blowing out the walls, exploded into the air. After burning *Invercy*, the soldiers gave the new castle (*Braemar*) also to the flames, then withdrew. Thus the Colonel was left a houseless wanderer.

After the burning of the castle, Mrs. Farquharson with her family went to live with the Colonel's brother Charles at *Balmoral.* Anne Ban got shelter in a cottage at *Ruigh-an-t-Scillich* in *Glen Ey.* The Colonel had a peculiar claim upon its occupants, as will be seen after. As for Colonel Farquharson himself, his residence was in the cave formerly noticed in *Glen Ey;* and to this place his favourite Anne often resorted, to beguile his weary hours.

At last death, relentless death, carried off that beautiful, high-spirited, but unfortunate girl. The Colonel greatly regretted her, and composed a deeply pathetic *Lament,* in which he deplored her loss, and wished that it had been his *first* wife instead of the second that had died, etc.

His wife, hearing this, was very much displeased ;

and at one time, when M'Dougal the Colonel's servant was at *Balmoral,* she bribed him to make a parody on the *Lament.*

M'Dougal agreed to do it, as he too was much annoyed to see the Colonel so taken up about a girl, instead of seeking to revenge the defeat at *Tullich* and the burning of the castle. Having succeeded in parodying the *Lament,* he took an early opportunity of trolling out in the most sonorous manner the following :

> ' Alas! thou art gone, Anne,
> Leaving me in deep sorrow;
> But never shall thy memory depart,
> Until I get bear bread and butter.'

He had parodied the whole, but the Colonel did not wait to hear more, but went and ordered all the butter and bear bread to be found in the two *In-vercys* to be brought to his presence. Then he ordered M'Dougal to appear. On entering the room he was ordered to sit down at the table ; and no sooner was he seated than the laird seized two loaded pistols and levelled them at his head.

'Eat !' cried the Colonel, pointing to the store before him. M'Dougal was filled with dismay, but began to eat ; and still he ate, and ate, but the laird's look relented not. It seemed to be not only eat or die, but eat and die ; and this went on until absolutely more would not enter, for up to that point the laird's tightening finger on the trigger stimulated his flagging energies.

The Colonel then kicked him out, expecting he would die. He did not die, however, but the new version of the *Lament* was never repeated. M'Dougal had touched the Colonel on a tender point, and the irritation occasioned by that touch was not easily allayed; and still wishing to get rid of him without incurring the odium of murdering, he sent M'Dougal with a letter to the young Baron of *Braichley*, stating that this was the man who shot his father. The scheme did not succeed: the sum of the Baron's answer was, 'that if he did, it was no fault of his.'

Shortly after this affair the Colonel had a narrow escape from falling into the hands of his pursuers. He had for some time been putting up in a house at *Altchlar*, and was on this day, from fatigue or some other cause, sound asleep. A party of dragoons, by some means informed of this (perhaps by M'Dougal by way of reprisals), came over by the ford at *Allenquoich* right down on *Altchlar*. Again the faithfulness of one of his people saved him, by shouting through the window, in phrase significant enough to the Colonel, though not understood by the soldiers. And starting up, he drove out a window to the back, and escaped into a wood behind the house.

'He was tired now of this work,' he said, 'and was resolved in some way to get rid of the villanous

Whigamores.' It was not very long until he got the opportunity of putting this resolution, whatever it was, into practice. A very large party of dragoons arrived at *Braemar ;* and as it was pretty late, they turned their horses into the castle park, and kindling fires, made themselves comfortable for the night.

Towards morning a yell suddenly burst from *Craig Choinnich,* and a noise was heard as if a multitude of men were rushing down its steep sides—men, too, bent on destruction, for the bullets in hundreds were hissing over the park. Another yell then rose, louder and wilder than before. So the Whigamores, as the Colonel termed them, mounted and fled ; those at least who could, and those whose horses had run wild were in evil plight. Many of them were thrown into the river, and asked to carry the Black Colonel's compliments to their commander in *Aberdeen,* or to " *Righ William na Gorit,*" *i.e.* King William the Cruel, in *London,* and say that the Black Colonel did not care a bodle for them. This was the last incident of note during the life of the Black Colonel. His exploits did not end with life, however ; so I may close this account of it with one or two of his posthumous feats.

On his death-bed he gave express orders that his body was to be laid beside Anne Ban, in the churchyard of *Inverey,* and not in the family buryingground at *Castleton.* His relations did not heed his wishes, but had him conveyed to *Castleton*, and buried there with all the usual Highland ceremonies. Next morning (so the legend goes) the coffin, with all its contents, lay above ground; and this went on for a time, the laird's remains rising through the night, and the relations burying them on the morning.

As they still refused to attend to his wishes, he began to pay them nightly visits; and such sights and sounds greeted their eyes and ears night after night, that they were glad at length to let him have his own way. So one morning all met in the church-yard as by appointment, each surprised at the sight of the other; but the gruesome looks of all revealed plainly that they had been favoured with a special visit.

As at least six weeks had passed in this contest, the exhalations from the body were such as to put serious obstacles in the way of its removal. But as they were now quite in earnest about it, they fell upon an expedient, which was to draw it up the *Dee* on a sort of raft; and at length it was safely deposited in the burying-ground at *Inverey*, beside his much-loved Anne.

As to the coffin really having risen night after night, no one can believe that; but it is a fact that after a lapse of six weeks he was towed up the *Dee* and buried at *Inverey*. One old lady, who died a few years ago, told me that her grandmother had seen the procession.

The other posthumous exploit of the Colonel was of a nature somewhat similar, and occurred only some six years ago. A travelling or beggar woman was found drowned near the *Linn of Dee;* and as the weather was very stormy, it was necessary to bury her in the nearest churchyard, or *Inverey.* Whether it was that the stone had been removed, or that no stone had marked the spot where the Colonel lay, I do not know, but it so happened that the grave which they opened was that of the Colonel. This they knew by the remains of the plate, etc. etc., which they found in it.

Two of the young men present, though forbidden by the others, took some of the Colonel's teeth by way of memento. The night after this, the sister of one of these young men—who, it is said, knew nothing of the taking of the teeth—had a visit from an old man who demanded his teeth.

I forget the particulars exactly ; but, so far as I remember, the visit to the sister not being effectual, the Colonel called on the delinquents themselves, and continued to do so until they were obliged to go and put the teeth again into the grave whence they took them.

Being somewhat amused with this account, I took some pains when in the locality to ascertain the truth as to the re-interment of the teeth. It really did take place ; but the young men who were the actors in the scene, feeling now somewhat ashamed of the affair, say as little about it as possible.

The death of the Colonel took place about 1700. His son Colonel Peter succeeded him. He was again succeeded by his son Finla, an imbecile. In the next generation the race became extinct.

To bring out more clearly the social usages of the period, I may give the legend explanatory of the peculiar claims the Black Colonel had upon his tenants of *Ruigh-an-t-Seillich.*

In the chapter regarding the surnames found in *Braemar*, I noticed a traditional account of the ' Fir M'Donalds.' One of that race acted as gilliestreine or groom to M'Kenzie, laird of *Dalmore.* And the laird having on one occasion received an invitation from Grant of *Tullochgorum* to be present at the wedding of his daughter, sent this gilliestreine with his excuse, as it was not convenient for him to be present. The marriage did not meet Dalmore's approbation. The reason was that the girl was young, very young, and pretty, while the would-be bridegroom was very old ; but his lands were broad and his purse heavy, and that with his intended father-in-law made up for the lack of everything else.

If Dalmore had any sinister intention in sending M'Donald, who was a very handsome young man, to *Speyside*, he was not disappointed. A severe snow-storm kept the two young people in perilous

proximity for some days ; and before he left *Speyside*,
plans were laid which eventually outwitted Miss
Grant's father and her intended husband.

Dalmore, on his groom's return, made his way into
the heart of the secret, by saying inquiringly, ' Pity
the lassie should be given to that nasty old bodach.'

' What say you, laird, if I took her from him yet ? '

' I say you shall have the best farm on the *Dalmore*
if you do.'

' It's a bargain, then,' replied M'Donald, and set off
to get his plans in operation. As M'Kenzie and
Grant were great friends, none of the *Dalmore* tenants
were allowed to render any assistance ; but it did not
matter. The Black Colonel, whenever he heard of
it, supplied as many men as were requisite for ' the
bit fun.'

On the marriage evening M'Donald and twelve men
reached a sheep-cot near *Tullochgorum*, where festivities were going on in real Highland style. A stranger
made his appearance in the course of the evening,
and was, as usual on such occasions, so warmly
welcomed, that he soon made himself quite at home.
And having asked permission to dance with the bride,
he slipped a ring into her hand, for which she had
been anxiously looking. It was a token that all was
ready.

She contrived to slip away unobserved ; and hastily
dressing herself for a journey, made her way as fast

as possible to the sheep-cot ; and very soon the whole party were on their way to *Braemar*. It was a new version of Jock o' Hazeldean, when the lady was missed. Unfortunately the snow on the ground discovered the secret of the flight ; and the command being given to arm, the whole bridal party set out in pursuit.

By this time the *Mar* men with their prize were far in advance. But as the snow lay deep on the ground, it was a weary road ; and the lady, quite overcome, was unable to proceed farther. They carried her then by turns, but, despite all they could do, were overtaken at the *Derry Dam ;* and drawn up on each side of the stream, both parties prepared for battle. But Alastair M'Dougal, the Colonel's henchman, came forward, and, swinging his ponderous battle-axe round his head, dared the best man among them to cross the ford. M'Donald also came forward, and addressing Tullochgorum, told him that his daughter was with them by her own consent ; and though there were an hundred instead of ten to one, it would be better for them to go quietly home than attempt to force a passage across the ford. So the *Strathspey* party wisely concluded to do so ; and James of the Fir had his marriage celebrated in *Braemar* on the following morning.

Dalmore, afraid of consequences, refused to fulfil his promise of the farm. But the Black Colonel again came to the rescue, and gave them that of *Tomlice* at *Corriemulzie;* and from that time the M'Donalds followed the Invereys.

The first Christmas after this event Dalmore spent with his ally, Grant of *Tullochgorum.* The succeeding one Grant came to spend at *Dalmore;* and when about to leave for *Strathspey,* M'Kenzie said he would surely never think of going home without seeing his daughter.

'A daughter,' he replied, 'that brought shame on her father's house little deserves a visit from Tullochgorum.'

'Toots, man! I carry my head as high as Tullochgorum, yet *I* visit her, and so does Inverey.' And finally M'Kenzie prevailed. The Black Colonel, hoping that Grant would be induced to visit his daughter, had supplied them liberally with all that would be necessary to give him a worthy reception. Mrs. M'Donald, thus prepared, was ready to welcome them in.

'A fine trick was that you played us, my lady,' was Tullochgorum's salutation. His daughter made no reply; but handing her little boy to Dalmore, she went out for her husband. M'Kenzie quickly transferred his charge to the grandfather's knee. The right chord was touched; and when the son-in-law appeared, a complete reconciliation was effected.

The Colonel, who had been on the watch, soon

dropped in, and the day was made one of great festivity. Before they parted, it was agreed that the Colonel was to give them the farm of *Ruigh-an-t-Seillich* in *Glen Ey;* and Grant was to stock it well with sheep and cattle. Hence the claim the Colonel could make on the M'Donalds for a shelter to his favourite after the burning of the castle.

There are a multitude of other collateral traditions ; but as a fair sample has been given in that respecting the abduction of Miss Grant, it is needless to multiply them. I will therefore only give, ere passing to the last great epoch in *Bracmar* history (the risings of 1715 and 1745), the traditional account of the M'Kenzies of *Dalmore.*

The origin of the family and their settlement in *Bracmar* has been already given in a former chapter. It will be observed that there is a discrepance between the traditions which state that *Dalmore* was the gift of James IV., and that which makes Kenneth M'Kenzie shepherd to Invercauld, and *Dalmore* the gift of Finla when Kenneth married his daughter. This difficulty I cannot explain, unless perhaps the king and Finla had settled it on the occasion of the incognito visit before mentioned. The fact, however, is certain, that Beatrix Farquharson and Kenneth M'Kenzie settled down on the place now known as *Mar Lodge*, their descendants possessing the estate until a little before the rebellion of 1745, when it was sold to Duff of *Braco*, for, it is said, the trifling sum of two thousand pounds.

M'Coinnich Mor na Dalach, who went to the rescue at the *Cairnwell*, was the son and successor of Kenneth ; Big M'Kenzie was again succeeded by his son John, and John by a second Kenneth, who died about 1710. His successor, *Seumas Mor na pluice*, and two of his sons, were killed by the Katrin in *Glen Ey* about 1725. The next and last laird of the *Dalmore* was Donald M'Kenzie, who sold his estates to the Duffs.

In the time of *Seumas Mor na pluice*, who was contemporary with Peter, son of the Black Colonel, occurred the stormy rising of 1715, which with that of ''45,' 30 years later, form a distinct period in *Braemar* history, from the important changes to which it gave rise. To some details of these risings, but especially the changes consequent on them, the following chapters will be devoted.

PART THE FOURTH.

REBELLIONS OF ''15' AND ''45.'

' Ill-starred, though brave, did no visions foreboding
  Tell you that fate had forsaken your cause ;
Ah! were you destined to die at Culloden,
  Victory crowned not your fall with applause.'

CHAPTER I.

Great Hunt of 1715—Gathering of the Clans, etc.—Results of the Rising.

ABOUT 1715, the ' *Clann Fhearchair*,' *i.e.* Clan Farquharson, must have attained the zenith of their power (numerically considered at least) in *Braemar*. This will appear evident from the following list of Farquharsons holding estates in it.

First of all, as chief of the clan, is Peter Farquharson, son of the Black Colonel, holding the estates of *Invercy*. His younger brother, James Farquharson, held *Balmoral;* Lewis Farquharson held the estate of *Auchendryne;* Donald Farquharson, that of *Coldrach* in *Glen Cluny*. *Allenquoich* had been possessed by Farquharsons from the death of Lamont, as before stated. John Farquharson had *Invercauld*. *Monaltrie*, *Micras*, *Tullich*, etc. etc., were all held by Farquharsons; and not only within the boundaries of *Braemar*, but many other small estates or lairdships at no great distance from it: for instance, *Brougdcarg* in

223

Glenshee, Whitehouse in *Cromar, Achrichan* in *Glen-livet,* etc.

Of the causes of the rising of 1715 I can say nothing; but the details of it, so far as connected with *Braemar,* and still in traditional existence, form legitimate subject-matter for the present chapter.

Previous to the rising, the Earl of Mar, to find out how the clans and Jacobite families stood affected, appointed to meet the nobles and chiefs at a great hunting in *Braemar* on the 27th of August 1715. That grand hunt, which was the pretence for reunion, has been thus described by Taylor, the Water poet, who was present : [1]—

'There did I find the truly noble and right honour-

---

[1] John Taylor, commonly called 'the Water Poet,' after going to school at *Gloucester*—where, he says, he could get no further than his accidence, which 'gravelled' him—repaired to *London,* and was bound apprentice to a waterman. Notwithstanding the laboriousness of this employment, he wrote a number of poetical pieces, for which he took the appellation of the King's Water Poet. An enthusiastic Royalist, he, upon the outbreak of the Revolution, went to *Oxford,* where he kept a tavern, which was much resorted to by the students. Taylor aided the Royal cause by his satires and songs. When *Oxford* surrendered he returned to *London,* and opened a public-house, setting up the sign of the '*Mourning Crown.*' This, however, he was obliged to remove; on which he hung up his own portrait, with the following verses :—

'There's many a king's head hanged up for a sign,
And many a saint's head too ; then why not mine ?'

He composed upwards of eighty pieces in prose and verse, which exhibit the workings of a vigorous but uneducated mind. These effusions contain many curious pictures of the time in which the author lived, etc.

able lords: John Erskine Earl of Mar, James Stewart Earl of Murray, George Gordon Earl of Engye, son and heir to the Marquis of Huntly, James Erskine Earl of Buchan, and John Lord Erskine, son and heir to the Earl of Mar, and their Countesses, with my much honoured and my last assured and approved friend Sir William Murray, Knight, of *Abercarney*, and hundreds of others; knights, esquires, and their followers;—all and every man in general in one habit, as if Lycurgus had been there and made laws of equality.

'For once in the year, which is the whole month of August, and sometimes part of September, many of the nobility and gentry of the kingdom (for their pleasure) do come into these Highland countries to hunt, where they do conform themselves to the habit of the Highlandmen, who for the most part speak nothing but Irish, and in former times were those people which were called Redshanks.

'Their habit is shoes, with but one sole a-piece; stockings (which they call short hose) made of a warm stuff of diverse colours, which they call tartan; as for breeches, many of them, nor their forefathers, never wore any, but a jerkin of the same stuff that their hose is made of; their garters being bands, or wreaths of hay or straw; with a plaid about their shoulders, which is a mantle of diverse colours, much finer and lighter than their hose; with blue flat caps

P

on their heads ; a handkerchief, knit with two knots, about their necks : and thus they are attired.

'Now their weapons are long bows and forked arrows, swords and target, harquebusses, muskets, dirks, and Lochaber axes. With these arms I found many of them armed for the hunting. As for their attire, any man of what degree soever that comes amongst them must not disdain to wear it ; for if they do, then they will disdain to hunt, or willingly to bring in their dogs ; but if men be kind unto them, and be in their habit, then they are conquered with kindness, and the sport will be plentiful. This was the reason I found so many noblemen and gentlemen in these shapes. But to proceed to the hunting.

'My good Lord Mar having put me into that shape, I rode with him from his house, where I saw the ruins of an old castle, called the *Castle of Kindroghit*. It was built by Malcolm Canmore (for a hunting-house), who reigned in *Scotland* when Edward the Confessor, Harold, and Norman William reigned in *England*. I speak of it because it was the last house I saw in those parts ; for I was the space of twelve days after before I saw either house or corn-field, or habitation for any creature but deer, wild horses, wolves, and such like creatures, which made me doubt that I should ever see a house again.

'Thus the first day we travelled eight miles, where

there were small cottages built to lodge in, which
they call *lonquhards*. I thank my good Lord Erskine
he commanded that I should always be lodged in his
lodgings ; the kitchen being always on the side of
a bank ; many kettles and pots boiling, and many
spits turning and winding with great variety of cheer,
as venison baked, sodden, roast, and stewed beef ;
mutton, goats, kids, hares, fresh salmon, pigeons,
hens, capons, chickens, partridges, muircoots, heath-
cocks, caperkellies, and termagants ; good ale ; sacke,
white and claret ; tent (or allegant), with most *potent
aqua vitæ.*

'All these, and more than these, we had continually in superfluous abundance, caught by falconers,
fowlers, fishers, and brought by my Lord's tenants
and purveyors to victual our camps, which consisted
of fourteen or fifteen hundred men and horses.

'The manner of hunting is this : Five or six hundred men do rise early in the morning, and they do
disperse themselves diverse ways, within seven, eight,
or ten miles' compass. They do bring or chase in the
deer in many herds (two, three, or four hundred in a
herd) to such and such a place as the noblemen
shall appoint them. Then, when the day is come,
the lords and gentlemen of their companies do ride
or go to the said places, sometimes wading up to the
middle through burns and rivers ; and then they,
being come to the place, do lie down on the ground

till these aforesaid scouts, which are called the tink-hell, do bring down the deer. But as the proverb says of the bad cook, so these tinkhells do lick their own fingers ; for besides their bows and arrows, which they carry with them, we can hear now and then a harquebuss go off, which they do seldom discharge in vain.

' Then after we have stayed there three hours, or thereabouts, we might perceive the deer appear on the hills round about us (their heads making a show like a wood), which being followed by the tinkhell, are chased down into the valley where we lay. Then all the valley on each side being waylaid with a hundred couple of strong Irish greyhounds, they are let loose, as occasion requires, upon the herd of deer, that with dogs, guns, arrows, dirks, and daggers, in the space of two hours fourscore fat deer were slain, which after are disposed of, some one way and some another, twenty and thirty miles, and more than enough left for us to make merry with at our rendezvous.'

Tradition adds another item to the above account. ' They went out by *Glen Cluny*, and hunted round the whole of *Braemar*, until they came down upon *Glen Quoich*. There a little jollification was held. The deep round hole at the *Linn of Quoich* was then entire, though now perforated. Some anchors of whisky, some gallons of boiling water, and some hundredweights of honey, were poured into it, and soon bumpered off, replenished and bumpered off, until the whole company felt comfortable.' So from this circumstance the hole was, and is still, named the *Earl of Mar's Punch-bowl;* 'and a proper good utensil it was, and capacious withal.'[1]

Such, then, were the scenes amid which the rising originated. Mar, it seems, had no little trouble to get some of them to enter into his plans; at least a few of the legends say so : for example :

Mar was conducting Grant of *Rothiemurchus* up *Glen Lui,* when he broke the news of the intended rising to him. Grant objected to the design, among other things, saying,

'Why, where are your men, my lord?'

'Men!' repeated the Earl ; 'I think you only need to look behind you to see a pretty fair sample in my present following.'

Rothiemurchus did look round. Some hundreds of *Braemar* and *Strathdee* men accompanied them.

---

[1] Hill Burton, in his *Cairngorm Mountains,* says: 'The Quoich, which . . . derives its convivial name from a peculiar cataract often visited by tourists from *Braemar.* Here the gneiss is hollowed into circular cavities, like those of the *Caldron Linn ;* and in one of these the guides will have the audacity to tell you that a bacchanalian party once made grog by tossing in a few anchors of brandy, and that they consumed the whole on the premises.'

This story is not so very improbable after all, considering the number of the party—fourteen or fifteen hundred ; but the punch or grog was more likely to have been made of Taylor's *potent aqua vitæ* than of brandy.

While this discussion went on, the men stood aloof; and the followers of Rothiemurchus, tall, powerful fellows, were each in turn lifting an immense block of stone that lay on the burn-bank, nearly to their knees, to brag the *Mar* lads, while they, after the most determined efforts, were unable to free it from the ground.

'Do you call these boys men, my lord?' said Rothiemurchus, taking advantage of the incident; 'why, not one of them can move that stone, that my lads can make a plaything of.'

The Earl looked exceedingly displeased. Invercauld, with others, was standing by; and observing this, he walked up to one of his men, a Finla Farquharson, and asked if he had tried it. He had not; so Invercauld asked him to go and try.

Mar, Rothiemurchus, and the rest of the company drew round, for all were now interested. Finla not only lifted the stone, but came forward with it in his arms, and asked what they wished done with it.

'Throw it over my horse's neck,' said the Earl. Finla did so, and turned away as if nothing had happened.

'What do you think of our *Mar* boys now?' cried the Earl triumphantly. 'Let us see if any of your *Spey* lads can play that again!' The argument was unanswerable apparently, for Rothiemurchus and his men were with Mar on Sheriffmuir.

Another version of this story is given ; but the principal difference between them is in the name of the hero, which it states was Nathaniel Forbes of *Dalnhandy,* who was afterwards a captain in the army raised by Mar.

A few days after, Mar raised the standard of rebellion in *Glenlivet.* An army of 3000 was soon collected, which marched to *Strathdon,* where it was joined by a few more. They next marched to *Corgarff,* where they encamped some days. There they not only were joined by a number of the inhabitants, but also obtained a large supply of ammunition, which they greatly needed. They next proceeded to *Braemar,* where the Earl erected his standard, to which multitudes flocked, of the natives and other clans, to the number of 10,000. Among them, according to the song, were :

> 'The noble chiefs,
>   The Drummond and Glengarry ;
> Macgregor, Murray, Rollo, Keith,
>   Panmure and gallant Harry.
>   M'Donald's men,
>   Clan Ronald's men,
>   M'Kenzie's men,
>   Macgillivray's men,
>   Strathallan's men,
>   The Lowlan' men
>   Of Callander and Airly.'

A more particular account of the raising of the standard is given thus : 'On the 6th of September

1715, John Erskine, Earl of Mar, having marched from *Glenlivet*, where he had proclaimed the Chevalier de St. George under the title of James VIII., erected his standard at *Castleton of Braemar*, amidst a great assemblage of his vassals.

'The standard was made by the Countess of *Mar* (Frances, daughter of the Duke of Kingston), and was of a gorgeous, bright blue colour, having on one side the arms of *Scotland* richly embroidered in gold, and on the other the brave thistle of *Scotland*, with these words underneath, " No Union," and on the top the ancient motto, " *Nemo me impune lacessit.*" The standard had also two pendants of white ribbon, on one of which was written, " For our king and oppressed country ;" on the other, " For our lives and liberties."

'You may judge if there was not shouting, blowing of trumpets, etc., when this brave standard was upreared, and its rich silken folds unfurled to the free winds. But even in that hour of triumph there occurred an incident which threw a visible gloom over the spirits of the superstitious Highlanders : the gilt ball which ornamented the top fell down to the ground,—an omen, as they thought, of evil bode to the cause they were that day engaged in.'—*Deeside Guide.*

This incident reminds one of another such which took place in England under similar circumstances :

—' In August 1642, Charles raised the standard of civil war at *Nottingham.* "Render unto Cæsar the things which are Cæsar's" was the motto he chose ; but little success at first attended his ill-advised challenge. During the first night the wind blew down his flag from the castle wall, where it had been fixed ; and when the herald attempted on the following day to find a place for it on the Castle-hill, rock presented itself everywhere, and a company of soldiers, two by two, had to hold the standard in its place.'

While this general gathering to the standard was taking place, the *Mar* men were not idle. Their chief, Peter Farquharson of *Inverey*, was chosen colonel, as his father, the celebrated Black Colonel, had been under Dundee. His brother, James of *Balmoral,* was made *aide-de-camp* to Mar. Peter, on receiving his commission, at once hurried out the fiery cross ; and soon the hills and glens of *Braemar* resounded with the war-cry of the clan, as they hasted to obey the summons of their chief.

John of *Invercauld* is said to have seized his claymore, and at once set out, crying, ' Follow me, my merry men !'—the Farquharsons of *Riverney* and *Loynmor* joining him, as both were descended from Robert, who succeeded Finla Mor in *Invercauld.*

Harry Farquharson of *Whitehouse,* with his three sons, Francis, Charles, and John ; with them all the men of *Cromar.*

Donald Farquharson of *Micras*, Lawrence Farquharson of *Cobbleton of Tullich*, with his brother Robert, all descended from Allenquoich; and with the three the following of that family.

Lewis of *Auchendryne*, with his sons and men. The following characteristic speech of Lewis shows the spirit in which they came: 'I'm old now, and can be of little use; but what reck,' said he, pointing to his sons, and showing a large pistol in his belt, ' if my lads should not do their duty, can I no *sheet* them ?' [1]

Donald Farquharson of *Coldrach*, with his son George, came with all their following. The *Broughdearg* Farquharsons, William and Alexander, with Peter of *Rochalzie*, also assembled; and with them all the men of *Glenshee* and *Glen Isla*.

Shaw Farquharson, and with him all the men of

---

[1] These warriors had come down from their fastnesses with a resolution to fight as their ancestors had fought at *Kilsyth* and *Killiecrankie*. They appeared before the lowlanders of *Perthshire*, who had not seen them since the days of Montrose, in the wild Irish shirt or plaid, which, only covering the body and haunches, leaves the arms and most of the limbs exposed in all their shaggy strength. Their enthusiasm may be guessed from a simple anecdote :— A lowland gentleman, observing among their bands a man of ninety, from the upper part of *Aberdeenshire*, had the curiosity to ask how so aged a creature as he, and one who seemed so extremely feeble, had thought of joining their enterprise. ' I have sons here,' replied the man, ' and I have grandsons; if they fail to do their duty, cannot I shoot them ?'—laying his hand upon a pistol which he carried in his bosom. ' Can I no sheet them ?' were the exact words.—*History of the Rebellion.*

Strathaven and *Glenlivet;* and finally, Rob Roy raised and brought all the men of *Gairn.*

There is another character also that I must not forget, *i.e.* Muckle Cattenach of the *Bealachbuidh.* A strong, brave man he was, proud of his physical force. His bearing, consequently, was not the most lowly, nor his manners the most conciliatory to his neighbours. Previous to the rising, some of them, by way of humbling him a little, reported him to the Earl of Mar as a 'reckless depredator on his moors and forests, and a great destroyer and hewer down of his noble trees.'

The Earl consequently wrote him a letter, reproaching him for his behaviour, and citing him to appear on his first visit to *Bracmar.* Cattenach, poor man, could not read himself; but he kept most carefully this precious letter until he met in with some one who could read it for him. Some time after, having to cross the ferry at *Carn-a-Chuimhni,* he went into the boatman's house—a sort of tavern. There he found a number of people, with Alexander Gordon, priest of *Gairnside,* whom they had taken prisoner.

This was an opportunity not to be lost; so, stepping up to the priest, he asked him to come along with him.

'The people won't let me,' replied the priest.

'Rise, sir! and come away; and let me see the

man that will hinder you.' And as none of them cared to interfere with Cattenach, the priest was let go. Having taken him home, Cattenach produced the letter, which Mr. Gordon read. Its contents, as can be easily imagined, made the mighty man very angry; and suspecting that Invercauld was at 'the bottom of it,' he resolved to be revenged.

An opportunity was not long of presenting itself. Farquharson had been at *Aberdeen;* and on the day he was to return home, Cattenach armed and went to the woods west of *Inver*, to wait his arrival. Fortunately Invercauld had learned what he had to expect, and so took the short cut through the hills by *Philagie*, to avoid the rencounter.

When his servant—who, to prevent suspicion, had proceeded by the usual route—reached the place where Cattenach lay concealed, he saw to his dismay a gun levelled at him; but with great presence of mind he raised himself in his stirrups, and turned round as if looking for some one. He was thus allowed to pass; and beyond gunshot, he gave rein to his horse, and was quickly out of danger.

I do not know how long Cattenach lay waiting the laird; but Invercauld for the future took care not to give him another such opportunity.

When Mar arrived, he was told how angry his letter had made Cattenach, and how dangerous a man he was; so the Earl sent a messenger to him, to say that he needed not trouble himself attending to the summons, as the Earl did not wish to see him.

'But I want to see the Earl,' replied Cattenach; and buckling on his sword, he set out, and forced his way into his lordship's presence, as he sat in the castle with a number of the gentlemen of the country about him.

'My Lord,' began Cattenach, 'it appears I have been accused of cutting down and wasting your wood; and it is true that I have taken a tree now and then, like others of your tenants; but, my Lord, there are those sitting there with you who have bought lands with the profits made by cutting and selling your wood.'

No one spoke; so Cattenach continued:

'Perhaps you would find them far less ready to help you in a strait than Cattenach of the *Bealach-buidh*, on whom it is attempted to lay all the blame.'

The Earl was wise enough to make a friend of Cattenach. He made peace also between him and Invercauld; so of course Cattenach hastened to join the Earl at the rising, and, it is said, distinguished himself at *Perth*.

The effects of this rash and ill-advised rising were, as all know, disastrous to those engaged in it. I only notice particularly its consequences in *Braemar*. Many of the brave men who marched away so gallantly, never returned. John Farquharson was taken at *Preston*, and kept in prison a considerable time. Many other Farquharsons also taken at *Preston* were *transported*, and most of them died in exile.

Those who were at *Sheriffmuir* fared little better. Harry of *Whitehouse*, after returning home, was with his two sons made prisoner, and confined in *Aberdeen*. Francis, his third son, had been taken at *Preston*.

Shaw of the *Achreachan* Farquharsons was killed. James of *Balmoral* suffered greatly until the general indemnity. Colonel Peter, his brother, fled to *France*, and remained there until the indemnity. He escaped having his estate forfeited, by being attainted under a wrong name.

But not only did the proprietors in *Braemar* suffer : the mass of the people also had to share in the common misery. A body of troops was sent into the country, which they completely wasted. It is said that not a single house was left standing in *Braemar*, except one belonging to an old woman at *Corrymulzie*. She did not, like her neighbours, fly to the hills when the soldiers approached, but kept beside them ; and as fast as they set fire to the thatch of her hut, she set to work and extinguished it. Charmed with her patience and courage, they at length desisted, and left her dwelling not much injured.

Before the people fled, they had forethought suffi-

cient to collect all the meal in the strath ; and having
tied it up in sacks, it was hid in the deep chasm below
the *Falls of Corrymulzie.* After the soldiers' departure it was found to be little injured : the water had
formed a sort of paste over all the surface, leaving
the interior dry. Thus the creatures were saved from
the additional horrors of famine.

Shortly after this general burning, *Braemar Castle*
was rebuilt, and a garrison placed in it. A second
garrison was placed in a house at the *Dubrach,* another in the castle of *Abergeldie,* and a fourth in the
castle of *Corgarff.* The soldiers had also orders to
disarm every fighting man in the district. These
orders were not very easily put in execution, especially as respected such characters as Cattenach, etc.
A particular account of his opposition is still in traditional existence.

He for a time put them all at defiance, and sometimes made very narrow escapes from the soldiers.
On one of those occasions he killed an officer in command of the party, and fled to the woods. While
lying asleep one day near his own house, a party of
twelve stole upon him. One of the soldiers who was
friendly to him made some noise as they approached.
Despite this warning, they had their hands on his
gun when he started up ; but the whole of them could
not wrench it from him. As more men were coming
to their assistance, he snatched at his dirk, and came

such a slash down the barrel of the gun as effectually
rid him of all further trouble.

The head officer, finding force of no avail, resolved
to try other measures. So he sought out Cattenach,
and explained to him the orders he had received,
and the necessity he was under to see them enforced.

' Now you see, Cattenach, I have a capital gun here,
of which I make a present to you ; and you, as a
man of honour, will return the compliment by coming
down to-morrow to the *Inver*, and in public presenting me with yours.'

Taylor's remark in regard to Highlanders is indeed
true, that ' they are conquered with kindness.' So it
was with Cattenach : ' This was a decent lad of an
officer, he was sure, and not to blame for the harsh-
ness shown to the Highlanders.' So Bealachbuidh,
resolving not to bring him into disgrace, accepted the
gun, and on the morrow, as agreed, handed in his
own at the *Inver*.

CHAPTER II.

Gillespie Urrasach and his brother Donald.

AFTER this general disarming of the people, and from the absence of so many of their leading men, the country sank gradually into a quiescent state. But fresh visits from the *Kern* roused them out of this torpor, and also brought upon the scene a new champion for the *Braes of Mar*. Champions perhaps I should say, as there were two brothers ; the eldest *Gilleasbuig M'Coinnich, alias Gilleasbuig Urrasach, i.e.* Archibald M'Kenzie, *alias* Archibald the Proud or Bold.

Gilleasbuig Urrasach belonged to the *Dalmore* family ; a nephew he was of the laird *Seumas Mor-na-pluice, i.e.* James with the Big Cheeks. He is said to have been a little person, well-made, with ruddy face and light brown hair. Though of no great size, he was wonderfully strong—' all life, activity, and vigour.' No one in *Braemar* was his match with claymore, targe, or dirk ; ' nor could any with pistol or gun so surely hit a given mark.'

Q

In character he was remarkable for cunning, power of enduring hardship and fatigue, inflexibility of purpose, presence of mind in danger, and coolness in carrying out the schemes his fertile brain contrived. To all this he added unbending fidelity to his chief, and implacable enmity to his foes.

But, with his surpassing bravery, he had an amount of pride which rendered him ridiculous. ' He would not stoop to agricultural labour ; aped the gentleman, as, when dining on brochan, porridge, or kail, he had to be served on table-cloth with cover, knife, and fork, whether needed or not,' etc.

He would not stir beyond the threshold without being armed to the teeth,—the ordinary complement being gun, broadsword, dirk, targe, a pair of pistols, a *skiandubh* stuck in the garter of each hose ; besides which he carried one in the sleeve of each arm, which, by a curious contrivance, came down of themselves when he bent his arms in a particular manner. ' This was to secure him from surprise, *however* an enemy might find him ; assure him of an arm defensive, even when fallen, or taken at close quarters unexpectedly by a foe of greater personal strength.'

A multitude of traditions exist as to his prowess. I notice only a few, for the sake of illustrating the state of the people at this period. In his early years, Gillespie with several others were driving wood south through *Glenshee.* As they were descending into the glen, a large party of *Glenshee* men, with their horses and currachs (a sort of creel made of wicker-work, which hung one on each side of the horse ; there were no such things as carts in *Bracmar* in those days), were scrambling up the brae on their way for a load of peats.

A kind of ' wordy war ' had for a long time existed between the inhabitants of the glens, which generally took the form of rhyme.   The *Glenshee* men being numerically strongest, took the favourable opportunity of letting their squibs fly without mercy on the *Strathdee* men below.   One rhyme began thus :

> ' *Gairn* men and *Mar* men,
> Eaters of the bear bread,' etc.

Gillespie, stung to the quick, sprang up the brae, a dirk in one hand and a skian in the other ; and beginning at the last horse, he cut the girths and tumbled the currachs down the hill-side, and so on until he had gone over them all—the *Glenshee* men standing aghast at his audacity.   Then retreating to some distance, he leaped upon a little hillock, and thus parodied their rhyme :

> ' Elves of *Glenshee*,
> Wicked fools,' etc. etc.

Then, by way of conclusion, he said, ' Now, men, after this, say nothing of the *Gairnside* and *Bracmar* men when they are fewer than you, or I'll cut up every one of you, as I've done your horse-girths to-day.'

Not long after, Gillespie, in the same employment, was passing through *Glenshee* alone. When crossing the *Blackwater* at the ford, a company of *Glenshee* men coming from the opposite direction met him about the middle of the stream.

One of the men in passing struck Gillespie's horse with his bludgeon ; and the horse making a plunge, deluged Gillespie with water. His dirk was out in a moment, and with one dig of it did serious damage to one of the aggressor's legs. And not satisfied with that, he pursued the man to the bank, where a desperate struggle ensued. The others came to the rescue ; and at length Gillespie, quite overpowered, and his victim, were both left for dead.

Some time after, when the bodies were being removed, it was found that neither were quite dead ; so they were removed to a house in the vicinity, and the one 'installed in a bed in the *but* end, the other in the *ben ;* and their wounds and bruises attended to.'

Both got on favourably ; and as the people's work had to be attended, they were left alone one day. About mid-day, when the ' good-wife ' came home to prepare dinner, to her great horror she found Gillespie lying in the passage between the two rooms. Unable to walk, he had crawled that length with his dirk between his teeth, with the intention of getting to the *Glenshee* man, to settle accounts with him. This revengeful purpose was happily prevented. He was forced to bed, watched, and as soon as possible removed to *Braemar*.

The affair was not yet ended, however. Dalmore, thinking that his kinsman had not been justly dealt by in *Glenshee*, required that condign punishment should be inflicted on the party who had ill-treated him. This the lairds of *Glenshee* refused to do; so war was declared, and both parties mustered their men.

Dalmore, as on a former occasion, sought the aid of his ally Invereshy. The messenger he employed was a bold follower called '*Cas Bhruite*,' *i.e.* Bruised Foot, who received instructions to march what men he could get with all speed to the *Cairnwell*, as there M'Kenzie had appointed to meet the lairds of *Glenshee*.

Cas Bhruite delivered his message, and Invereshy at once promised eighteen men; and pitying the lame messenger, he bade him rest a day before he returned.

'Nay,' said *Cas Bhruite*, 'I will show the nearest way.'

'Where they will be to-day, you will be the morn,' returned the laird.

Bruised Foot made no reply, but quietly taking up his place in the rear, set off with the party. By and by he was tramping in the middle. In a little he had gained the van. Without rest or pause, through wet road or dry, long heather, mosses, and rough moor, that desperate march was continued without a word being spoken.

They crossed the *Monadh Ruadh,* came down by the *Geldie,* on by the head of *Glen Christie* and *Glen Conna-feidh,* over by the *Alltan Odhar,* the *Baddoch,* and *Loch Brotachanside,* and appeared on the scene of conflict as the combatants were preparing to meet. Seeing a second army coming against them, the lairds of *Glenshee* agreed to the terms dictated by Dalmore. 'As to *Cas Bhruite,* his fame rang at every hearth in *Mar* and *Badenoch;* even yet, the terrible march he conducted that day is not forgotten.'

From a multitude of Kern adventures, by which Gillespie won for himself a name and laurels, I select only one. Some time previous, the lairds of *Braemar* had appointed twelve men to keep watch against the incursions of the Kern, with Gillespie as their general-in-chief; yet one morning the *Inverey* folks found their pens and stalls empty. No sooner was this known, than Gillespie and his men set out on the track of the robbers, and overtook them at the '*Bothan Leathan.'*

The Kern, seeing the pursuers in force equal to themselves, signified their willingness to come to terms. The two parties therefore joined each other, and began to talk together in small groups, as the matter was to be arranged amicably; and Gillespie with the Kern chief had gone aside a little, to agree on the terms of arrangement. After much wrangling an understanding was come to.

'Shake hands on it,' said the Kern chief, holding out his open palm.

'Willingly,' replied Gillespie, stretching out his hand. The Kern chief took the extended hand, and cunningly manœuvred with it until he had Gillespie firmly by the wrist.

'Now, *Lochaber* men,' cried he, 'let the kail and the bear bread out of these *Braemar* men's stomachs for them ; I have the best of them by the hand.'

Gillespie was not outdone. By means of the *skiandubh* in his sleeve, and the curious contrivance by which he got it into his left hand, he in turn cried, 'Now, *Braemar* men, let the stolen beef and mutton out of these *Lochaber* men's stomachs for them, as I have the best of them on my knife.' And with that he plunged it into the Kern's heart.

The *Lochaber* men, on seeing their chief fall, were disconcerted ; and the Braemarians took such advantage of that circumstance, that only two escaped to tell the tidings in *Lochaber*.

With all his greatness, Gillespie enjoyed a frolic occasionally. For instance, the priests being still under interdict, they had to meet with their people in quiet places ; and one day, while some old women were waiting for him in one of the upper glens, Gillespie took a fancy to act 'father confessor' to them. He succeeded in making them believe that he had been commissioned to act for the priest; so all retired from the room but one, and she commenced in the usual manner.

Gillespie listened with the gravity of a judge for some time. At length he started, and with extraordinary emphasis exclaimed, ' What! did you really do that ?' The thing was very trivial.

' Yes,' replied she, sobbing, ' and may God forgive me for it.'

' Pardon you !' cried Gillespie. ' Never! that's a sin for which there is no pardon in this life, nor in the life to come.'

With that she began to wring her hands, and be in great despair; and Gillespie, unable longer to restrain himself, had fallen back on his chair, and was laughing unrestrainedly. And just at that juncture the priest made his appearance. Gillespie's was a very grave offence; and however it fared with the old woman and the pardon of her sin, he had no little trouble, through penance and otherwise, to get rid of his.

Another Kern incident, and the last I shall notice, brings out in bold relief his inflexibility of purpose. It was late autumn, and the summer shielings of the *Alltan Odhar* being deserted by the return of the people to their homes, the Kern found refuge in the huts they left. Spies, which they sent over the country, observing that Dalmore's cattle were less guarded

than the others, gave information to that effect. The
whole band came down and swept the place clean,
and before morning had the whole safely lodged with
them in the *Alltan Odhar*.

Seumas Mor na pluice sent a message to Gillespie,
then ascended the *Ey* with his two sons and a small
body of retainers. Having come to open rupture
with the Farquharsons, he was unwilling to risk an
engagement with the marauders, and perhaps lose
his men : so he instructed his sons, with all his followers, to make a circuit and climb a hill overlooking the Kern's camp, and thus cut off their retreat
from *Braemar*. He was then to go singly to them,
and try to make arrangements. If not successful, he
was to give a signal—namely, by raising his hand to
his brow—on seeing which they were to fire.

M'Kenzie then went on ; and calling the chief to
parley—it was the renowned *Cathfhearnach Dubh*,
i.e. the Black Man of the Battles—endeavoured to get
back his cattle for a sum of money, which he offered.
The two chiefs stood a little in advance of the principal shieling ; and while in the heat of the bargain,
Dalmore, forgetting himself, put up his hand to right
his bonnet. His men mistaking this for the signal,
fired ; a sentinel who guarded the shieling fell. The
Kern chief thinking himself betrayed, seized the gun
of the fallen sentinel, and shot *Seumas Mor na pluice*.
A cairn of stones was afterwards erected on the spot

where he fell, near the hunting shiel of the Duffs in the *Alltan Odhar.*

A short contest followed. The sons with their party left their vantage-ground; both the young men fell, and the rest were put to flight. In the confusion that followed their deaths, the Kern escaped with the cattle; and Gillespie, who now arrived, not having sufficient force to pursue them, only succeeded in shooting down some stragglers. On returning home, his wife told him that they had also stolen his own grey mare.

'Weel,' Gillespie replied, 'I could pardon them for that ; but this day they have killed the laird and his two sons in the *Alltan Odhar,* and I swear that I will not sleep twice in the same bed, nor drink twice of the same well, till I have avenged their death, and received full value for my grey mare.'

His wife tried hard to turn him from his purpose ; but no—Gillespie was inflexible. So, dressed in beggars' rags, his arms below them of course, and a wallet over his shoulder, he set out for *Lochaber.*

His great difficulty was to find out the chief who shot the laird ; for, having seen him but imperfectly at the *Alltan Odhar* affair, he could not distinguish him from the rest of his countrymen. Two years passed in the fruitless search ; still his purpose remained unshaken, and he went on begging, attending also steadily fair and preaching, marriage, late wake, baptism, burial, feast and meeting of every kind. At a festive gathering one evening, while the dance was going on with great spirit, one of them jostled another rather awkwardly.

'Take care, man,' replied the other, 'or I'll serve you as I did *Seumas Mor na pluice.*'

'They were dancing round, ye ken,' said my informer, 'and Gillespie waited until the man came back again, and was dancing with his back to where he sat ; and just in a moment he drove his dirk into his back up to the very hilt, and fled before the bystanders got owre the start. Then the whole band set out in pursuit, but no Gillespie could be found. An' whare dee ye think he was a' the time? Just on the head of the house. It wasna very high, ye ken ; so he just lap up, and lay there among the lang girse till near morning ; and when they were a' back and quiet again, he came doon an' set away hame.'

Such is the account I had from a descendant of the Dalmore family. There is another version of the story, however ; but the one I have just given is likely to be the most correct. The other is more circumstantial, and reads better. It runs thus :—

'His fruitless search had continued for three years, when a great meeting of the fighting men in *Lochaber* was arranged to take place in a tavern, in order to concert a raid, and also to divide the black mail levied on subject districts.

'The inn where the meeting was to take place was a wide, long, low building, with a flat roof covered over with weeds and long grass. Three holes in the side walls, half closed up with sods, served the place of windows for the great hall. A huge table of rude masonry, covered over with flat stones, stretched from end to end, leaving a space for passage between the wall and the seats, which were also built of stone, and covered with moss and heather. A hole in the roof served for the egress of smoke, and a large opening in the front wall for a door; and along the wall strong juniper roots were inserted, whereon to hang their arms, etc., while they took refreshment. A partition divided this primitive hall from the innkeeper's dwelling, equally primitive. Through a small wicket the refreshments were served to visitors.

'To this inn Gillespie repaired in good time, and so insinuated himself into the landlord's good graces that he was permitted to sleep in a corner of the hall, covered up with heather.

'When night descended, the Kern assembled in great force. A blaze of split pine roots burning on the table enlightened the whole company. The bag of black mail lay conspicuous beside the beacon. The guns, swords, dirks, and targes on the wall reflected the blaze fantastically. After the company had ate and drank plentifully, they began to amuse themselves: they talked, and roared, and laughed,

and sang; but Gillespie lay as still as if he heard
them not. In this half-drunken humour they began
to boast of their deeds. And as each was trying to
get a hearing for himself, the chief rose up and
ordered silence; then proposed that each man should
in turn tell the most remarkable adventure of his
life. The proposal was received with cheers.

'One after another then rose and told his tale: a
medley as wild as the assemblage, and as varied,
each more fearful than the preceding.

'"Silence!" shouted the chief, as he rose to tell
his tale. It was the *Cathfhearnach Dubh* himself.

'"I too," he began, "have done many remarkable
things in my life; but what I account my greatest
feat, was the taking away of *Gillespie Urrasach's*
grey mare while he was at supper; and the best shot
that ever I fired was that which laid low *Seumas
Mor na pluice.*"

'Gillespie leaped midway from his bed to the
table: his beggars' rags fell from off him, while the
barrel of a pistol glanced in his outstretched hand.

'"Was it better than that?" he roared, as every eye
glared upon him. A sharp report and bright flash
followed. The blood spouted from the chief's breast,
as, leaping up in the air, he shrieked out, "*Gillespie
Urrasach!*"—then fell backward dead.

'The Kern seemed petrified into the stone on which
they sat. Gillespie kicked the beacon through the

hall; then seizing the bag of black mail, he glided like a shadow through the open door ; and as soon as he cleared it, he put his hand upon the edge of the low roof, sprang upon it, and as the night was dark, lay concealed among the low grass.

'The Kern, on recovering themselves, made a tumultuous rush to the door, and searched in every direction, but without success. After hours of weary pursuit they returned to the tavern, and called over their names, to see that their number was complete. Thus assured that there was no ambush in the way, he slipped quietly down and set out for *Braemar*, as they began to intone the first notes of the coronach over the *Cathfearnach Dubh.* He never halted until he reached *Dalmore.* Once there, he delivered up the black mail to the new laird, not forgetting, however, to pay himself for his grey mare.'

The subsequent history of this bag of gold is interesting. The laird of *Dalmore* hearing that lands in *Cromar* were for sale, resolved to lay out his gold in their purchase. On going to inspect them, however, he quite changed his purpose, and determined rather to keep his gold in its hiding-place. Not satisfied, however, with its present place of deposit, he shifted it to another ; so it found its last resting-place in a height on the south side of *Ben-Macdhui.*

M'Kenzie's mode of selecting his hiding-place was original : he left his home by night, so as to reach

Ben-Macdhui before morning ; having reached a certain point, he waited there until the sun rose, and there, below the first spot which its beams illuminated, he buried his gold.   His object of course was to mark with precision the spot where it lay, as any external mark might have served to others as a clue to its whereabouts.

It was not until M'Kenzie lay on his deathbed that he revealed the secret to his sons.   But although he was most particular in telling them the day of the year on which he buried it, and the particular spot on which they were to wait until the sun arose, all their efforts to obtain the gold have been unavailing ; so the *pose* on the *Meal-an-oir, i.e.* Hill of the Gold, is yet undisturbed.   It is not many weeks yet since an intelligent old lady belonging to the M'Kenzie family assured me that she had not the slightest doubt of the truth of this account, or that the gold is yet in its hiding-place on the south side of *Ben-Macdhui.*

Gillespie lived to a good old age ; and some stories regarding his conduct on his deathbed are equally quaint with those pertaining to his life.   But death is too serious a matter to jest with.   His younger brother *Donald Urrasach*, or Donald the Proud, has already been immortalized by Sir Thomas Dick Lauder, in his legend of *The Miller of Glen Cuiach.*   That legend, except in a very few particulars, is perfectly correct, as an old man still living in *Castleton* remembers the miller, whose name was James Ley, and the gusto with which he used to relate the story, and also how heartily he used to laugh at Donald's discomfiture.

CHAPTER III.

Changes in *Braemar*—Earl of Mar's Estates sold—The *Ephiteach*.

WHILE *Gillespie Urrasach* and his brother Donald were pursuing their adventurous course, many important changes were taking place in *Bracmar*, some of which I now proceed to notice. On the 15th of July an Act of Grace was passed, which released those who were in prison, and the others from fear of further punishment. John of *Invercauld*, and all who had been in 'durance vile,' returned home; Colonel Peter Farquharson of *Inverey* also, who had been in *France*. But most of those who had been transported to the *West Indies*, etc., died abroad.

The next great event was the disposal of the sequestrated estates of the family of Mar. A full account of that transaction, so far as the lairds of *Braemar* were concerned, is found in the following letters of Lord Grange, who with Lord Dun had the disposing of the property and rights:—

R

LORD GRANGE TO THOMAS ERSKINE OF PITTODRY.

'EDINBURGH, 22*d March* 1730–1.

.   .   .   .   .   .

'The parting with those things in *Aberdeenshire*
gives me a great deal of uneâsyness. But what can
we do? Better to part with some, and save the rest,
than lose all. . . . The bargain about the forest has
gone so oddly, that you should know it.

'We resolved to give the offer to the gentlemen
whose lands lay nearest to it,—namely, *Inverry* and
Dallmore. The first came here himself, and the
other commissioned his brother about it. Lord Dun
thought fit to call Invercauld hither to give advice,
and to him allso he proposed to buy the *Davach of
Castletown*, who was for it, but regreated he was to
have no share of the forrest for grazing to it. Dallmore's people have shunned me, as afraid ever since
the impertinence of James last deceast, and applyed
wholly to Dun, and Lord Dun in this affair trans-
acted all, both with Dallmore and Inverrey; and the
price he asked, by Invercauld's advice, was fifteen
years' purchase of the rent it has been set at these
two years passt. At length Dun, with Inverry and
Charles, came to me; and his share of the forrest,
and what he was to pay for souming and rouming of
the shiels and gleimings, came to ten thousand merks.
They pretended not that it was too dear, but said

that they were not able to pay for it, and had even
on that pretence proposed before to Lord D. to let
them have all for five thousand merks; and Lord D.
believing that if they did not, none else would purchase it, nine thousand merks was agreed to on both
sides. The proportion of this for his part of the
forrest (the same that he has in tack) was four thousand five hundred merks. Dallmore, after much
jangling with Lord D. for that part he has in tack,
would not give the seven thousand five hundred
merks, which at fifteen years' purchase it amounted
to, and Dunn gave up with him, which he told me in
the forenoon; and I told my Lord that I would not
consent to his getting another offer for it, but let
Invercauld have it, who had been more useful to us,
and might be so still, and proceeded more hand-
somely, to which Lord Dun agreed. And I assured
Invercauld in the afternoon that he only should be
the man. He no sooner parted with me than he
told this to Dallmore's brother, who came to me
almost out of his wits, and said he did not think he
had given up with Lord D.; that his brother might
leave the country if Invercauld got this, and insted
of fifteen had better give fifty years' purchase than
want it; and almost with tears begged me to let
him have it still. I told him how unworthy he was,
knowing the value of it so well, yet to strive so much
to beat down the price, that he had had it several

times in his offer at that low price, and rejected. He
answered that it was only to learn whether Inverrey
should get an abatement, that he might ask it too.
I replyed that it was nothing to him though we had
sold it to Inverry for sixpence ; and since he had
been thus on the sharp with us, he had been de-
servedly trapt ; that I had given my word to Invercauld, and would not break it at any rate.

'Then Lord Dun and I met with Invercauld and
Inverrey, and his brother Charles and he and J.
Thomson were to draw minutes ; and Lord D. to
go from town next day. The minutes Charles made
were perplexed nonsense, like his looks, and, I believe, like the inside of his head too. Therefore, just
after Dun went away, I drew the minutes myself,
and sent them to the lairds and their writer, and met
with them about two hours afterwards. They were
displeased with them, and none more than that bitter
little villain Charles. I added some things on the
margent, which pleased them. So we parted, and were
to meet next day and sign, when the minutes were
transcribed on stampt paper. When I came from
them, a gentleman, exceedingly responsible, told me
he heard of the bargain ; that I was vastly cheated
by these villains ; that he was not at freedom to tell
me his man, nor did I need to care, for he would
give me for Invercauld's part seven hundred guineas
above the seven thousand five hundred merks. I

told him I suspected that Dallmore was his man, who therefore was still the greater villain, since he had strove to cheat us even of a part of the seven thousand five hundred merks. He would not tell me his man ; but, in short, he offered me four thousand five hundred merks above the seven thousand five hundred, and to give me his own bill for it, payable for it at Whitsunday next ; and assured me of a merchant for Inverrey's part, at a proportionally higher sum than Inverrey's. I told him, had I known as much when they impertinently and sawcyly jangled with me about the minutes, I could have broke with them, but now could not honourably do it, should he give pounds sterling for merks Scots ; that I had never broke my word in any bargain, and never would.

'When Invercauld came to me next day I told him this, and that we were ill-used by all of them, and expected it not at his hand, and would think it very odd if he came not up to the price, or at least make a handsome compliment ; but he was deaf. The thing began to be talked of ; and Sir H. P——ne happening to meet the two Invers, told them so, and that it filled everybody with indignation to see Lord M.'s family in the present circumstances treated so by those who ought, least of all men, to do so. . . . Inverrey and his brother seemed not a bit moved. Invercauld was in a sort of agony, and his lip trembled (as you know it does when he is in great concern), and he hasted to get away from him. Much pains was taken to persuade me that I was not tyed in honour ; but I hate to drive too near that point, or to do anything that looks like shirking, or playing fast and loose, whatever be the consequences.

'At length I again met with the two lairds and writer, the minutes being ready for signing. I composed myself to great calmness, and observed it, though inwardly very angry. But I told them calmly and plainly that I was a frank dealer, as they knew, and would without any commotion tell them the truth ; that I was ill-used by them, and Lord D. and I plainly imposed upon by those that, as gentlemen, and who had received not a few former favours, and still profest great kindness and respect to the family, would not have hurt it so signally in its present circumstances. They said the rent would never answer in money to the agreed price, and that they would gladly give a nineteen years' tack at a smaller rent ; but they acknowledged that they valued the priviledge of killing deer and roe, being heritably deputy-forresters, and thereby entitled to the generall's warrands for carrying arms, and were afraid of strangers, and especially men of power, getting the forrest, which hurt them vastly ; and hoped I would be so good as not to do it. I answered, that as their goodness to me had been very extraordinary, it was merry enough to talk so on this occasion ; that if all these things

were so valuable to them, and that others would pay
for them, why should not they ? And they knew
the family could not spare such summes at present.
That by holding me to my word, Lord Mar losst on
the forrest about £500 sterling ; and since I took not
the legal priviledge of resiling, if they came not up
to the price, or made a handsome compliment, I
would declare them the most ungenerous men alive ;
and that I hardly believed there were other two
gentlemen in the shire of *Aberdeen* who would use me
so. Their answer was, that I had made the bargain
with them already. In short, we signed the minutes,
and left them with that worthy gentleman, Charles,
the writer (whom I may probably remember), to be
sent to the country to Lord D. to sign them. As I
left them, Invercauld was so modest as with trembling
voice to entreat me still to get Alnaquoich and some
servants of his kept out of the Porteous roll, which
before he had desired of me without any concern.
When I left these three, they got their cousin, young
Fenzean, and went to the tavern, and made merry.

· · · · ·

'Let me end this long story by another passage.
When Lord Dun proposed the *Castletown* to Invercauld, he made some objections to the terms, but it
was plain he was for it. I told Dun we should end
that with him before he got the forrest, without which
he thought none would buy the *Castletown* for want

of grass ; and therefore, if both were not ended at once, he might think to put his own terms on us for the *Castletown*.   But Lord Dun seemed not touched with this, and hurried out of town.   When I spoke with Invercauld about the *Castletown*, after I saw he was resolved to hold me fast about the forrest, he told me plainly that he would not come up to our terms.   But he will be disappointed, for I think to get our own terms, though his honour should have the forrest ; and if another will but give as much as he, can any mortal say that his honour of Invercauld should be the man after what has passt ?'

LORD GRANGE TO THOMAS ERSKINE OF PITTODRY.

'EDINBURGH, 14*th* *June* 1731.

'I believe your conversation with Invercauld has made him ashamed of the affair about the forrest, for Lord Dun tells me he gave up his minute.   I am glad on't, on account of his own character, for I think him the best of the set.'

LORD GRANGE TO THOMAS ERSKINE OF PITTODRY.

'EDINBURGH, 18*th* *June* 1733.

'I hear Monaltrie has owned his being in the wrong to Captain Grant, and has given bond for the bygones, etc.   He might once have had a better bargain.   He certainly must be what he called himself, "a very weak man!"   But I am glad that affair is at an end, and I wish that they may now be very good friends.'

The end of all this altercation was, that all the three lairds, Invercauld, Inverrey, and Dallmore, got the property they wanted. The lands thus disposed of, an offer was made to the proprietors of *Deeside* above *Culblean*, that each should buy up the feudal rights of the lord superior over their different holdings, and pay in all, between them, for these the sum of £1000. A meeting of the lairds was called at *Pannanich Lodge* to take the offer into consideration, and, if they should decide on accepting it, to assign what proportion of the sum each should have to pay. The proprietors had, I may state, a right to every third tree on their estate, to the whole pasture, divots and peats. They were hereditary foresters, and therefore allowed to carry arms and kill game : the military service, and the small tribute of money as an acknowledgment of superiority when the lands changed hands, were of little moment. So they ended their deliberations by refusing the offer ; and Duff of *Braco* became the purchaser. At this point, therefore, another noble family comes upon the scene, a slight sketch of which I give ere proceeding further with the legends.

The following account of the noble family of Duff, of which the *Braemar* legends speak at first somewhat slightingly, as narrated to me, was professedly taken from a MS. history, written originally in Latin, and translated into English about the year 1746.

'The country of the Vermicenii, or, as it is sometimes called, Venricons, that whereof the kingdom of the Picts chiefly consisted, was at first called *Ross*, which, in the ancient language, signified a peninsula, which agrees exactly with the nature of the place, as it is separated from other counties of the island by the *Ochil Hills*, the *Firths* of *Forth* and *Tay*, and the *German Ocean*. At length it was called *Fife*, from a prince named Fifus, who governed the land. He was cousin to Kenneth II., by whose valour the Picts were entirely subdued ; and as a signal mark of royal favour, and in reward of his extraordinary services against the Picts, was by His Majesty made Thane, Governor, or rather Prince of *Fife*, in 838.

'This Fife, surnamed Duff, continued during the life of Kenneth II. and his brother Donald V. to enjoy his exalted position, and used his power so as to be lamented by high and low when he died in 858. Duff M'Duff succeeded him in virtues as well as in honours and estates, in the reign of Constantine II., and died with him, fighting against the Danes in defence of his country, 878.

'Fife the warrior was the third thane. He made great havoc among the Danes during the reign of Gregory, whom Fife survived even to the reign of Donald VI., and was then succeeded by Duff, who

held the dignity during the reigns of Constantine III.
and Malcolm I., and died in the reign of Indulph.
Colban, Malcolm, and Constantine held the dignity
successively, with all the glory of their ancestors.

  'To Constantine succeeded M'Duff—"a man who
surpassed all encomiums." In 1056 he slew the
tyrant Macbeth at Lumphanan, and set Malcolm III.
on the throne of his ancestors ; and was afterwards,
in a public convention of the Estates, created by him
Earl of Fife. He was also made general of His
Majesty's forces ; and when he died, was buried among
the kings at *Icolmkill.* He was succeeded by his
eldest son, Duff II., who flourished during the reigns
of Edgar and Alexander, and on his death was interred in the royal sepulchre belonging to his father.

  'Constantine, second of that name, and third Earl,
died young, and was buried at *Iona*, and was succeeded by Michael, son of Galeus, "a man justly
admired for his virtues ;" and was chosen by His
Majesty as tutor to the prince who, for the beauties
of his mind, was termed "the angel incarnate." He
was succeeded by his son Duncan, who in noble
endowments, etc., if possible, surpassed his father.
He died in 1154, and was succeeded by Duncan,
who was made Lord Justiciary of *Scotland*, and, on
marrying a niece of Malcolm IV., received large addi-
tions to his estates. After founding a convent of
nuns at *North Berwick*, he died in 1203.

'He was succeeded by Malcolm, second of that name, and seventh Earl, who founded the *Cistercian Monastery of St. Servian* at *Culross*. He married Maud, daughter of the Earl· of Mar, and with her obtained large possessions. He died at *Culross* 1229, when his estates and honours devolved on his nephew Malcolm III., who married Winifred, daughter of Llewellen, Prince of *Wales*. Colban, the next and ninth Earl, after a short possession of the dignity, gave place to his son Duncan in 1270, who on the death of His Majesty Alexander III. was appointed Regent of *Scotland*. He was slain by the Abernethies in 1286. Duncan V. of that name, and eleventh Earl, died in battle 1299, and was succeeded by Duncan VI., who married Maria Mortimer, niece to Edward of *England*. This marriage proved the ruin of the illustrious family, as from that day they aided the English.

'Duncan VII. of that name, and thirteenth Earl, was the author of a lampoon termed *My Letter*, which was presented to Pope John XXII. by the Scottish nobility in 1320. Duncan was made Governor of Perth by Baliol, but was apprehended by the Brucian party, and conducted with his wife and daughter to *Kildrummy Castle*, where he died in 1336. Isabella, his daughter, married Walter Stuart, a prince of the blood-royal ; but as both died without family, the honours and estates devolved on his brother the

Duke of Albany, and regent of the kingdom. He
was succeeded by M'Ducus his son, who was beheaded by James I. So ended for a time the Thanes
and Earls of *Fife*, who had flourished for a period of
498 years.

'In 1401, David Duff, a collateral branch of the noble
family of Duff, obtained from Robert III. the *Barony
of Muldavit*, and was afterwards made Earl of Fife.'

In July 28, 1735, William Duff, who is connected
with the *Braemar* traditions, was created Lord Braco
of *Kilboyde;* and on April 26, 1759, he was created
Viscount M'Duff and Earl of Fife, at which point this
brief sketch of the Duff family closes, as the few
traditions given of it occur about or after that period.

Braco, shortly after his purchase, came to *Braemar*
with a number of workmen to cut down some of the
wood. Looking about, he determined to begin in
Glen Quoich. Allen-Quoich accompanied the wood-
men through the glen, and saved every third gigantic
pine from their hatchets. When they had cut down
some sixty, they began to consider how they were to
be got to the *Dee*.

'Ay, ay, Braco,' said Allen-Quoich, 'there is your
wood; shoulder it, and away ye go; but mark you,
I won't allow earth to be broken on my land, or
my pasture destroyed. Do you it therefore at your
peril; and meanwhile there is an interdict.'

This was no joke; and Braco, completely nonplussed, had to return home, minus wood of course. But, according to current traditions, he soon and often returned to *Braemar.* On these occasions he assiduously cultivated the acquaintance of all the proprietors, but especially that of Allen-Quoich. This resulted first in a great change in the old laird and family's style of living ; secondly, in embarrassed circumstances; and ultimately in the sale of *Allen-Quoich* to Braco, who was his principal creditor.

A saw-mill was soon established on the *Quoich* after Duff's accession ; and as there was none now to serve an interdict, or save every third tree from falling, the woodman's axe made quick work among the forest glories.

There is yet another story regarding the manner in which *Dalmore* was acquired by Braco. A sort of wordy war had for some time existed between the followers of Inverey and those of Dalmore. As was customary in the *Highlands,* each great family had its bard ; that of the M'Kenzie family had his nose cut off at *Sheriffmuir.* The bard of *Inverey* was one of the *Marcaich* M'Intoshes. So the two companies used to encounter on the banks of the *Dee.* Each party, keeping its own side, hailed across the river the praises of their own chief.

These ' tournays of poesy ' had an unhappy effect. From the praises of his own chief, the bard generally ended in the bitterest satires on the rival family.

This war of words continued to rage until it took the more material form of feud and lawsuit ; and somewhere between 1726 and 1733 it came to open war. Both parties—M'Kenzies and Farquharsons—levied their fighting men, and met in *Corrie Bhui.* When it came to the point, the sages in both camps wished for a peaceable termination, and deputies passed between them with the intention of effecting this. But among the M'Kenzies 'one voice was still for war.' A tall, dark, powerful man kept pacing up and down, demanding blood, 'as little good,' he thought, came of the battles that ended in peace.

Invercauld, who was at the head of the Farquharsons, wished to know who that wild fellow was.

'That,' replied the deputy, 'is the *Ephiteach ;* and he has sworn that if a ball be shot to-day, it will be his endeavour to send the second through your heart.' *Donald Dubh an-t-Ephiteach, i.e.* Black Donald the . Egyptian, had the reputation of being a 'crack shot ;' and as Invercauld felt that he was at an unchancy near range, it was found quite possible to come to an understanding.

But the days of good fellowship between the families were at an end. They soon after went to law, instigated, tradition says, by Braco. The legend of this affair concludes by saying : 'One court of law was tried after another ; and as their means got done, Braco's purse supplied them both. M'Kenzie always lost, but on getting a fresh supply began again. But there is a limit and an end to everything ; and the limit came in M'Kenzie's means, and an end in his complete defeat by Inverey. The lawyers were now to pay. Inverey, in repayment of his supplies, gave over to Braco his costs against Dalmore. As for M'Kenzie, it was the case of *Allen Quoich* over again ; and for another £2000, which would have been about a penny for every tree on the estate, Duff came in, and the laird stepped out. M'Kenzie got a tack of lands on *Gairnside* from Aboyne, and set up at *Lary.*

Some of the M'Kenzies, however, remained in *Braemar:* among them was the *Ephiteach,* or Egyptian, so called from having been in *Egypt.* He was something of a character ; and with his cousin *Domhnull MacRobaidh Mhoir, i.e.* Donald, son of Robert the Mighty, succeeded *Gillespie Urrasach* and his brother Donald in the championship of *Braemar.*

CHAPTER IV.

Rising of ''45'—Battle of *Falkirk*—Second Gathering—
Culloden and its Results, etc.

OW wonderfully deep and abiding,' writes an old Highlander, 'was our love for Prince Charlie!' And it was indeed something extraordinary, that after suffering so much as a people at the recent rising of ''15,' the Braemarians were again found so ready to face suffering and death to support the claims of the 'Pretender.'

This last rising of ''45' seems to have been even more of a popular movement than the former one. There was now no Earl of Mar to summon them out as lord superior. Yet so strong was the current of popular feeling in favour of the Pretender, that neither his successor Lord Braco, nor the Earl of Aboyne, nor the laird of *Invercauld*, though all on the side of Government, could stem it. That this was the case, the following extracts from the *Legends of the Braes of Mar* make evident:—

'Lord Braco, who supplanted Allen Quoich and

Dalmore, was a favourer of the established Government. Invercauld himself was an old man, and what influence he possessed he freely used for the same party as Braco: his son had a commission in the Black Watch. But these two proprietors' opposition was of little moment. The whole of the district was Jacobite—rich and poor, young and old, men and women.'

The thought forcibly strikes one, that some cause must have existed, of strength sufficient to produce this state of feeling. Paragraphs like the following give some inkling as to what it might have been :—

'And how about the Rev. Alexander Gordon of *Gairnside?* Why, he accompanied all the following of *Balmoral* as chaplain ; and perhaps the "bra' lads'" hearts were none the less daring, from knowing they would have his services on the battle-field. And perhaps the swords of Mar were none the less efficient, that he besought the Lord of hosts in their behalf.

'The men of *Gairn* under Fleming of *Auchintoul,* and the three Macgregors with their followers, convened at *Dalfad.* Besides his arms and accoutrements, each man carried only a bag of meal sufficient for three days' vivers, and a spare pair of new brogues. As they went out, the *Glaschoille* Macgregor of *Inverigny,* after doubtless meditating on their bare and unprovided condition, exclaimed, " A soldier, my lads, should always go away poor and come home rich."

'"When men go forth to battle, Inverigny," returned Mr. Gordon the priest, "there is a store of other riches besides those of this world to be thought of and striven after."'

The effects of such teaching on minds so little cultivated can be easily appreciated. They were fighting not only for 'Charlie,' but also for the re-establishment of Popery.

But to return. The chieftainship of the Clan Farquharson belonged of right to Finla, son of Colonel Peter Farquharson of *Inverey*, lately deceased. But Finla being an imbecile, his uncle, James Farquharson of *Balmoral*, took his place. Balmoral was joined by Francis Farquharson of *Monaltrie*, commonly named the *Baron Ban*, or Fair-haired Baron, and Charles Gordon of *Blellack* and *Pronie Gairnside;* these three being the great leaders of the movement.

Braemar at one time, like many other places in the *Highlands*, had the advantage of one living in it who could not only see into futurity, but also occasionally tell them when events of importance were transpiring in places at a distance, just at the exact time, or perhaps a little before.

Accordingly, it is stated that 'on the 25th July 1745, the seer of *Glen-Lui*, Duncan Calder, intimated to the men of *Mar* that Prince Charlie was that very day landing at *Moidart*. One of the incredulous lairds of the district despatched a messenger to verify the tidings, but ere he returned the country was ringing with the din of arms.' Be that as it may, the tidings of 'Charlie's' arrival soon reached *Braemar*. Again the Farquharsons mustered in all their strength. The place of meeting was probably *Carn-a-quheen*.

Lewis Farquharson of *Auchindryne* was now dead ; but his three sons, Alastair, William, and James, assembled with all their followers, the Farquharsons of *Tullochcoy* in their company.

Among the men of *Dalmore* and *Allen Quoich*, the *Ephitcach* and his cousin *MacRobaidh Mhoir* shone pre-eminent. Lord Braco, though opposed to it, could not hinder his men from rising. Nor Invercauld, it seems, either ; for his daughter even, 'the Lady M'Intosh,' took the field, and in her train were many of her father's followers.[1] She figured largely in the battle of *Falkirk*. A little before it began, the following conversation took place :—

---

[1] 'The M'Intoshes had been raised under somewhat remarkable circumstances. . . . The chief or laird, usually called M'Intosh of *M'Intosh*, was, or affected to be, loyal to the existing sovereign, and personally appeared in arms on that side. At the same time, his wife, a young woman of high spirit and resolution, raised the clan for the Chevalier, and adding to it three hundred Farquharsons, formed a very good regiment.

'The strange proceedings of this lady caused her to be distinguished by the jocular appellation of "Colonel Anne." It is said that at a subsequent part of the campaign, M'Intosh himself being taken in the capa-

' " Balmoral," said Lochiel, " why did you not bring Invercauld with you ? "

' " Invercauld, you see, thinks differently from us," answered Balmoral ; " but there is the less to regret, as I see his daughter the Lady M'Intosh here ; and some of the men following her, I could swear, live not ten oxgangs from *Invercauld.*"

' The lady was then passing at the head of three hundred gallant lads, wearing a man's bonnet, a habit of tartan richly laced, and having a pair of pistols at her saddle-bow.' Here I may notice also, that on a subsequent occasion the Prince owed no less than his life to this lady.

To return to *Bracmar.* Cattenach of *Bealleachbhui* was still in fighting trim, and 'went out' with his son-in-law, Malcolm Durward of *Mullach.* Harry Farquharson of *Whitehouse* also gathered with his *Cromar* men ; Patrick Fleming of *Auchintoul,* with several M'Gregors and all the *Gairnside* men, as in ' '15.' In short, all in the district, except Lord Braco, Invercauld, and the Earl of Aboyne, hasted to throw off their allegiance and join the standard

city of a loyal militia captain by a party of the insurgents, was actually brought as a prisoner into the presence of his wife, who was then acting a semi-military part in the Chevalier's army. She said with military laconism, " Your servant, Captain ; " to which he replied with equal brevity, " Your servant, Colonel." Lady M'Intosh was a daughter of Farquharson of *Invercauld,* a friend of the Government.'—*Chambers' History of the Rebellion.*

of rebellion ; and any who remained at home were compelled to contribute of their substance. For instance :

On the 26th November Lewis Gordon writes from *Huntly* to Moir of *Stonywood* thus : ' I have a letter from Blellack, who has execute his orders to very good purpose, notwithstanding the opposition he met with from Inver-call, whose people, as well as Lord Braco's in that country, he has obliged to comply in paying a " cess " for the Prince.'

On the 9th December Blellack writes from *Tarland* to Stonywood : ' I would have given Mackie the party ye desair, if Munaltry and I had not sent a good many of the men we had upon fitt with Mr. M'Gregor of *Inverenzie* to *Aberdeen*, which will be with you before this comes to hand. . . . I have sent the list of the *Ses Lonmay* inclosed to Munaltry up the country, where he is just now, who will certainly ack conform to the directions. I am just now sending a part of our men to *Aberdeen*. . . . At my desair the Earl of Aboyne's tennants sen in their *ses* by the bearer.'

It would be tedious to give the details of all the doings of the men of *Mar*, but one or two short traditions respecting their exploits at the various engagements may be interesting.

The battle of *Falkirk* was fought on the 16th January 1746. The traditional account of it is as follows: 'The 16th January was a wild, stormy day; but what mattered the weather to men who had often passed the most inclement nights of winter by the shelter of a stone in the open air? It was a steep rough climb up the heights of *Falkirk;* but what mattered it to the hunters of the deer through the wilds of *Braemar?*

'Opposed to Balmoral was Munro's regiment of horse. Balmoral drew up his men in the form of a wedge, thus: he marched at their head, two men followed in the second rank, three in the third, and so on to the rear.

'"Now, my lads," cried he, "march in silence. Fire not a shot till you can discern the colour of the horses' eyes, then give one volley all together; throw down your guns, and rush upon them; cut the bridles, hamstring the horses, and we will then arrange with the men."'

At this moment Colonel Munro was galloping up and down before his regiment, conspicuous for the splendour of his harness and plume floating gracefully in the breeze.

'Is there no deerslayer among you, lads?' cried Balmoral back to his men as they advanced in silence. Down at once on their knees dropped two or three of them. A sharp knell followed, the clouds of smoke rose into the air, and Munro's horse galloped away with empty saddle.

With bonnets tightly drawn down,[1] and plaids streaming in the wind, they pressed up the heights. In evil hour a bullet hit Balmoral in the shoulder.

'Four men,' cried his henchman, 'to carry our wounded chief to the rear!'

'Never!' cried Balmoral the Brave. 'Four men to carry your chief at the head of his children into the thickest of the fight!'

A dread hurricane was sweeping over the heights of *Falkirk*, but one still more dread of carnage and death swept over the combatants, as a volley that scattered destruction flamed out from the advancing wedge, who then with claymore, etc., rushed furiously to their work of death. Hundreds fell and rolled down the heights together, horse and rider, friend and foe.

Alastair Farquharson of *Auchindryne* had borne the standard of his clan up the heights; at length, overpowered with fatigue, wind, and rain, he could do no more.

'*Am beil Uilleam againn an sin?*' i.e. 'Is our William there? Tell him to come and take the standard.'

'*Imrich thu fhein do luideag Alastair; s'iomadh baistidh math a dh'ithe thu, nach d'ithe mise riamh;*'

---

[1] It was the custom of the Highlanders, before an onset, to *scrug their bonnets*—that is, to pull their blue caps down over their brows, so as to ensure them against falling off in the ensuing *mêlée*.

i.c. 'Carry yourself your standard, Alastair; many a good bread plate you have emptied that I never did;' meaning that his brother was older, and therefore better able to stand the fatigue.

In all, the battle of *Falkirk* lasted but a quarter of an hour. The close fire and terrible charge of the Highlanders could not be withstood. The dragoons were broken, and fled amain. 'So ended *Falkirk*, with glory, honour, and fame to those who went away from *Mar.*'

It seems as if, according to the usual custom among the Highlanders,[1] the *Braemar* men had gone home after the battle of *Falkirk*, as their second and last gathering took place at *Castleton* on the 15th of February 1746. As Balmoral had been severely wounded, Francis Farquharson of *Monaltrie*, or the Yellow-haired Baron, took the command. They had been successful in their last campaign, and they were going out exulting in the idea that they would be so again. But while all were thus indulging in the bright hope, the seer of *Glen-Lui* suddenly exclaimed —'You are going away, men, hearty, merry, and cheery; but, alas! alas! you will return sad, and sorrowful, and heart-broken.'

---

[1] The strictly feudal obligations obtained in *Braemar;* one of which was, that whenever summoned they should attend their superior with fighting men according to the extent of their fees or holdings, for six weeks, at their own expense.

Monaltrie was so provoked at this outburst of discouragement, that he struck down the now aged, bent, and hoary seer; the deed was no sooner done, however, than he bitterly repented of his rashness. 'Honour and loyalty,' said he to his men as he led them away, 'call us out, be our return what it may.'

Harry of *Whitehouse* and Gordon of *Blellack* had the *Cromar* men all assembled at *Tarland* when Monaltrie arrived there from *Braemar*. They rested for the night; and next morning early, with banners displayed, and bagpipes playing the '*Rough Tykes of Tarland*,' they marched three times round the Auld Kirk, then departed in the direction of *Kildrummy*. Three hundred Farquharsons were in this company; yet a short time after, perhaps a month, William Farquharson of *Auchindryne* returned to *Braemar* to raise more, and had succeeded in raising another hundred, when the news reached him that the Duke of Cumberland had left *Aberdeen;* so William with his new recruits hurried away through *Badenoch*.

On the morning of the battle, William and his company reached a small farm not far from *Culloden*, where he rested for a little to refresh his men. After breakfast some of them began to dance. While thus engaged, the thunder of the cannon on *Drummossie Moor* reached their ears. Then it was up and away. But it was too late. The Highland army was completely routed, and all was over with the '*Suaith-ucas-ban*'—the House of Stuart—and for ever.

'The history of the battle is but too well known ; I concern myself, therefore, with the men of *Mar*. Our lads were stationed beside the brave M'Intoshes on the right, and rushed forward with them in their chivalrous attack ; and with them, sword in hand, cut their way back again, when all was lost. The army assembled there should have gained Prince Charles Edward Stuart a very bright crown ; but through dire mismanagement and bad generalship it was cut to pieces, and with it perished for ever the hopes of the Stuarts and the power of the *Highlands*.

'The Baron of the yellow hair, who led on the Farquharsons, lost seventy-nine men, with sixteen subaltern officers, and was himself taken prisoner. He was carried to *London*, and with three brother officers condemned to death. On the night before the execution, a reprieve came for Monaltrie. His three companions met their fate on the following day. He was the last detained in prison for the affair of the "'45."'

The gallant Harry of *Whitehouse* also fell on *Drummossie Moor*. Eighteen men, who lived between the two bridges in *Glengairn*, also fell on the same fatal field, and many more from other parts of it. The priest of *Gairnside*, Alexander Gordon, was taken prisoner and died in confinement.

M'Gregor of *Inverigny* and Fleming of *Auchintoul* fell wounded side by side ; a ball had broken one of Auchintoul's legs. In the evening, while both lay writhing with pain, some soldiers passed, and seeing M'Gregor move, drove his bayonet through his shoulder; and thus died the laird of *Inverigny*. Fleming wore a pair of excellent new boots, which caught the eye of one of the soldiers, who proceeded instantly to possess himself of them. He lay still while the boot was drawn off the sound limb ; but alas when the operation was repeated on the broken one ! He bore the pain, however, unmoved ; and when unbooted, let the broken member fall to the ground, as if lifeless. The fate of his companion was a warning to him. 'I have been in danger,' he used to say, 'and I have seen death face to face ; but my fortitude and courage were never more severely tried than by the undoing of my boots on *Drummossie Moor.*'

'Malcolm Durward of *Mullach* saw his two brothers fall by his side, at the moment the clansmen broke through the first rank of the red-coats. He himself got unhurt out of the confused *mêlée* of the rout. In his flight he met a convoy for the English army, and without a word he cut out with his sword the first horse of the train, and mounting him, rode off. Not one of the drivers, though armed, durst interfere : his size and apparent strength terrified them.'

The prediction of the seer, Duncan Calder, was

now amply verified. A broken remnant only reached home; and no sooner had they done so, than the 'red-coats,' as they termed the soldiers, were at their heels. All fled to the hills and various hiding-places. Charles Farquharson, son of Andrew of *Allergue*, with several others, had their hiding-place in *Craig Cluny*. Then it was that he heard the revelling of the soldiers in his own house, during their unsuccessful visits in search of him. The houses of *Auchintoul, Inverigny, Monaltrie*, and *Auchindryne* were burnt to the ground. Garrisons also were re-established at *Corgarff, Abergeldie*, the *Castle of Braemar*, and at the *Dubrach*, to enforce the various enactments consequent on the defeat of the rising.

In what tones of deep dejection have the results of that day, so fatal to the hopes of the Stuarts, been recorded by some local chroniclers!—'that dreadful 16th of April, a day of bitterness, a day of death, a day stained with the blood of the brave,' etc. 'Scarcely,' says one, 'had the boom of the cannon ceased, when another cry of anguish arose throughout the *Highlands;* and what wonder!—the ruthless soldiers were at the door. Old men were butchered without mercy. Our children were tossed on the bayonet's point, and our houses made a heap of blackened ruins.'

Naturally and strongly as our sympathies flow out to the vanquished and suffering, yet the con-

clusion in this instance cannot be avoided, that
the disastrous results of that day have been beneficial—that the great and evil events of the period
have been overruled for the general good of our
country.

CHAPTER V.

Disarming of the People—Contests with the Soldiers—The
last Rebel in Scotland, etc.

OME of the new measures introduced were
very obnoxious to the Braemarians. One
of them thus writes : ' Not only would the
soldiers put down the "'45 " men, but they had orders
to deprive the Highlanders of their arms ; their im-
memorial right to hunt and fish ; ay, and even of the
liberty to wear their ancient costume. These tyran-
nical measures the men of the *Braes of Mar* resisted
most stoutly.' That they really did so, will be made
sufficiently manifest by relating the traditions yet
extant regarding the returned malcontents.

The surviving leaders of the rebellion seem to have
given little trouble. With the plebeians it was different.
Blellack, for instance, practising a piece of ' Scotch
policy,' rented a farm from Lord Aboyne, who, being
on the Government side, protected him from the red-
coats ; and by having his letters addressed to ' Charles

Gordon, farmer at *Gellan*,' the Government could not discover that they were for the laird of *Blellack*.

After his return from *Culloden* he took refuge at his farm ; while his henchman M'Connach by some means got to be keeper of the canteen in the Government castle of *Corgarff.*

Balmoral, after his wound at *Falkirk*, retired with his lady to his estate of *Auchlossan*, where he remained in hiding to his death ; or, as others have it, in the *Abbey* in *Edinburgh*.

Invercauld was no less accommodating to his relatives than Aboyne had been to Gordon of *Blellack*. More so, indeed, as he went the length of harbouring some of the returned rebels in his own house : one of them at least—Farquaharson, laird of *Broughdearg*.

This *Fear na Bruach, i.e.* Man of the Braes, as he was commonly termed, the laird of *Broughdearg*, was one of Prince Charles's surgeons. The legend giving some account of his history, and how he acquired his professional qualifications, beats all the others for extravagance :—

'*Fear na Bruach* was sent by his parents to *Italy* to study medicine. When he returned home, father and mother were both dead, and his affairs entrusted to a tutor. After his return, the famous Cagliostro, the celebrated physician under whom the young laird had completed his studies, informed his pupil by letter, that he could see from *Italy* a white serpent going

daily at noon to drink from a well at the bottom
of *Coire Chronic*, or the *Dubh Choire*—the Corrie of
Echoes, or the Black Corrie. He instructed *Fear na
Bruach* also to catch this serpent, by laying out for
it a repast of fresh cream, and having caught it, to
bring it forthwith to *Italy*.

'The laird followed the physician's directions,
caught the white serpent, and sailed away. After
his arrival he was ordered by Cagliostro to boil it in
a caldron ; but, on pain of death, not to touch the
contents, or let them boil over. With care and dread
Fear na Bruach stirred round the seething decoction ; but despite all his endeavours, the liquid came
up, hissing and spurting even to the brim. The
temptation to taste was now too strong for *Fear na
Bruach*, and quick as thought he dipped in his finger,
raised it to his mouth, then fled amain.

'Pursuit followed. It seems to have been unsuccessful, as bloodhounds were brought into requisition ; and in the despair which seized him, when he
heard their bay loud and close upon his track, he
leaped forward, and struck in his fall the side of a
huge tree. To his amazement it burst open, and
he fell breathless into a great hollow within the
trunk. With great presence of mind he rose and
re-adjusted the door which had admitted him, then
lay concealed there for twenty-four hours. Finally
he slipt on board a ship, which was just ready to

T

sail from a harbour near by, and returned home again.

'The tasting he had permitted himself of the decoction rendered him omniscient in medicine, so that no disease could baffle his skill, neither could he ever fail in effecting a cure. Some will wonder that he and his generation are not still in the land of the living; but old age is no malady. Death then is but the falling of ripened fruit.

'After the wars, in which such a skilled physician must have been of the greatest value, and while he harboured at *Invercauld, Fear na Bruach* often spoke of another well in *Craig Choinnich*, the waters of which would render physicians unnecessary, by having virtue to cure all diseases. This well also had a serpent, for in the night-time he could see it, he said, from the dining-room windows of *Invercauld*, on the face of the hill near the well below a bush of rushes, lying on a flat stone; but neither he nor any one else has found it.'

Extravagant as this legend is, in former years its authenticity, by some at least, was undoubted. In proof of this, I may state that about sixty years ago, an elderly woman living in *Braemar* prevailed on a young girl of fifteen, who is still living, to accompany her to *Craig Choinnich* in search of the treasure.

The search was continued until they came upon a well quite answering the description; for beside it

were the rushes, flat stone, etc. In consequence of a
dream, the woman expected, in addition to the serpent, to find a wallet full of gold below the slab.

So the two, having found the place, also succeeded
in raising the stone, when the digging for the gold.
commenced in right earnest. For hours and hours
they dug, until the girl, quite exhausted, struck work;
but the woman, strong in the faith of the gold, dug
on. At length she also had to give in ; and, said the
girl, now an old woman, to me lately, ' I dinna ken
what *she* was, but *I* was glad enough to get home.'
So vividly are the place and incidents of the day
stereotyped in the tablets of her memory, and so
graphically does she relate them, that her grand-
children, oftener than any other, ask her to tell them
the story of the *Wallet of Gold*.

Of the rest of the leading men, Farquharson of
Monaltrie, or the *Baron Ban*, was in prison ; Patrick
Fleming of *Auchintoul* was in concealment near
Culloden; Charles Farquharson of *Cluny*, and some
others, were in the hiding-place on the *Craig.* So of
course none of them made any resistance to the new
measures introduced. As before stated, it was not so
with the plebeian portion of the people. The *Ephiteach*
in particular, his cousin, and several others, gave an
immense deal of trouble to the soldiers. Racy accounts of their doings are still given by the old people.

So very obnoxious had the two Donalds rendered

themselves to the soldiers in the castle, that many schemes had been resorted to for their capture. One sergeant in particular distinguished himself by his vexatious pursuit. The *Ephiteach's* mother, who was a widow, lived in *Auchindryne ;* and this sergeant often broke in upon the lone woman, hoping, of course, to catch her son, and on such occasions would boast of what he would do to him if he could only get him alone.

One day the widow, instructed by her son, informed the sergeant that in a certain part of *Coirenam-muc* (a hollow in the side of *Morrone*) he would meet the *Ephiteach*, provided he went alone, and without fire-arms. The sergeant at once threw down his gun, and set off.

The *Ephiteach*, who had been perched on the top of his mother's box-bed, quickly descended from his hiding-place, and was in time to keep the soldier from waiting. Both drew their swords in silence, and fell too with all their might. The *Ephiteach* was the victor. He first disarmed the sergeant, then brought him to the ground with a blow from the pommel of his sword ; and before he had recovered his senses, had his hands tightly bound behind his back.

' Now, sergeant, suppose you had me as I have you, what would you do ?'

' I would kill you.'

' Well, as you have been so honest, I will spare

your life ; but you shall remember the *Ephiteach* to the longest day of it.'

Then he undid the sergeant's clothes, fastened them in a bundle, and hung them round his neck ; and having cut a number of birch twigs, greatly accelerated the sergeant's return to the castle by their aid. He never after shone in attempts at capturing *Dubh an-t-Ephiteach.*

The soldiers had orders to prevent the Highlanders from fishing as they did formerly. This was a great grievance ; and they persisted in doing it, despite all the vigilance of the soldiers. One evening the *Ephiteach* and his cousin were fishing by torchlight at a deep place in the river, near where the Established Church now stands. The soldiers had observed them, and came stealthily down and fired upon them, as one was holding the torch and the other using his spear. So narrowly did the *Ephiteach* escape, that a ball struck the pole of his spear as he was in the act of using it, and snapt it in two between his hands. The Donalds were obliged to run ; and they did so, vowing that that shot would be a dear one to the soldiers.

Next evening they fixed a torch on a pole, and stuck it into the ground by the side of the river, near the place where they were the previous evening. When the soldiers came down to catch the supposed poachers, they found nothing but a pole ; but, by the light of the torch on it, the two Donalds saw to take aim. They fired, and two of the soldiers fell—one dead, and the other severely wounded. Another version of this story is, that the *Ephiteach* had several guns, and fired them quickly one after another, and that a *number* of the soldiers fell ; and that the rest, believing there was a large party of the rebels, fled in disorder. The first version I was assured was the true one ; but whichever way, the place was called, by way of remembrance, the ' *Putan Sassenich.*'

One night, when the *Ephiteach* paid a stolen visit to his mother, he found her in great distress : her only cow had been taken away by the soldiers. No doubt they had left money equal in value for the cow, but that did not make up her loss. The soldiers took what they wanted from the people, but in return always gave what they considered its value in money. As they who have but one cow generally take good care of it, have plenty of food, etc., so the soldiers, thinking the widow's cow would be especially good, helped themselves to it ; and of course the *Ephiteach* was greatly exasperated.

A short time after, he learned that Captain Millar, or ' Muckle Millar,' one of the officers, intended to convey his wife to the south through *Glenshee ;* so he hurried away to wait them on the *Cairnwell.* And as Captain Millar, mounted on horseback, with his wife behind him, was passing along, in a moment the *Ephiteach*, with levelled gun, started up before them.

' Swords, and fair play!' cried Millar.

' Such play,' replied the *Ephiteach*, ' as you order your men to give me and my countrymen ; and that is, Shoot them down, bayonet them, shoot them down!' He fired. The captain was only wounded ; so he reloaded, and shot him dead. The grave of Captain Millar is still pointed out on passing the *Cairnwell*.

M'Kenzie then seized the bridle-reins, and mounting into the vacant place, conducted the lady on to the *Spittal of Glenshee ;* then set off on foot for *Glen-Lui*, and remained there in hiding until the soldiers found out his whereabouts. He narrowly escaped being taken, as they came upon him at midnight ; but they were disappointed. He fled to the *Dee*, cleared the *Linn* at a leap, and retreated into the wilds of *Upper Glen Ey*.

Both he and his cousin were at length taken, and brought in shackles to *Invercauld*. As the head officer happened to be in *Aberdeen*, they could not be shot until his return ; so they were safely lodged in the ' donjon ' until his return.

Invercauld was in no ways fond of seeing his countrymen treated in this manner, though he might have been excused for bearing the *Ephiteach* a grudge on account of the affair at *Corrie Bhui*. So, after having made his arrangements, he caused the two prisoners in the donjon to be warned that, in the evening and throughout the night, there would be revelry, feasting, dancing, and drinking, to celebrate the king's accession.

'They did keep it up in style ; and Invercauld, who then, like other lairds, had a still of his own, made the waters of life abound. . . . The sentinels carried on the waltz as well, and all was maudlin mirth and madness. When matters were come to this pass, the two prisoners split the donjon door and came out. On hearing the noise, the commandant's secretary—who, suspicious of treason, had avoided joining in the debauch—rushed down stairs and seized a gun from one of the sentinels, who, prostrate on the floor, was singing with all his might :

> " George is a merry boy,
> Long may he reign," etc.

But as he made a charge down the corridor at the handcuffed heroes to drive them back to their prison, Invercauld's butler tripped him (by mistake of course). The two jumped over him, and away to the hills, or rather to the blacksmith at *Auchindryne*, who soon made them both free.

'As they were receiving the congratulations of their friends, a messenger in hot haste from Invercauld arrived to say that the secretary had taken horse, and was gone to *Aberdeen* for his commandant ; and that Invercauld was afraid a serious charge might be made out against him.

' " Let us go after him, *MacRobaidh ;* we'll surely catch him before he reaches *Aberdeen.*"

' " Before he reaches *Aboyne,* you mean," replied he, striding away with a gun, brought by one of his friends, and a dirk, of which he had taken the loan.

' " Messenger," said the *Ephiteach,* "tell Invercauld, if he see a bonfire on the top of *Craig Cluny* on the coming night, he may be sure we have stopped the secretary." Then helping himself to a sword, he strode away after his cousin. Away they ran through *Philagie* and *Aberairdar, Crathie* and *Micras,* and on reaching the foot of *Gairn* they saw the secretary just entering the *Pass.* . . .

' *MacRobaidh Mhoire* and the *Ephiteach* could hear the clatter of the horse's hoofs as they rushed out of the pass and bore forward on *Tullich.* When they left *Tullich* behind, the secretary, looking back from *Tomnakiest,* saw in the grey light of the morning the two Highlanders hurrying after him. He knew the sight boded him little good, so he hurried forward at the utmost speed to *Culblean.*'

When the two Donalds came down the height behind *Camus O'May,* the secretary was only a gun-shot ahead. Down went *Robaidh Mhoire* on his knee, levelled his gun, and fired. The horse rolled on the road ; but the rider, disengaging himself from it, started on foot. Alas ! the race must be short now. The *Ephiteach* was at last blown, but the terrible

MacRobaidh Mhoire flies forward like the wind. In a few minutes he is on his victim.

'Spare a defenceless man !' cried the *Ephiteach* from behind. The other heard, but heeded not, for he hewed the secretary down with one blow. When reproached by M'Kenzie, he only replied, 'Dead men tell no tales !' That evening, according to promise, the two lit a fire on *Craig Cluny*, which considerably eased the anxiety of Invercauld.

'When the commander returned, the soldiers could give but a very confused account of the escape of the prisoners. Invercauld could not make the matter a whit plainer. The death of the secretary was, naturally enough, laid to the hatred the country people entertained for the soldiers. Still the officer had his suspicions, and from quartering on Invercauld, went to the castle, now repaired and fitted up to receive them. But he made frequent visits in force on the laird, besides keeping him often little better than a prisoner within the castle.

'The *Ephiteach*, on hearing of these annoying proceedings, began to consider how he could restore the laird to favour. At last the opportunity presented itself. While Invercauld was undergoing one of the customary detentions in the castle, the officers from *Abergeldie, Corgarff, Dubrach,* and *Glenshee* were invited to a feast there. At table the laird was known to sit always at the same seat, behind which a window opened, looking towards *Invercandlic.* Before the festal day, he was warned by *Donald Dubh* that he must, as if accidentally, get himself replaced there by one of the guests from the other garrison, or let the place be empty.

'The laird doubtless managed the matter well, and waited also somewhat impatiently for what was to happen. While at dinner, the company were startled by a loud report, and crash came a bullet through the window where Invercauld used to sit. The bullet, after carrying away part of a waiter's thumb, lodged itself in the opposite wall.

'The whole party ran to the windows. A tall dark form stood on the opposite side of the river, who waved his gun triumphantly, and called loud enough for them to hear:

'"That's for the traitor Saxon laird of *Invercauld*, from me, *Donald Dubh* the Egyptian." Then he turned up the way of *Glen Candlic.* Donald's generous purpose was fully accomplished. Seeing how narrowly the laird had escaped death at Donald's hands, it could not longer be supposed that he had connived at his escape. He was again received into favour with the Saxons, and remained from that time in good repute. The *Ephiteach* was never again taken, but died peaceably at a good old age.'

There were many other characters who were equally obstreperous with the cousins, and of course numerous legends exist regarding them. But what has been given will sufficiently illustrate the spirit of the people, and the difficulties the soldiers had to encounter in the enforcement of their order ; so it is needless to multiply them. A much more pleasing theme will be found in still later changes.

The last relic of the rebellion passed away in the person of Peter Grant, who lived to the extreme age of 110, and died in *Braemar*, 11th February 1824. For some years before his death, this solitary rebel received fifty pounds annually from Government, yet he never made his submission ; nor could any one induce him to drink the king's health, though many for amusement and otherwise tried to do so. Though thus liberally supported, he was proof against their kindness, as much as of their harsher measures. Nothing would subdue him : he died, as he had lived, a rebel.

He had been an extremely handsome man. Some of the old people still retain a vivid recollection of his beautiful appearance even in extreme old age. His hands, in particular, I have often heard commented on for their whiteness, symmetry, and freedom from wrinkles,—a peculiarity of his face also.

'Oh, but he was a bonnie man, as ever I saw,' said an old friend from whom I have culled many of the foregoing legends ; 'and when I was a youngster, I used to sit and hear him tell stories till my hair would have been almost standing on end ; and when I grew up a bit, mony a time I treated him to a glass, just to set his tongue a-going. He was fu' o' stories ; and oh, I liked weel to hear them.' Not a few of Peter Grant's stories are found in the foregoing pages.

CHAPTER VI.

Priest Farquharson—Last Chief of the Invereys, etc.

NE of those who left *Braemar* in '45,' to return no more, was Alexander Gordon, priest at *Gairnside.* His successor was Charles Farquharson; and some account of 'Father Charles' and his brother *Maighistir Jan, i.e.* Master John, also a priest, brings down the traditional history of *Braemar* to 1799.

John and Charles Farquharson were the sons of Lewis of *Auchindryne*, younger brother of John the Black Colonel. He was at first intended for a minister of the recently established Protestant Church; but while pursuing his studies for that purpose, he became a convert to the Roman faith.

After that event Lewis seems to have been more inclined to a soldier's life than a clerical one; but his two sons, John and Charles, supplied his lack of service, as both became priests and Jesuits.

Alastair, the eldest son of Lewis, was killed at *Falkirk.* His son, a youth, succeeded to the estates;

and William, the youngest son of Lewis, became
tutor to the young laird his nephew.

John Farquharson, the elder of the two brother
priests, was a missionary at *Strathglass.* He had
not gone to the wars in ''45,' like priest Gordon ;
for about that period his spare time seems to have
been occupied in making a collection of Gaelic
poetry—the first ever made—but which unfortunately was lost at *Douay*, where John lived for a
number of years. He had hard times of it while he
was in *Strathglass.* But his history, though interesting, is not connected with my subject ; so I merely
notice concerning him, that he spent the last years
of his life as chaplain to his nephew Alexander
Farquharson of *Inverey*, *Auchindryne*, etc., and died
at *Balmoral*, 22d August 1782.

'Both the fathers, John and Charles,' says one of
their own persuasion, 'were held to be saints. Many
persons possessed by devils were brought to them
from far and near, and by them restored and cured.
They had also, we are told, the gift of prophecy.
Their piety gained them the veneration, their learning
the esteem, and their urbanity the love of all who
knew them.'

My old friend in *Braemar*, who remembers him
very well, says of Father Charles : 'He was a great
big man, with long white hair curling down his back,
and a bonnie man as ye would have seen. A clever

man too ; for he had learned *philosophee* and *astro-
nomee*, and understood things so weel that fouk
thought he had the second sight : he could have told
them even when a storm was coming, etc.

'He had great fame, too, for casting out spirits.
There is a case that I min' weel, for I saw it wi' my
ain een ; an' that was three stout men that brought
their brither from *Athole*, possessed wi' an evil spirit,
as they thought. They had a rope about him, an'
ane o' them gaed at the back wi' a great stout cudgel
to belabour him, for he broke out sometimes terrible.

'Weel, they took him to the priest's door, and he
came out to them, an' they telt him what was the
matter. "Pit him into my room," says he. "They
couldna dee that," they said, "for he was so out-
rageous." "Pit ye him in," said he, "an' leave him
to me ; I'll manage him." So they pat him in, and
gaed awa owre to the inn, for the priest said they
would need to leave him twa or three days. An' in
little mair than that time, I min' as weel as onything o' seeing him gang doon the road hame, *as weel*
as ony o' them.

'That was a great case wi' the fouk, o' casting out
the deevel. But his housekeeper telt me after hoo
he did. He examined a' his head, an' then he pat a
blister on the back o' his neck. Then he mixed up
some herbs and gae him to drink ; and that was the
way that the evil spirit was cast oot.'

As the laws against the priests were very stringent, and pretty well enforced about *Bracmar*, Charles had not a few difficulties at the beginning of his ministry. One escape from capture is thus related :—

'As Invercauld and his coachman were coming along the banks of the *Dee* one day, they saw on the opposite side Father Charles sitting among the trees at the foot of *Craig Choinnich*. The coachman proposed to arrest him, and gain the Government reward. Invercauld durst not oppose. So the man crossed the water at some little distance ; and going up stealthily behind the priest, took him by the collar, saying at the same time,

' "You are my prisoner in the king's name."

' " Stop a minute, then," said he, " till I finish my prayers." So he went on quite leisurely, until he came to the end ; then shutting the book with a slap, he stared the man hard in the face as he repeated very sonorously, "*In nomine Patris, et Filii, et Spiritus Sancti. Amen.*" Then he rose up to go with his capturer. But he would not enter the river, to cross over to the other side, but at one particular place. So the coachman gave in to that, and they plunged into the water together.

' It was not the shallowest part of the river certainly, for they were soon up to the arm-pits ; then in a moment Father Charles seized the man by the collar and nether garments, dipped his head into the

U

water, allowing him to kick and struggle at full scope. Then, letting him breathe for a minute, he dipped him in again, and continued the process until he was within an inch of his life ; and carrying him in that state through the water, laid him down beside his master, who sat on the bank witnessing the whole transaction in an agony of laughter.'

Many of the sayings and doings of Father Charles go far to prove that he had a considerable spice of humour in his character. His mode of giving reproof also was often very original. One example will make this evident :—

'One of his own people, a Mrs. Gordon, had a terrible fashion of prigging wi' fouk that gaed to see her, to eat, eat, till they couldna even get eaten for her. Weel, the priest was at her house ae day, an' she was just, as usual, tormenting him about eating. So he turned to one of the servant lads that was sitting at the fireside, and said, " Gang out, Alastair, an' see if my pony is taking onything." In a minute the lad comes back, an' says, " The pony has plenty o' hay, and it's eating fine."

'" Ay, you see," said the priest, looking to Mrs. Gordon, "the pony has mair sense than its master : it can eat *without* a bidding."

'Oh! mony a mony a time has she telt me that story, and loughin' owre it ; but it didna cure her,' said the old man who told me this quaint account.

As a physician, Charles was little behind his relative *Fear na Bruach.* His mode of treatment was original; but detail would not be very pleasant. Cancer he could cure without any operation, simply by applying a lotion prepared from herbs by himself. A gamekeeper of Lord Fife's, Munro by name, is said to have been cured by him, after he had been treated by the most skilful doctors without effect. Pity he has not left the prescription.

The end of Priest Farquharson's life was more settled than the early part of it, as he got a little croft at *Ardearg,* where he was permitted to live without molestation.

The Bible of Father Charles—the *Douay* version of course, with lengthy notes—is still in the possession of some relatives in *Auchindryne,* and bears evidence of careful perusal. At length he died at *Ardearg,* on Nov. 30, 1799, and was buried in the churchyard at *Castleton.*

After the death of Farquharson laird of *Balmoral,* and of Finla the imbecile laird of *Invercy,* the estates pertaining to both passed to the laird of *Auchindryne,* the son of Alastair Farquharson, who fell at *Falkirk.* Under the tutorship of his uncle William, he had grown up as strongly Jacobite as any of his ancestors. There was, however, no way of showing this now, but by resisting the innovations introduced after ''45.' This he did not do in his own person, but by encouraging his tenants to resist as far as possible the stringent enactments against poaching, fishing, etc.

Alexander seems to have been what the people say of him—'a real old Highland chief, a man according to the people's hearts ;' the last one also, occupying as it were the transition point between the genuine feudal system and that regular state of matters which after his death was induced. And under his auspices, the broken remnants of the past, sullen and sore, wearied themselves in fruitless efforts to break the toils which held the old system in death-grasp.

From many stories relating to this point, one example may not be tedious :—

'Alexander of *Auchindryne* by no means agreed with Duff of *Braco ;* neither did the *Braemar* people generally. In olden time they were welcome to go out and bring home a bird, hare, or even deer, " to keep the pottie bilin." But it was changed times now ; for any of Braco's own tenants caught poaching were at once expelled the estate, and those of other landowners fined or imprisoned. Alexander of *Inverey* and *Auchindryne* was greatly disgusted at such proceedings.

' " Never mind, billies," he would say, " poach, poach away on Duff's lands as much as you like ; but oh, boys, have clever feet. Only get to the middle of the *Dee* when his keepers are after you, and I'll stand good for you."

'The tenants were not slow to take such advice, and poach on Duff's moors and forests they did with a vengeance. Some of them were caught from time to time, and sent into *Aberdeen ;* but Alexander, true to his word, was there to pay the fines, and take them home with him again.

'"Just try yourself, Duff," he would say ; "you may put them *in,* but I'll take them *out* as fast as Braco." And so he did.'

One laughable little episode occurred during one of these rencounters. 'A number of young men were out one evening, doing the laird's bidding ; and Lord Fife's head gamekeeper came upon their track, gave chase, and finally fired upon them. One of the young men narrowly escaped death. The rest of them resolved to give the keeper a fright, as he had no right to *fire* upon them. He had taken his stand upon a "fell dyke," possibly to reconnoitre. Observing this, one or more of them fired, aiming at the wall, exactly below where he stood. A perfect cloud of dust was raised, and part of the wall displaced. Losing his balance, he tumbled over, shouting at the same time,

'"Murder ! murder ! I'm shot, I'm shot !" etc.'

'You may be sure,' said the octogenarian who gave me this account, 'we didna wait to help him up. They tried sair to fin' out wha had deen't, but we keepit gey quiet. But mony's the guid lauch we took to oursels on the heads o' it.'

But though Alexander was thus unscrupulous in regard to the property of others, he did not like to be encroached on himself, as the following letter of his will show. I copied it from the original letter a few months ago :—

'BALMORAL, 14*th May* 1777.

'DEAR UNCLE,—The bearer James Lamont in *Dalagowan*, tells me that Margrat Gordon in *Dalvoror*, and her son John ffarquharson, are, in Difiance of all the orders I have given to the contrary, keeping their sheep in my fforrest of *Conyvron*, by which means I am like to lose my glen rent, as nobody will send cattle to graze when it is eaten with their sheep. I have wrote to John Gordon, my ground-officer there, to seize on them and poind them ; but I am afraid that perhaps he may not execute my orders right. I hear his wife is very bauld. I must therefore beg of you, that when the bearer requires it, that you'll take with you three or four of the *Auchindryne* tennents, as I can trust in them, having you at their head, and seize upon their sheep, or upon the sheep of any other person you shall find within the bounds of my fforrest, and bring them down directly here, and I shall take care of them till they are relieved. I desire that they be brought *here*, as I'll be sure they won't steal them away till they relieve them by paying for them as the law directs. You may tell the men you bring with you, that I'll mind them for their trouble, besides being obliged to them. I was at first thinking of going up myself to take them ; but on second thoughts I reckoned it would be better to send you in my place, as perhaps, if they saw me and a few men with me going to the glen, they might take them out of the fforest before I reached. But they won't suspect you ; only it is necessary to keep this order secret till you have execute it. I beg you'll behave yourselves like men, and not let me be affronted.—I am, dear Uncle,

' Your most affect. nevew,

'ALEXR. FFARQUHARSON.'

The *finale* of the *Auchindryne* history is thus given :—

'James, the laird's son, was, alas, not of the same stamp as his father. He associated with the Duffs ; and their son, a James also, taught him expensive habits. . . .

'This did not at all please the old man, who foresaw a dark future; but he could not change his lad's heart. But what he could do, he tried. He offered every one of his tenants leases of their holdings while grass grew or water ran, at the same rents they then paid. But they little understood his generosity or true motives. They thought the laird must see that land was to get cheaper, and they feared they might be ruined. Only one of them, the farmer

of *Dalbreckachy*, Alastair Lamont, could be prevailed
on to accept a lease of the kind.   Having prevailed
with one, he did not give up with the others.   So
every time they came to pay their rents he renewed
his offer, but in vain ; and even Dalbreckachy, who
had accepted, often begged the laird to cancel his
lease, and put him on the same footing as the others.

'"Na, na, keep it, laddie," the laird would reply ;
"it will do you and your family good when I am in
the mools.   Keep ye it, laddie."

'He had sore misgivings ; but he kept it on, just
not to displease the good old man.   By and by
word reached *Braemar* that the laird was dying.
Lamont took alarm, and hurried off to *Balmoral*
with the obnoxious lease.   He was ushered into a
room where the old man sat alone in his chair, very
"wae" and sad.

'"O laird!" cried the farmer, "as ye hope to meet
God in mercy, tak' this lease off my hands, for it will
be the ruin of me and of my family."

'"Well, well," said the poor laird, with a sigh of
resignation, "God's will be done."   And he threw it
into the fire.   "But, Alastair," he continued, "the
day will come when the men of the *Braes of Mar*
would dig me out of the grave with their teeth, could
they get such leases as you all refuse.   God protect
ye, my bairns, for I'll soon be away."

'Too soon that day came, alas!   James succeeded

in his place. He had before his accession contracted a debt of eight thousand pounds, due the greater part to the Duffs. They came for a time to a kind of settlement, by James letting the Earl have part of his hill *Craig an Fehithich*, opposite *Mar Lodge*, which the Earl planted to beautify the view from his windows.'

The sum which the Earl allowed for it was then considered extravagant; and when some one expostulated with the Earl on his prodigality, he is reported to have said very jocularly, 'That he knew what he was about, as that hill would serve as a key to the rest.'

'The evil day came at length. Pressing demands were made by the Earl of Fife, and James determined to sell off the estate and clear away his debts. The tenants, on learning this, came forward in a body and offered themselves to clear off the debt to the Duffs, provided James would not sell his lands. But it would not do. In spite of all their devotion, the estates were sold to the Earl of Fife, and Inverey left *Braemar*. He gave *Ballater* and *Tullich* to Monaltrie for his estate of *Bruxie*, whither he himself retired.

'Afterwards we read in the newspapers: "Died at *Jock's Lodge* (near *Edinburgh*), James Farquharson, the last of the Invereys."

'Lewis Farquharson, his brother, who had married

the heiress of *Ballogie*, was once present at the *Brae-mar* gathering, and he was made very welcome for auld langsyne.   The hearts of the people yearned to him ; and they felt sad and wae when the memory of old times came over them.   But it was Mr. Innes with them ; Mr. Innes this, and Mr. Innes that.

' " Not Innes," replied he ; " I am *that* at *Ballogie ;* but I am Farquharson in *Braemar.*"

' That went to the people's hearts ; there was a tear in every eye.   But they cheered him ; yes, they did it heartily, though their cheers were like to choke them ; and then he went away.

' The next thing—ay, there it is, as I picked it from the blank leaf of a missal belonging to the family :—" 27th September 1830. — Obiit Dominus Ludovicus Innes (quondam Farquharson de *Inverey*), novissime autem de *Balnacraig* et *Ballogie*, anno ætatis suo 67." Lewis had a son, who died young and unmarried ; and so the race is nearly extinct.'

CHAPTER VII.

Social Usages of the Braemarians—Dress, Food, etc.—Last Case of
Witchcraft—Cheese-peel.

THE next and last point of interest in *Brae-mar* history was the auspicious event of it becoming again, as in days of old, a royal residence—a change conducive to its highest interests.

But, before touching upon that subject, I may notice briefly the state of the people as to social usages, dress, food, etc., about the end of the eighteenth century, as at that time the old habits, customs, etc., had but begun to give way by the introduction of Saxon usage and modern improvement.

And first as to dress. After the defeat at Culloden the soldiers had orders to *oblige* the people to lay aside their ancient costume. This in *Braemar* they entirely failed in doing. But a kind of compromise was made. The kilt they *did* not, and *would* not lay aside; but they agreed to have it of other material than tartan. They adopted instead a greyish sort of colour, with a few narrow stripes of white round the bottom, by way of border. This was a great concession ; for in *Braemar*, as well as in other Highland districts, they had attained to a great proficiency in the production of those beautifully bright and permanent colours, for which very old tartans are famous.

It has appeared to some surprising that the Highlanders should be able, from the scanty materials which their country afforded, to produce such brilliancy of colouring. In those days, good housewives distinguished themselves not only by the superior quality of cloth they produced—for all was home-made—but also by the brightness and variety of their colours. From the descendants of one thus distinguished I had the whole secret ; and a simple one it was, both as to the process and material of dyeing.

Black was produced from *aurn ;* green and yellow from heather, the green being first dyed blue with indigo. From 'white crottle,' a species of lichen, a beautiful crimson was produced. The 'crottle' or lichen producing this colour had to be kept in soak for at least a twelvemonth before use. A more common red was produced from madder ; brown from 'rough crottle,' another species of lichen : the fixing matter for all these colours being of the most primitive nature.

Shoes also were of home manufacture, being made out of skins prepared by themselves, in very primitive fashion, sewed in the inside and turned over.

The number of the people at that date was much greater than at present : for instance, in *Glen Cluny* there were forty-one families, now only six ; in *Glen Ey* nine, now only one, a gamekeeper's ; in *Glen Lui* there were six, now there are none ; in *Glen Dee* eight, now I think none ; in *Glen Quoich* eight, now none. This was exclusive of those dwelling in *Strathdee*, *Castleton*, *Auchindryne*, etc. Eight meal mills were also required at that time ; now there are only two, and one would be sufficient for the work required. One of the mills was at *Invercauld*, one at *Allen Quoich*, *Invercy*, *Kill-a-Coll*, *Auchindryne*, *Castleton*, *Coldrach ;* and the eighth at *Stron*, Gaelic *Stroon-een.* The millers were paid with so much of the meal.

' How was it,' I inquired on hearing this account, ' that so many could subsist then, when the few now, with a much better system of farming, can scarcely manage to live ? ' The answer to my question was given as follows, brought out fully by one or two other queries :—

' Weel, it has been supposed, and *said*, that it was principally through poaching in the woods and rivers that they contrived to subsist. Now, that was not correct ; for at the time when so many were in the country, James Farquharson, the fifth laird of *Invercauld*, and last of the direct line, had all his tenants sworn in not to touch his wood or water ; and the tenure by which they held their lands was, that it

was to be term-day when they were found doing
either. They had no other lease, and never were
removed but in the event of such trespassing; and
then he was inexorable : no man needed to plead for
them.

'I min' well a gey queer story of this kind. There
was a man they ca'd Grigor Riach, and ane o'
his laddies was at a place they ca' the *Red-banks*,
where Major Ross's house is building, gathering
tapins ae day: that is a kind o' supple twig that
sometimes springs from the bottom or root of the
birch-trees : it was to mak' a creel or something. The
laird, he happened to be riding that way, and saw the
boy, who ran. But the laird gave chase; and having
found out who he was, his parents were immediately
ejected. And though the people went and pleaded
for him that the tapins were of no use, and that he
was but a boy, and that his father did not know of
him taking them, etc., the laird was not to be moved :
they had to remove to *Glenshee*, and the father died
there soon after. That was the way poachers on the
very smallest scale were dealt with; and, of course,
those on a bigger scale were not treated more
leniently.

'Now how could the woods or the water serve
under such circumstances to keep people alive? No,
the real secret of it was this : every croft or small farm
had so many sheep. They had so many of what we

call withers, so many hogs, and so many ewes, kept
in their different enclosures. These enclosures were
never cleaned but in spring, when the ground was preparing ; and then the manure was taken out, saft and
warm, and laid upon the ground, and ploughed in,
or delved in, and then the bear was sown. And it
was nathing uncommon to have twelve bolls for every
boll of seed. The heads would a' been *that* length
(measuring about half a foot on his hand) ; and the
sheafs that heavy, that one would not have stood up
till ye brought anither to pit aside it at the harvest,
but would fa' doon wi' the weight o' the ears. And
then it was a' cut wi' the hook ; there was nae scything.
It was a' bear that was sown maistly, except only the
weest puckle oats ; for there was no oatcakes used
but at Christmas.

'Weel, then, as I was tellin' ye, there would be a
grand big kailyard, and that served generally for
dinner. First they were boiled, and then some brose
made of the bree, and then the kail would be chapped
sma', an' supped after. In the morning, for breakfast
it would be brose and milk to them ; and if there was
nae milk, it would be raw sowins. For supper it
would be sowins again, boil'd, or knothing, or something like that ; and of course it was only at extra
times that there would be a sheep killed, or onything
of that kind. That was the way they lived, an bra'
men they were, stronger and better - looking than

mony to be seen now-a-days. For instance, the twa brithers, the Invereys, that selt *Balmoral* about fifty or sixty years ago, the ane was sax feet four, the other sax feet twa, and stout in proportion. Of course there would be a' sizes ; but strong, stout men they were generally.'

'They would have few dainties then,' I said jocularly ; 'they would not drink tea in the morning, I suppose ?'

'Na, they didna dee that,' said the old man, laughing ; 'I could tell you gey funny things about the tea when it cam' first in fashion. There was a woman lived up by there, Bell M'Gregor they ca'it her : she had been a servant to the Farquharsons of *Allen Quoich.* When the two sisters were left, Miss Peggie and Miss Nancy, *Allen Quoich* was selt, an' they gaed to *Edinburgh,* an' had a house in *George Street.* They were auld maids, ye ken, but had plenty to keep themselves comfortable. I used to wonder often that Miss Peggie was never married, for she was as fine a looking woman as ye would hae seen : the ither wasna that.

'Weel, when I gaed to the south wi' my sheep, I aye called on the Misses Farquharson ; an' as regularly as I called, I got a *pun'* o' tea for an auld schoolmaister in *Glen Cluny.* There was fouk that I thoucht mair o' than that man ; but I wouldna refuse to tak' it for a' that. Weel, there was ae year they asked

if I would tak' half a *pun'* o' tea to Bell M'Gregor
also, as she had been a faithful servant to them, and
they wished to send some token of remembrance to
her.   Weel, I took the tea to Bell.

'"Heich!" said she when I gae it to her, "they
micht a sent something that would a been o' mair
use."

'"Weel, hoo cam' ye on wi' the tea, Bell?" I speir'd
some time after.

'"Heich, the tea!" said she.   "I kenna what's the
guid o' that stuff.   I pat it into a pottie, an' boiled
it, an' boiled it; but never a bit safter grew it.   Syne
I pat in a good slake o' butter, and boiled it again;
but it was just as teuch as wands after a'."'

'Did she pour out the liquid?' I inquired.

'Weel, I *did not* speir; but that was her *very words*
to me.   I assure you I did not wait to speir muckle
mair, but made oot as fast as I could, an' took a guid
lauch to mysel'.'

About 1782 the first 'English-speaking' family
came to settle in *Castleton*.   They must have had
considerable difficulty in communicating with their
neighbours, as up to that period Gaelic universally
prevailed.   A laughable instance of the difficulty
they had in communicating their ideas was thus
related to me: 'The brither of the new innkeeper
and one Alastair M'Donald had a great wark wi'
ane anither,' said the old man; though the one could

X

speak no Gaelic but a few words he had picked up since coming, and *vice versa.* The incomer taught this new friend to smoke—no common thing in those days. When any accident happened to the pipe, it was rather a serious matter to get a fresh supply. Such accident happened to the Braemarian one day : he broke his pipe, and soon as possible sought out his friend, to see if he could help him in the emergency.

'"Oh, my cuttim pipe!" said he with great vehemence, "*I'll brak him!*"

'"Hoots, man," replied the other, "what for would ye brak yer pipe? you'd better nae dee that, in case I ha'na anither."

'"But I'll brak him *already!*" cried Alastair, pulling out the fragments, to make the extent of his misfortune manifest. Of course the only response was a hearty burst of laughter ; but it did not disturb the harmony between the friends, as their mistakes were mutual.'

Somewhere about this period an English teacher was settled in *Braemar.* 'An' a' body,' said my old friend, 'was *so* anxious to learn English. We were forbidden to speak Gaelic ; an' when we were at the school, mony a threshing did we boys get for deein' it aye. We thoucht it was gey *hard,* and it our mither tongue.'

A curious custom prevailed also in regard to teaching : only the eldest son and youngest daughter of a

family were taught to read. The schoolmaster's fee
was a peck of meal in the year—I suppose for every
child in the family. In respect to his fee, the
teacher was quite on a level with the tailor and
blacksmith, who also had a peck of meal from every
family for doing *all* their work for a year. When
any one wore out their clothes sooner than usual, it
was not the parents who provided the material that
made any complaint, but the tailor, who was bound
to do *all* the work of the family on the terms stated ;
and he used to grumble sadly when they were not
careful.

The blacksmith's duties, however, could not have
been very onerous, as the horses used for agricultural purposes only got shoes for their fore-feet once
a year, when the spring labour commenced. Ploughs
were all made of wood, excepting the ' *sock*,' *i.e.* share.
When any one took a job to the blacksmith, he remained until it was finished, however long. He was
expected also to take food enough with him to supply his own wants, and the blacksmith's too, all the
time he remained.

At one time the belief in witches, fairies, ghosts,
etc., was universal in *Braemar;* now such ideas are
all but exploded. A few, however, still think more
about these things than they care to confess. One
man with whom I conversed not long ago, attributes
this great change to want of faith among the people.

Their forefathers, he thought, were remarkable for the greatness of their faith, which fully accounted, he believed, for all the supernatural appearances, etc., of former times.

The last case of witchcraft in *Braemar* occurred in this wise : The innkeeper had sown a large bed of onions, in which a neighbour's hens made sad havoc. As his frequent requests that they should be kept out of the way for a time were quite unheeded, he resolved to rid himself of the nuisance by shooting them. But as the woman had the reputation of being a witch, he could not get either his sons or servants to meddle with the hens. One lad was at length prevailed on, by the promise of a sixpence, to shoot either one or two of them.

Having shot them among the onions, he had to carry them to the woman, and tell her why it had been done. 'He was terrible unwilling.' At last he took them up, went to her door, and threw them in, shouting at the same time his message not over politely.

'Shortly after the young man grew ill, an' pined away ; naebody could ken what was the matter.' So they came to the conclusion that he was witched. The only remedy, therefore, was for the lad to draw blood of the witch *above the breath.* 'And I think,' said my old friend, 'that the funniest thing I *ever* saw was the lad watching like a cat for his opportunity ; and when he had got her in a suitable place, tearing the mutch aff her head, an' scratching her face till the bleed cam'. He grew better after it, tho' ; and I can assure ye that it was looked upon as a case o' *real* witchcraft.'

It is pleasing to turn from this instance of credulity to one of very opposite character—that of a strong but totally uncultured mind bursting the shackles of superstitious belief which at that time held the mass of the Braemarians in thrall. I give the account in her own words :—

'The first place I gaed till, they had a great fear of the fairies coming down the lum through the nicht an' takin' awa the bairns. So I got strick orders every nicht afore I gaed to my bed, to pit a bit fir in the links of the crook. They thoucht the spirits and fairies cam' doon the lum, but when they came to the bit fir they couldna get farther. So I began to consider, lassie as I was, that if they couldna come owre a bit fir, they couldna hae power to dee a body muckle ill ; but then, ye see, being a servant, I had just to dee as I was bidden, but that was my ideas o' it.

'Then they had a great wark about dogs *seeing things*, *i.e.* spirits or ghosts. ' Weel, there was ae day that we were coming along the road, and there was some rags hung up on sticks for a " *tattie bogle.*" The dog, he was trotting on the road afore us bravely; but whenever he saw the bogle, he crouched awa in at our backs, and seemed quite in a terror.

'"Noo," says I to them, "dee ye see that? Ye say dogs see things that fouk disna see. Weel, we see the bogle, an' we ken what it is, and it disna trouble us. The dog, he sees't tee, and it's fu' o' terror to him, because he doesna understand it. Noo, that's the way that they see things,"' etc.

Another curious practice existed. In summer the flocks and herds were taken to the upper glens to have the benefit of the richer pasture they afforded. The women and children tended them; and a sort of temporary dwelling was put up to shelter them, called 'shiels.' Most of the men remained at home to labour the fields, etc., but paid many visits to the shiels in the evenings. They also repaired to them on Saturdays, and remained till Monday.

Many customs then obtained which we would now think very curious; for instance, at nights there would be a promiscuous gathering of fourteen, fifteen, or more, into one bed,—not constructed, of course, on the same plan as our modern ones. They extended along the whole breadth of the shiel, and were formed of heather packed very closely on end. This afforded a resting-place deliciously soft and fragrant.

Into this style of bed were convened at nights the heads of the family, the children—young and old— servants, and visitors; and yet, at the time when this

custom prevailed, the morality of the people was high
to a degree unknown in modern times. An old man,
still living, who had thirty years' experience of this
glen life, ere it became a thing of the past, says that
during all that time not a single breach of modesty
occurred, at least not to his knowledge.

There was, when he was quite a boy, one man
whose life was suspected of not being so pure as it
ought to be : he was consequently looked down upon,
and avoided particularly by the young ladies. There
was one very pretty girl he had quite a fancy for, and
would have paid her frequent visits while in the glen,
but was prevented in the following manner :—

' This young woman,' said my old friend, ' was very
good and kind to the herd-boys, giving them a drink
of milk, cheese and bread, etc., occasionally. She
was consequently a great favourite. One day she
came up to us, and said, " Now, boys, I'll give you
a good dish of curds and cream if you'll stane ——
owre the hill when ye see him coming the nicht."

' We had no idea then *why* she wanted us to do
that ; but it didna matter : we were willing to please
her, and win our curds and cream. So we gathered
two or three great heaps o' stanes ; and whenever we
saw him coming, we set tae and pelted. He tried sair
to get by us, but we mastered him. I suppose he
was puzzled to know why we did it ; but at ony rate
we got our curds and cream. It wasna for some

years after that I understood the true meaning o' the
stoning ; and it was just that she thoucht mair o'
hersel' than hae the name o' a licht character like
him coming about her.'   It is very different now.
Yet still, in the scale of morals, they are much in
advance of Lowland districts.

With another droll little incident I sum up this
account of glen life.   When the season was over, the
cheese, butter, etc., which had been made during the
summer, were taken home and stored up for winter
use.   On one occasion, when a servant-man had
brought home his cart full of such treasures, he asked
his master *where* he would put them.   There must
have been something unusually provoking in the
question, or the ' good-man ' must have been in an
unusually cross mood, for the answer was :

' Into the *peel*,' meaning the deep pool in the *Cluny*,
near the Established Church.

The servant, who no more lacked fire or contuma-
ciousness than his master, went straight to the place,
took the back-door out of the cart, and tumbled the
whole into the water.   ' Ye may be sure nae little ado
was made ; and the place was aye called the " Cheese
Peel " after.'

This incident must have taken place subsequently
to the year 1796, as about that time carts were first
introduced to *Braemar*.   They were of very primitive
structure—just a framework of wood, with rapes or

ropes made of tow, pob, or horse-hair twisted round it, to keep in the load, of what kind soever it was. There was not a bit of iron on the wheels or any other part. The price of the whole was also very moderate, as the first three carts used in *Braemar* cost, horses and all, only two guineas.

CHAPTER VIII.

Braemar becomes a Royal Residence—Highlanders' Love to the
Queen—Prince Consort, etc.

HE last great events of importance in *Brae-mar* history took place in 1848, when Prince Albert purchased the reversion of the lease of *Balmoral Castle*, held by the late Sir Robert Gordon, from the Earl of Fife ; and in 1852, when *Braemar* became, as in days of yore, a permanent summer residence of Royalty.

After these auspicious events, many other changes took place of minor importance. The old castle disappeared, and the new one which superseded it is considered the *ne plus ultra* of castles in the eyes of the Braemarians. The old castle, however, was not the only structure which gave place to one much superior. Schools, dwelling-houses, etc. etc., underwent to a great extent the same beneficial process of resuscitation.

But a higher and still more wonderful change has passed over the spirit of the people since the political storms of ''15' and ''45,' when they so willingly fought and bled for Prince Charlie.

As to the causes of this change, they are various.

The old race which took an active part in the rebellion has died out ; a great number of their descendants emigrated ; while the asperities of the remainder were considerably softened down by time, the great mollifier, previous to the arrival of the Queen and Prince Albert to sojourn in their midst. And what has transpired since 1848 has dissipated for ever all remains of antagonistic feeling to the Royal house, which superseded their favourite one of Stuart.

In confirmation of this statement (as some maintain that the people are still Jacobite, though covertly), I may adduce some few testimonies from the people themselves ; not given to serve any purpose, but just in the course of ordinary and easy conversation, and without knowing that what they said would ever be made use of :—

'Ay,' said an intelligent old Highlander with whom I was talking one day on the exploded Jacobitism of the people ; 'ay, had ye come here maybe forty years ago, ye would have seen a gey difference in the state of the people. They were rouch, rouch (in the sense of being disaffected) ; but I could say now, to my certain knowledge, that there's nae a man in the country but would lay down his life for the Queen, if there was the needs be.'

From many such testimonies I select another somewhat amusing. In conversing with a really superior Highland woman one day, I asked,

'Are there any Fenians among you ?'

'Na, they needna come here.'

'Wouldn't they find much sympathy ?'

'I'm thinking *no*. I doot there would be a stout battle if they came this gate.'

'Would you turn out in defence ?'

'That we *would*, men and *women*. It wouldna be,' she added with increasing energy, and a peculiar intonation of voice which threw a world of meaning into her statement ; 'it wouldna be as lang as there is life in our bodies that they would touch ae hair o' her head. Na, it wouldna be that,' she continued ; 'for we're nae feart for a feicht, if they would only come to that wi' it. What we dinna like is that sleekit ways o' theirs, maybe twa or three o' them comin' o'er the hills, an' doing mischief afore we kent o't. But they're nae like to hae the chance o' that either noo, for fouk has their e'en about them.'

'You seem to love the Queen very much.'

'We dee that.'

'As well as ever you liked Charlie Stuart ?'

'Ay ! *every hair o't.*'

'This may be the case of those in the immediate vicinity of *Balmoral*,' was the remark of a southern gentleman ; 'but in the remoter parts of *Braemar* the people are Jacobite still.' To correct that and similar ideas, I give the following perfectly reliable statement from a professional gentleman, intimately acquainted

with the people in the parts of *Bracmar* most remote
from *Balmoral* :—

'Some ladies, belonging to one of the old Jacobite
families, from a different part of the *Highlands*, came
to sojourn for a time in *Bracmar*. Never doubting but
they would meet with sympathy for their strangely
cherished feelings of antipathy and opposition to the
present Royal line, they spoke of them freely, but, to
their great chagrin, met everywhere with rebuff. They
went then to the village of *Inverey*, where the people
were formerly red-hot Jacobites, assuring themselves
that there at least it would be different. Their disappointment, however, was greater than before; for the
people pretended that they did not even know who
was meant when they mentioned the name of Charles
Stuart.'

'The line of demarcation that separates sovereign
from people,' writes one in a weekly newspaper some
little time ago, 'at once forbids the union of a
common tie. The right divine is an impassable
boundary. Ordinary humanity cannot reach it, but
must stand aloof to admire and do homage to the
regal power above it ; or it may rudely gaze, but not
dare to claim the crowned head as a link in the great
chain of human feeling. The glow of sympathetic
union does not exist ; for the regal performers possess
the sad prerogative of being able to clasp no man's
hand in the fellowship of mutual joy or sorrow.'

Wherever such a state of matters exists, it certainly is not at *Braemar*, where the Queen for a time exchanges courtly splendour and ceremonial for her quiet Highland residence, and a life unostentatious almost as that of a private lady. How much she enjoys the temporary release, is made known by the publication of the beautifully simple record of her domestic life during these short periods.

It ought to be stated, however, that condescending as Her Majesty may be in her intercourse with her Highland subjects, and however much she may and does make them feel that she is their friend, she never so descends as to become anything less to them than their Sovereign and Queen. And it is the beautiful blending in her of the assured firmness of one born to rule, with much of the simple, loving, tender woman, which has taken such hold of their hearts,—a hold still further deepened by the excellence of her moral character, her name being an embodiment of everything honourable, pure, and good. Deeply do they feel what Tennyson has so well expressed in his lines :

> 'A thousand claims to reverence close
> In her as Mother, Wife, and Queen.'

An old woman one day, while giving a most graphic account of her own and others' earlier interviews with the Queen, their extreme nervousness, etc., said, with inimitable pathos,

'But she' (the Queen) 'said she didna want us to feel like that, for she was *just a woman* like oursel's.'

One or two instances of their nervousness on first meeting the Queen, etc., may at least have the merit of being amusing, as given in their own words :—

'Shortly after the Queen came to *Balmoral*, as I was on the road to *Crathie* one day, I met a lady and gentleman coming walking away up. As I guessed in a minute wha it would be, I fell a-shakin'. There was nae way o' getting aff o' the road, so I thoucht I would just try and keep as far frae them as possible. But they came straught up to me, and the Prince asked if I could tell them where the man lived who built the bridge. I kent weel aneuch where the man lived ; but I couldna tell him, I was shakin' at sic a rate. He thoucht I didna understand him, and asked again ; but it was just the same. Then the Queen speired, an' she spak' *real plain ;* but it didna matter, I couldna get oot ae word.'

'And did you not speak at all ?'

'Not a single word could I say, and I suppose they thoucht there was nae use of fashing themselves mair wi' me, for they went away lauchin'.'

Another instance, equally amusing, was that of an elderly woman on meeting the Queen for the first time. Like the former, while on her way to the village of *Crathie*, she met the Queen and a lady walking on the road ; and finding that there was no way of getting off, resolved to keep as close to the opposite side from that on which they were walking as possible.

'Hech me! but if I wasna a *bonnie* woman that day! I'm thinking that I got my colour up; and I didna grow better, I can assure ye, when I saw them leave the side o' the road, an' come walking awa up to the middle o' it. An' syne the Queen came richt in afore me, an' looked into my face an' said,

'"It's a fine day."'

Here the old woman stopped abruptly; but I queried, 'And what did you say?'

'I said YES.'

'Nothing more?'

'Nae ae word.'

The inexpressibly droll manner in which she made the last two statements made it impossible to keep from a laugh, in which the old woman joined as heartily as any of us.

It would be easy to multiply instances also of the Queen's condescension, or, as they phrase it, 'goodness,' were it right to drag forth acts done in the sweet secrecy of her Highland retirement, and place them under the glare of the public eye.

Not less strongly did the affections of the people twine round Her Majesty's Royal Consort. Very vividly indeed is the simplicity, manliness, and purity of his character still remembered and commented on; and how keen even yet their sense of loss! ' The name of the righteous,' it is said, ' shall be in everlasting remembrance;' and truly his hallowed memory is yet green and fragrant, though his outward form be seen no more.

As I have in every instance, when I could lay my hand on the material, given a brief sketch of the descent, character, and doings of the *Braemar* proprietors, the series will be fittingly closed by slightly sketching in like manner that of the late proprietor of *Balmoral—' Albert the Good.'*

Towards the close of the last century there dwelt in the castles of *Ehrenberg* and *Rosenau,* Francis Frederick, the then reigning Duke of *Saxe-Coburg Saalfeld,* with an interesting family of six children. The monarchy represented by this ducal house was, in comparison with surrounding powers, unimportant. Yet since that time these six young princes and princesses have, either in their own person or through children, taken important places among the Royal families in *Europe.*

One of them, Princess Victoria Maria Louisa, by her marriage with the Duke of Kent, became the mother of Her present Majesty, our own beloved Queen. Ernest, the eldest son, succeeded his father on the ducal throne in 1806. And of the two sons afterwards born to him, the youngest, Albert Francis

Y

Augustus Charles Emanuel, contracted the happiest
and most brilliant of all the Coburg alliances;
and never perhaps did the United Kingdoms of
Great Britain and Ireland rejoice more heartily than
on the day when he led to the altar Victoria, his
cousin and our Queen.

Sometimes our nation has rejoiced when subsequent events have proved that there was little real
cause to do so. In this instance, however, the nation
had not to regret its joy as premature. Wisely and
well did he fill the high position to which he had
aspired, and much true service did he render his
adopted country. But as it does not come within the
scope of the present work, I can enter on no detail.
I may, however, be permitted to notice in passing,
how favourably he contrasted in most respects with
the husbands of former queens regnant—Philip of
Spain, for instance. No monument exists in all
our land to perpetuate his odious memory, nor sculp-
tured tablet to record or commemorate a good deed.

How different with the lamented Prince Consort !
And while the various towns and cities throughout
the empire seemed to vie with each other in loading
his memory with honour, his Highland tenants of
Balmoral, Birkhall, and *Abergeldie* also spontane-
ously united to erect an obelisk in the grounds near
the castle ; while the Queen, in response to this
genuine outburst of affection, caused a bronze statue

of the lamented dead to be placed in its close vicinity.

Coming yet further down the hurtling stream of time to the husband of Queen Anne, Prince George of *Denmark*, we will again find that contrast is favourable to the Prince Consort. Though Prince George was no monster of superstition and cruelty, nor unfaithful to his adopted country, like Philip, and though he lived in harmony with his wife the Queen, yet in an intellectual point of view how inferior!—his abilities being so slender as to render him contemptible in the eyes of his wife's relations, one of whom used to say sneeringly, that he had tried Prince George in every way, but found '*nothing in him.*'

Not so was it with Prince Albert, the late proprietor of *Balmoral*, who not only possessed great intellectual powers, but also used them freely in promoting the best interests of his adopted people. It only, however, comes under the scope of the present work to illustrate by some few facts and incidents, how he brought these powers to bear on the moral and physical improvement of his Highland tenantry of *Birkhall*, *Abergeldie*, and *Balmoral.*

Much good was in the first place done indirectly, by affording on a large scale employment to the people. His fertile genius projected many improvements on the *Balmoral* estate, while his sound judgment and elegant taste had ample scope in carrying them into practical effect, by building, enclosing, and remodelling all that was awry or become *effete.*

More, however, was done directly. Under his supervision three schools were erected : one a female school near the village of *Crathie;* another for boys and girls at *Strathgirnock;* a third, also for boys and girls, near *Birkhall,* the property of the Prince of Wales.

Previous to the erection of the school at *Girnock,* there had been one supported by a society in *Edinburgh;* but for a considerable number of years before the arrival of the Queen and Prince Consort at *Balmoral,* its support had been withdrawn, and in consequence the school had fallen into decay. The building and endowing of a school in that locality was a great boon to the inhabitants of the district, as they were some five miles distant from the parish school.

The intellectual improvement of the people was still further sought by the establishment of a library, from which the tenants who wished it were supplied gratis with books once a-week.

In addition to the building of schools, the village of *Crathie* underwent a complete transformation. Many tasteful and commodious dwellings were erected, while the old ones were so altered as to be placed almost on a par with the new in point of appearance.

I may notice, lastly, the very deep interest he took in his numerous *employés.* Not only did he put money into their possession by providing work for them, but also seemed anxious that they should use it in such a way as to be of real service to them. He took pains, I was also informed, to acquaint himself with the character and circumstances of each, and then contrived in a judicious manner to give every encouragement to the industrious and well-conducted.

Under such *surveillance,* almost fatherly in its care and goodness, drinking and every species of immorality was discountenanced ; while, by the example and influence of high morality, and by the esteem and veneration with which his character had inspired them, they were stimulated to high purpose—namely, the determination to merit his approbation. And now that he is passed away, not a single dissonant note is heard among the sweet harmonies which his singularly excellent character produced on the heart-chords of his humble tenants of *Balmoral.* ' He was noble, great, and good,' says one; ' His very appearance showed what *he was,*' said another. ' Oh, he was a fine character,' says a third, ' with a degree of consideration for others rarely met with.' One fact mentioned by this person in support of his statement as to the considerate element in the Prince's character was this, that such of his servants as would by others have been paid every *six* months, were by him paid at the end of every *third :* this with the view to prevent any necessity for contracting debt, of running up accounts on the one hand, or allowing people to lie long out of their money on the other.

Another thing which strikes one forcibly while talking with them about their late proprietor is, that almost invariably their remarks are interspersed with phrases indicating their deep sense of the irreparable loss sustained by Her Majesty, and particularly the Prince of Wales, in being deprived of the wise and skilful guide of his youth. How truly in this unselfish manner, not with the loud sound of formal sorrow, but with the deep-ringing tones of personal feeling, they did, and do still,

> ' Mourn for a noble Prince—
>   A Prince of Royal race;
> Mourn, that in yonder palace-home
>   Death made one vacant place,
> And laid with unexpected blow
> A husband and a father low.
>
> ' Mourn for their widowed Queen—
>   Bereaved—who stands alone !
> Though loved by every British heart,
>   And Sovereign of the Throne ;
> Whose early love, whose hope, whose stay
> In manhood's prime has passed away.'

Our *finale*, however, must not be too much in the baritone; so I cannot conclude this volume better

than by quoting some lines written by an old Scotch-
man, who dearly loves his Queen and country:

'In rural peace and privacy,
　　'Mong nature's landscapes grand,
Surrounded by true Highland hearts
　　Amid the mountain land,
Far from the glare and gauds of state,
　　In happiness and glee,
Long may Victoria freely roam
　　Beside the "bonny *Dee!*"

'Amid our mountain scenes sublime,
　　Afar from courtly care,
Oh, may the loftiest of the land
　　Life's noblest blessings share!
Safe in her princely Highland home
　　May she live blithe and free,
And Britain's honoured Queen long bless
　　The beauteous banks o' *Dee!*'

LEGENDS